Praise for **supercorp**

"This is the book that the world has been anxiously waiting for, perhaps Kanter's most notable, certainly one of the most important books of this decade. This is a must-read for all our current and future leaders who will profit enormously from her lessons on how organizations can succeed in these perilous times."

—Warren Bennis, University Professor at University of Southern California and author of *On Becoming a Leader*

"Rosabeth Moss Kanter has done it again! She breaks new ground in *SuperCorp* by envisioning the corporation of the future that creates long-term value through breakthrough strategies that help solve intractable social problems. This is a must-read for anyone concerned about where capitalism needs to go."

—Bill George, former chairman and CEO of Medtronic and author of *True North*

"For decades, Rosabeth Moss Kanter (Is she the new Peter Drucker?) has been at the cutting edge in helping corporate leaders understand how to master turbulent changes. Now she returns with innovative insights on how companies—and their leaders—can be at the vanguard of the twenty-first century. *SuperCorp* shows how corporations big and small can not only succeed in a globalized economy but can also rebuild public trust. Timely, informative, and uplifting—all of the qualities of a great read!"

—David Gergen, CNN senior political analyst and White House counselor to four U.S. presidents

"Rosabeth Moss Kanter puts a new and welcome human face on the many ways companies can serve a public purpose while also prospering financially and building an enduring culture of success."

—Andrea Jung, chairman and CEO of Avon Products

"Kanter presents us with a thoughtful review of the ways in which companies can grow and create financial opportunity for their clients and shareholders while at the same time fostering societal

good. Some have called it 'doing well by doing good,' but Kanter's careful analysis goes beyond the platitudes by offering solid examples and important insights."
—Samuel J. Palmisano, chairman, president, and CEO of IBM

"In the present time of unprecedented challenges, Rosabeth Moss Kanter's new book is so timely. Society will accept corporations only if they fulfill societal objectives and needs."
—Klaus Schwab, founder and executive chairman of the World Economic Forum

"*SuperCorp* is a brilliant report from the front lines of companies creating the future by accomplishing the seemingly impossible: driving profits and growth while being in synch with the demands of a new generation of employees and a public fed up with Enron-type excess and scandal. Here is the practical game plan every business needs to pursue to build a profitable future through a capitalism based on progressive ideals."
—Daniel Vasella, chairman and CEO of Novartis

"*SuperCorp* is a meaningful resource for executives learning the keys to unlocking growth and innovation in today's challenging global marketplace. The research and case studies are insightful, liberating readers to go beyond the structured models that have historically guided business. Kanter makes a compelling case about the role played by corporate culture, values-based decision making, and larger societal issues in the creation of sustainable success."
—Ivan Seidenberg, chairman and CEO of Verizon Communications

"Society demands that the business of business be more than just business. Unless your business is also serving a social purpose, you miss an opportunity for innovations that bring profits. Rosabeth Moss Kanter, one of our most outstanding scholars, excels in her characteristic manner by taking the lead and developing practical ideas for the leaders of the future."
—Ram Charan, coauthor of *Execution*

supercorp

ALSO BY ROSABETH MOSS KANTER

America the Principled:
6 Opportunities for Becoming a Can-Do Nation Once Again

Confidence: How Winning Streaks and Losing Streaks Begin and End

Evolve! Succeeding in the Digital Culture of Tomorrow

Rosabeth Moss Kanter on the
Frontiers of Management

Innovation (coedited)

World Class: Succeeding Locally in the Global Economy

The Challenge of Organizational Change (coedited)

When Giants Learn to Dance: Mastering the Challenges of Strategy,
Management, and Careers in the 1990s

Creating the Future (coauthored)

The Change Masters: Innovation and Entrepreneurship
in the American Corporation

A Tale of "O": On Being Different in an Organization

Life in Organizations: Workplaces as People Experience Them (coedited)

Men and Women of the Corporation

Work and Family in the United States

Another Voice (coedited)

Creating and Managing the Collective Life (edited)

Commitment and Community

supercorp

HOW VANGUARD COMPANIES CREATE INNOVATION, PROFITS, GROWTH, AND SOCIAL GOOD

Best wishes,

rosabeth moss kanter

CROWN
BUSINESS
NEW YORK

All rights reserved.
Published in the United States by Crown Business, an imprint of the Crown
Publishing Group, a division of Random House, Inc., New York.
www.crownpublishing.com

CROWN BUSINESS is a trademark and CROWN and the Rising Sun colophon
are registered trademarks of Random House, Inc.

Library of Congress Cataloging-in-Publication Data is available upon request.

ISBN 978-0-307-38235-1

Printed in the United States of America

Design by Robert C. Olsson

10 9 8 7 6 5 4 3 2 1

First Edition

In memory of my wonderful parents,

*And in celebration of Matthew, Melissa, Alison Lily,
and generations to come*

CONTENTS

contents

PART IV. AGENDA FOR THE FUTURE

supercorp

introduction

ONE BRIGHT SPOT in the otherwise grim and gloomy financial news in January 2009 was IBM's profit announcement, which exceeded financial analysts' expectations—no small feat in good times, much less bad. IBM had a profitable end to 2008 and a strong profit outlook for the quarters ahead, leaping ahead of the competition. Furthermore, during a year in which world stock markets plunged, with the NASDAQ composite index dropping by 36 percent and Microsoft by 41 percent, IBM shares were down by only about 16 percent for 2008. IBM's stock price rose on the positive earnings news, which was released on the day of Barack Obama's inauguration as president of the United States, a day on which U.S. stock markets plunged again.

IBM is a bright spot for an additional reason. It is among the progressive companies I investigated, including Procter & Gamble, Banco Real, and Publicis Groupe, that have achieved the seemingly impossible: high levels of business performance—innovation, growth, and profit—and social good. They have mastered a tough challenge: building a resilient culture to flourish in turbulent times while leaving a positive mark on the world. While the short-term fortunes of any company, IBM included, can change precipitously, a high-performance humanistic culture provides the foundation for sustainable growth, profit, and innovation over the longer term.

For years, lip service has been paid by many corporate leaders to achieving high performance and being a good corporate citizen. What I have discovered in my research, however, is that the two issues, business performance and societal contributions, are, in fact, intimately

1

connected. Service to society, guided by well-articulated values, is not just "nice to do" but an integral part of the business models for companies that I call *the vanguard*. They use their unique strengths to provide innovative new solutions to societal challenges such as early childhood education, water safety and sanitation, employment for people with disabilities, small business development, energy conservation, and disaster relief. Societal initiatives undertaken largely without direct profit motives are part of the culture that builds high performance and thus results, ironically, in profits.

Values and principles, which include respect for people and concern for the environment, contribute to numerous capabilities: sensing opportunities and innovating; enhancing customer success and value for end users; making effective acquisitions; attracting and motivating top talent; working collaboratively to react or change quickly; and tapping the potential of an extended family of business partners for new ideas or market reach. These companies attempt to raise social and environmental standards in the countries in which they operate and also within their own workplaces, which tend to be flexible and family-friendly as well as increasingly diverse and green-oriented. Overall, they derive benefits in both innovation and execution.

Let me be clear from the outset that this is aspirational. Even the best companies do not meet their ideals all the time, and they do not do it perfectly—they have vulnerabilities and blind spots and can be mired in bureaucracy. Their leaders are not soft-hearted do-gooders. The companies mount and defend lawsuits, push the limits of their market dominance and pricing power, compete aggressively, and lobby governments for favorable treatment. But they live up to high aspirations often enough to put them in the vanguard of a new paradigm for business.

This new paradigm is particularly timely as the world struggles to recover from financial crisis and also faces ongoing challenges of climate change, educational and economic disparities, political uncertainties in conflict-ridden regions, and the potential for border-crossing pandemics. For the past decade, the latest waves of globalization have caused enormous turbulence everywhere, in growth regions as well as in mature societies. But the vanguard companies have mastered the turbulence of technological and geopolitical change by making critical internal changes from which other companies can learn, and they have lent their business capabilities to produce social innovations from which the general public can benefit.

In the work for my 2004 book, *Confidence: How Winning Streaks and Losing Streaks Begin and End,* I saw that turnarounds are based on psychology as much as economics; people must have confidence that positive outcomes are possible before they invest their money, effort, or loyalty. Thus, in the midst of chaos, financial free-fall, and scandal caused by the misconduct of some, the good conduct of vanguard companies can provide optimism about the future—that there are many companies in the United States and the world doing the right thing and doing it with a sense of mission that enables them to deliver what their customers want in a way that is significantly better than their competition.

The transformational enterprises that form the vanguard set a new direction for business in the future: companies that are successful and prosperous in their own right while forces for good in communities and the wider world. They are role models with much to teach, including:

- how to build an enduring culture for the long term that enables continual change and renewal, as well as rapid response to crises
- how to use values and principles as a guidance system, for self-and-peer control
- how every step of the innovation process can be enhanced by a strong social purpose and connections with society
- how humanistic approaches can smooth the tensions of mergers and create productive new collaborations
- how workplaces can incorporate tools and approaches of the digital age, including remote work from home and self-organized social networks, to unleash employee energy for both daily tasks and making a difference in the world
- how people of diverse origins, races, and ethnicities can be encouraged to find common ground while expressing rather than suppressing their identities
- how community service can build relationships and reputations and how business capabilities can contribute to the public agenda

• how to minimize the negative consequences of globalization and involve companies in addressing societal problems while understanding the limits of reliance on the private sector

• how leaders and potential leaders can cultivate the skills to master the challenges of the globalizing world of the future

The vanguard model is not only good for business and society writ large but is also good for individuals. The newer generations of professionals and managers want satisfying work and a paycheck, certainly, but they also want to be members of an institution that contributes to the common good. This desire for positive meaning is apparent in the groundswell of world approval for the election of a new American president who stands for an idealistic call to service and the spirit of positive change.

america and the world: origins of the search for the vanguard

BARACK OBAMA'S election as president of the United States in November 2008 meant that Americans traveling abroad no longer had to pretend to be Canadians.

Witticisms like this about loss of respect for the United States in the world are no joke. During a research trip to Egypt in 2006, a guide driving my researchers and me toward a security checkpoint said he would tell the guards we were Canadians. If he said we were Americans, he told us, we would have to wait while the police organized a motorcycle force to escort us. The government was bending over backward to ensure the safety of Americans—implying that we were potential targets.

This book is about globalization and new business models. But writing it was stimulated, in part, by changes in the world and America's role in it during the opening years of the twenty-first century.

I have long been interested in the interplay between the economy and society. In addition to the financial functions performed by businesses, companies are social institutions, producing jobs and shaping lives through their products, services, norms, and operating standards. Through numerous research projects and consulting engagements (described in my previous books such as *The Change Masters, When Giants Learn to Dance, Evolve!, Confidence,* and *Men and Women of the Corporation*), I illuminated the role of the human element in effective business strategies, whether modest innovation or major transformation.

In 1998, as part of the Initiative on Social Enterprise at Harvard Business School, colleagues and I convened a national forum, Business Leadership in the Social Sector, with many high-profile elected officials, progressive company chief executive officers (CEOs), and experts, including an exchange with Hillary Clinton via videoconference from the White House. We considered how major companies could go beyond being "responsible" and accomplish so much more if they used their core business strengths to address significant societal needs, such as public education and job creation in poor inner cities. They would not be a substitute for government action but innovators adding their unique capabilities as a partner to government. The forum featured, among others, IBM and its innovations developed in partnership with public schools, called Reinventing Education, which had started in the United States but had not yet been taken around the world.

That forum was a time of celebration of the best that American-style capitalism could be. A few short years later, the millennium ushered in additional significant challenges, including terrorist attacks and a backlash against American companies for accounting scandals, with recession and low esteem for America made worse by the invasion of Iraq. Yet expectations were also growing for the role of business in the world. The United Nations was trying to enlist major corporations to sign up for a global compact to support its Millennium Development Goals to end poverty, improve global health, and educate children in basic skills. Could companies possibly rise to these heightened expectations? And which metaphor did companies most resemble—business as devil exploiting helpless communities or business as angel raising standards to improve lives?

Having talked with progressive companies in the United States, I wondered about the impact of multinational companies on the ground in many other countries, including those that were not particularly U.S. friendly, where populist sentiments were antagonistic to American-style capitalism. In 2002, I sent a team to Egypt to take a look; one member was a native Egyptian studying at Harvard. Their report, "The Role of Trans-national Corporations in the Development of Human Capital in Egypt," tried to pin down the mechanisms through which foreign companies influenced society. One striking discovery was that Procter & Gamble had contributed to the creation of Egypt's first health maintenance organization, in part so that P&G could offer its local employees benefits comparable to those offered in the United States.

I also saw that my ideas about leadership, change management, innovation, and regional competitiveness resonated in developing countries where I was invited to speak or consult, including Turkey, Mexico, South Korea, Brazil, India, and the United Arab Emirates (both Dubai and Abu Dhabi). In some cases, the companies that invited me were leaping ahead of American multinational competitors or buying U.S. assets. That furthered my interest in how business has been changing.

I began a systematic research project guided by broad overarching questions aimed at understanding companies wholistically, as they operate in many parts of the world. For example:

• Are companies responding to changing expectations about the role of business in society, in a contradictory era of privatization accompanied by challenges to the legitimacy of global capitalism? Can societal considerations contribute to effective business and product strategies?

• Can companies that are leaders in setting and exemplifying world-class standards leverage their social investments to maintain marketplace advantages in the new global competitions? Can they both provide public benefits and also improve their own performance?

• Are companies engaging more deeply with suppliers, customers, and communities as members of an extended family of partners? Does this nourish the business and provide laboratories for innovation?

• Can new kinds of social involvements help companies build their brand locally throughout the world, ensure favorable market conditions (stable governments, educated consumers, suppliers and distributors operating to high standards), and make a positive difference to diverse communities? Can this have a high impact and be sustainable over time?

• What are the new workplace challenges associated with progressive business practices, as employees bring new expectations to their jobs in a globalizing world? Can workplaces be empowering and inclusive, meeting the needs of men and women, parents, and minorities? What skills and qualities are necessary for mastering these challenges? Who becomes a leader; who is likely to rise to top positions?

My starting point was these grand questions, posed at the ten-thousand-foot level of theory. But after more than three years and 350 interviews and observations in twenty countries, I have written this book to provide a variety of down-to-earth answers. The new model for business comes from my experiences with IBM, Procter & Gamble, and others among the world's best companies.

First, for those concerned about making their companies more competitive as well as more socially constructive, the book offers numerous practical lessons for managers and professionals at all levels. The vanguard model that I put forth runs through strategy and operations and can improve innovation, mergers, teamwork, and relationships with government and the public. Senior executives should be able to learn from the CEOs in this book. But one does not have to be the CEO to see how vanguard principles can change business practice.

I also have a broader audience in mind beyond business. I try to explain global change to the general public and convince informed citizens that, with the right leadership and values, companies can make unique contributions to help produce a better world. I hope that general readers will find good stories that illuminate trends and possibilities. After all, most people in the world do not work for large companies. But everyone is affected by business trends as consumers, community members, and citizens. And some find their well-being and livelihood influenced by the ripples of companies through supply and distribution chains: people in small companies who are suppliers or distributors for larger entities; members of nonprofit and nongovernmental organizations who operate on behalf of communities touched by business; and educators teaching the next generation of potential leaders.

At this moment of global financial meltdown, it is important to add that the vanguard companies highlighted throughout this book have generally escaped the worst of the crisis, outperforming their industries even as markets declined. Since that group includes several banks outside the United States, it is heartening to know that positive role models can be found even at the worst of times.

I hope that the messages about the potential for principled businesses to lead the vanguard of change will inform and inspire readers throughout the world. I hope to show that "business leadership" is not an oxymoron and that if corporate executives follow the models in this book, enlightened companies can drive positive change.

The world applauded President Obama on his election because he represented the power of hope and the potential for change. Perhaps this book can make a contribution in that direction. The challenges facing the world are daunting, and for some people business has seemed part of the problem. Now is the time to ensure that business becomes part of the solution.

There has long been a sterile debate between economists who argue that the only purpose of a business is to make money and activists who demand that companies invest resources to address social and environmental issues. The former find it irresponsible to shareholders for companies to take on social causes, the latter irresponsible to other stakeholders not to embrace those causes. This book offers a third way, one that combines pragmatism and idealism. The new paradigm for emerging vanguard companies enables them to pursue their everyday business opportunities in a way that reflects humanistic values and the promotion of high standards. This, in turn, helps them grow quickly and effectively with solid profits and equally solid reputations. While some may start reading the next chapters with skepticism, the proof is in the evidence I have gathered for this book.

part one

the opportunity

chapter one

the wave

WHAT IF TRENDS in the world economy, such as global mergers and consolidation, environmental degradation and overpopulation, should lead to the entire world food supply being controlled by one giant monopoly? Imagine that the enormous conglomerate produces the only remaining edible protein, which it calls Chicken Little, in a high-rise factory in South America. Chicken Little's source is a massive mass of cultured chicken breast, kept alive by algae skimmed by low-wage workers from multistory towers of ponds. The ponds are surrounded by mirrors that focus the sunlight onto them, which is environmentally friendly but otherwise totally artificial. Slices of Chicken Little are cut by machine and shipped all over the world to people who have no choice but to swallow the foul synthetic fowl.

This is a science-fiction fantasy, served up by Frederik Pohl and C. M. Kornbluth in their best-seller *The Space Merchants*. But it is not far off from the way many critics think about business. Today's reality can easily reinforce that negative view, when headlines herald food shortages in some places (e.g., Africa), overconsumption and obesity in others (e.g., America), product safety concerns (e.g., toothpaste from China), bank failures (e.g., Lehman Brothers and Washington Mutual), and outright corruption (e.g., the forced resignation of Samsung's chairman in South Korea).

As bashing goes, big-business bashing is socially acceptable and politically correct. A century ago, the term *bureaucracy* emerged to describe faceless impersonal vehicles that run like clockwork and run roughshod over human feelings. A half century ago, the military-industrial complex and organization-man conformity were named and scorned. Today, greed is attributed to Big Oil profits and derivatives-peddling banks that caused a massive global financial crisis. Critics can always find reasons for the unease that the public often feels about big companies. Even revered entrepreneurial Google is vulnerable to being dubbed an evil empire after growing big enough to dominate the online search field and Internet advertising.

But another model is on the rise, and it is already changing the image of what business is and can be. I call that new model the vanguard company.

Vanguard companies are ahead of the pack and potentially the wave of the future. The best of this breed aspire to be big but human, efficient but innovative, global but concerned about local communities. The best have business prowess and clout with partners and governments but try to use their power and influence to develop solutions to problems the public cares about. They sometimes serve as an alternative to inefficient or oppressive states or religions by standing for high universal standards of openness, inclusion, and transparency. The leaders of a vanguard company espouse positive values and encourage their employees to embrace and act on them.

Vanguard companies have the power to contribute to the world in positive ways, and they want to do so. This new business model has been arising in recent years but is still a work in progress. It is no longer a sideline activity or an afterthought, such as check writing to give away a few leftover crumbs, but a mainstream imperative that infuses every aspect of the business. It is becoming the wave of the future because the public demands it and employees want it, especially the highly educated new generation that wants to work for companies in sync with their idealism. Furthermore, the capabilities of vanguard companies enable them sometimes to take action more quickly than governments. Or they work with governments to add great value to solving problems that matter to the general public, such as education, health, or the environment.

A vanguard company might even fly to the rescue when disaster strikes. That is what IBM did in India and Asia following one of the deadliest natural disasters in history, the December 2004 tsunami, just as the company had done after earthquakes, terrorist attacks, and other major emergencies. This story shows what the new model looks like in action. It is not just "do-goodism" but a whole new way of working, a new model for strategy, innovation, employee empowerment, and leadership that is good for business and, ideally, good for the world.

tsunami

ON THE DAY of the tsunami, Shanker Annaswamy was close to the beach in his hometown of Chennai with his family. Annaswamy was an engineer who had joined IBM as chief executive for India six months earlier. It was raining too hard on that late December day to walk the beach, so he took his family to a temple a few kilometers from the ocean. Driving back to his relatives' house, he saw chaos in the road and people leaving their homes. He thought this was perhaps a film shooting, which always attracted crowds. At the house, he switched on the television and learned that there had been a tsunami. The full impact was not yet clear. When he returned to Bangalore that night, he was shocked to hear about the extent of the damage.

The next day in his office, Annaswamy received a visit from one of his managers, Sunil Raghavan, a long-time IBMer with responsibilities for protecting data security. Raghavan declared that IBM could and should do something to help. "I said, 'How can you help?'" Annaswamy recalled. "He said, 'Shanker, I have done this in the Bhuj earthquake before. IBM has capabilities.' The only thing I said was, 'What can I do for you?' He said, 'You being the head of the company, you know some of the governor's people. Can you talk with the IT [information technology] secretary of Tamil Nadu?' So I called this gentleman, Vivek Harinarain. When I reached him, although he could not connect IBM and tsunami, he said, 'Okay, why don't you send them. I have no time to think how they can help. But send them.'" At the same time, a team in New York led by Robin Willner at Corporate Citizenship and Corporate Affairs had prepared a memo requesting approvals by IBM senior leadership to deploy significant technology and talent to coordinate relief and recovery efforts on the ground.

It soon became clear that the tsunami, caused by an undersea earthquake in the Indian Ocean, wreaked enormous destruction in at least eleven countries, killing more than 225,000 people. Most tsunami damage occurred in Indonesia, Sri Lanka, Thailand, and India. In India, about ten thousand people were killed, and hundreds of thousands were rendered homeless. Annaswamy did not have to wait for the final toll nor for instructions from corporate. He immediately supported any IBMer's desire to help.

One reason a vanguard company takes direct action and does not merely write checks nor wait to join a bandwagon is that employees want it. Employees have been empowered to think for themselves and to advocate for decisions they feel make sense in their corner of the world. They know best how to argue on the basis of company values, even when there is no direct company self-interest, and how to tap company capabilities to do something unique, which other volunteers cannot accomplish. That is why IBM India mobilized so quickly—action was self-organized by employees. This was not the first time that IBMers had invoked IBM's humanitarian values to get support for a significant IBM role in the aftermath of a disaster. The company had done it in Kosovo, after the terrorist attacks in New York City in 2001, and following the Gujarat earthquake the same year.

FLASHBACK: EARTHQUAKE

To show that IBM India had experience relevant to the tsunami, Sunil Raghavan told Shanker Annaswamy about the earthquake near the city of Bhuj in the state of Gujarat, which happened in January 2001, before Annaswamy joined IBM. IBM's highly valued contributions following that earthquake gave Raghavan confidence that IBM could do something equally positive after the tsunami.

The Gujarat earthquake, like the later tsunami, did not affect IBM directly. The area is a remote, sparsely populated place of desert and marshland on the extreme western end of India, not far from the Pakistan border; IBM's closest sales office was about three hundred kilometers away. But though IBM was not impacted as a business when the earthquake struck, "as people we certainly were," Raghavan recalled. "You see all those horrific images on TV, and you say, hey, we must go and do something. So that was the trigger. It was not so much driven by linkages to our supply chain or our customer base."

Sunil Raghavan's role in the global delivery business gave him a vantage point for viewing IBM India's growth and role in the world. Customers around the world were, for strategic business reasons, increasingly sending work to India, and they needed strong assurances that the work they sent to India was secure. India itself was playing a more strategic role in IBM. Risk management expertise was essential. Raghavan understood how to pull a team together and move quickly, a vital skill cultivated in a vanguard company. Using this skill after the earthquake felt much more significant than saving data; the group in India felt they could save people's lives. IBM's values were not confined to dealings with customers; its values included making a difference in the wider world. IBMers were grateful that the company gave them that opportunity. Values help a vanguard company build extraordinary emotional ties and loyalty.

Thus, upon news of the Gujarat earthquake, Raghavan approached his boss, Amitabh Ray, vice president of global delivery for India, who supported Raghavan's zeal for action. IBM had connections with the state government in Gujarat, which made it possible to link Raghavan's group to relief efforts. Numerous nongovernmental organizations (NGOs) and companies were donating equipment and sending out volunteers; IBM did that too. In fact, large numbers of IBMers wanted to go to places affected by the earthquakes and help the crisis management team; senior leaders had to pull them back out of concern for their safety.

The team in Gujarat asked a more strategic question, one that guides the choices of a vanguard company: how to help in ways that used IBM core competence, its technology expertise—the business equivalent of its superpowers. The IBM team also sought involvement of business partners, drawing on a large network of close relationships—another key asset of a vanguard company that enables creating big coalitions to achieve big goals. Raghavan drove back and forth between Bhuj and Ahmedabad, the Gujarat state capital. At a meeting of IT vendors and dealerships, he spoke about the IBM effort and sought contributions of equipment and supplies. The next question was how to know where those goods should go. That is where IBM technology could help.

In a precursor of IBM's Smarter Planet initiative, an IBM system was quickly developed to track material flow at each entry point to the disaster area—roads, train stations, the airport. But phone lines and cell towers were down, so how could the data be transmitted? The determined and imaginative IBM team put a laptop in a car and drove it from place to place to move the data across the stations. Though time-consuming, this was a better tracking mechanism than anything else around to guide decision making by government and other relief agencies. "I think they were very happy, because afterward they were able to trace what went where. They were able to retrieve some material from place A and send it to place B. Given the level of chaos, there was just no other way they could have done that," Raghavan said.

Tracking and handling medical supplies is vital after an emergency involving thousands of people. Because the government hospital in Bhuj collapsed in the earthquake, the area was bulldozed clear so a tented hospital could be set up. Big containerloads of medicines had come in from all over the world, but ground personnel could not read the foreign-language labels, so they did not know what they had. Moreover, the containers were in the sun; blistering afternoon temperatures of 40 degrees Celsius (104 degrees Fahrenheit) could cause deterioration quickly. IBM established a system that documented the generic names of medicine in many languages. Medical inventory management system code, written in the United States, was adapted quickly in India and connected to the Internet. IBM volunteers sat down with three or four pharmacists brought in from other locations to go through the medicines container by container. They took inventory and put the data into the system. Users could then key in information from the label, which would tell them what the medicine was. And inventory numbers indicated a surplus of some medicines that could be sent to other places where they were needed.

Later, after the team left, the IBMers knew that their inventory management system lived on. Local users continued to download code updates as they rebuilt the district hospital and the surrounding small health centers.

One big disaster behind them, IBMers gained confidence in their ability to use their core technology to make a difference, and that became important after the tsunami. Indeed, the whole country gained confidence. After the Gajarat earthquake, the government of India made disaster readiness a priority. By the time of the tsunami a few years later, the government felt confident enough to refuse U.S. help.

THE TSUNAMI RESPONSE

Sunil Raghavan saw the tsunami as even more devastating than the earthquake. Once again, IBM sites were not affected. But when the magnitude of the tsunami disaster was clear, he was confident that IBM would want to help. First, he placed another early-hours call to his boss, Amitabh Ray, requesting a team for the next three days. Ray recalled, "This team spontaneously said we would like to participate in the relief work. Nobody from corporate told them that they had to do this." In the morning, Raghavan walked into Shanker Annaswamy's office and got his support, as well as a go-ahead from the government IT official for the state of Tamil Nadu.

Despite the danger of a repeat tsunami, Sunil Raghavan and his team packed water and emergency supplies in their cars and headed for Nagapattinam in Tamil Nadu, the southern state that bore the brunt of the impact. They went in an exploratory mode. Rather than pulling solutions off the shelf, they had to learn what would add value—the same ears-to-the-ground listening mode used by a vanguard company to trigger innovation. As they toured the area, they immediately saw differences between this disaster and the earthquake. While the earthquake had wiped out large areas and destroyed infrastructure, the tsunami devastation was concentrated in the first few hundred yards from the shore. Farther out, conditions appeared normal; even streets of shops were still standing. The IBM team attended a meeting with about two dozen NGOs about what these various relief groups were doing and how they were coordinating their efforts, to see how IBM might add value. That evening, the state IT secretary invited Raghavan and colleagues to dinner at his home; all the hotels and restaurants had closed down.

One challenge was straightforward administration, to manage the volume of relief supplies. In one day, the enormous inflow of material filled up all the space government officials had for outdoor storage, and supplies were diverted to Madras. IBM provided a temporary material receipting system. Soon it was clear that there were problems coordinating data coming in from other places along the coast, so IBM set up a website to post data and updates, borrowing bandwidth from an IBM customer, a local Internet service provider. About a half-dozen small projects like these were done, using standard technology. IBM made it clear up front that it wanted no publicity and was not looking for money. If business leads might follow, IBMers were not coming in to chase them. "That makes it far easier to engage, because people then are comfortable that you're not coming in with ulterior motives. So it has translated into goodwill for sure. It has translated into what we think of ourselves as IBMers, that we're pretty serious about playing our role as citizens," a team member said.

After leaving good systems in Tamil Nadu, in January 2005 IBM India leaders shifted to challenging problems in the Andamans and Nicobar islands, remote places with great strategic significance to India (and none to IBM). This next phase provided opportunity for significant innovation—the chance to develop something new intensifies the motivation of vanguard company employees. Much of Nicobar had gone underwater, destroying homes, buildings, and infrastructure such as harbors and telecommunications. In a few months, the spring rains would start and not let up for eight months, providing a natural April deadline for shelter for displaced families. The government had to ship in everything it needed. To respond, IBM developed another Smarter Planet demonstration, an unconventional supply-chain system to track what was shipped, whether it came in by air or sea, and its location in a variety of stocking points. It could reconcile inventory when items came in tons or truckloads and were then dispatched in bales or cartonloads. People could call in lists and have them keyed into the system.

A vanguard company gains its powers primarily from the ability to integrate its pieces, to combine people, to get the action moving quickly. IBM's emphasis on teamwork across the whole extended enterprise helped the tsunami efforts. Field activities, from discovery to deployment, used a collaborative approach. People worked across IBM units, tapped business partners, and involved NGOs. (That is the difference between arm's-length transactions, such as donating supplies, and implementation of systemic solutions that leave the recipient better off later.) In the Andamans, IBM trained students from a polytechnic institute in Port Blair in open source and Linux programs, deploying the students to collect data the way IBMers had done after the Gujarat earthquake. Joint involvement in service solidified or built relationships. Business partners were useful sources of knowledge, helping identify an appropriate resource for a particular situation. Later, IBM helped the Indian Institute of Technology in Kharagpur near Calcutta establish a disaster management and relief center. Everyone was getting smarter.

The satisfaction for the IBM team members came from their desire to serve and the knowledge that if they did not maybe nothing would get done. When a vanguard company encourages employees to look outside the company, to society, to understand markets and supply chains, its people also see where there are gaps, underserved populations and unmet needs, for which they feel responsible. "The mandate was to serve," Raghavan said. "It was not 'figure out how we can make more money off this in the future.' Otherwise we would have never gone to the Andamans, a remote chain of islands with tourism as its main business. I think the reason we were keen to go there was simply because it is so inaccessible for people from the mainland to go there, so the normal NGO presence that we would have found there, we did not find in this case. So I think it was that much more important for us to go and make the difference."

The support that made this project possible was just one of many examples of employee autonomy and managerial trust, another hallmark of a vanguard company's new way of working. That is not surprising to IBM senior managers involved with the tsunami efforts. Amitabh Ray, Sunil Raghavan's boss, said, "Trust is one of the IBM values, right? That's why this tsunami project was so important to me. It was not corporate directed. It came from people who believed in IBM values; they said this is what we ought to do. If you strongly believe that you have a solution that can help the people on the ground, you approach your manager. And I can bet that any of our managers will say okay, unless that person's doing something that is very client critical. Then obviously we'll have a group meeting, because there could be a very serious impact on the client side. But we will provide all the support to the client team to ensure that we can release that person."

IBM was careful about its commitments because there was still a business to run, so it did not overpromise on these so-called Blue projects—projects done under the IBM banner (its ubiquitous blue logo) without a revenue-producing ("green") customer. As the business unit head, Amitabh Ray was asked by Raghavan for approval, because the tsunami effort would have to be funded from the global delivery organization's own budget, for the software development and for the time of IBMers to implement the system district by district.

Leaders figured out how to sustain the effort. A vanguard company is measured not on declarations but on results, which means making longer-term commitments and sticking with them. "Even when we started as a voluntary effort," Shanker Annaswamy said, "it was not the one-day effort, right, where you go in and then you do your magic and you come out and everybody's happy? If you go in, you are committing your teams for a little bit longer time. And then the utilization pressure of their time comes in, and that's where my leadership team members and the global teams come and help. And if that person has to be released for a certain time to go and do their job and come back, then an alternative person steps in. So the one good thing about IBM is IBM does not jump in and do without thinking. The effort is not done with compromises of a customer solution. But you very knowingly commit your time, plan for that, and contribute."

The ability to deploy people flexibly and their willingness to give their personal time make it possible to have big impact with modest resources. Backing up the IBM India teams in the field were many people back home in the offices, each giving a little something. People from a variety of functions got involved in an operations center in Bangalore managing the movement of relief material, including Inderpeet Thukral, director of strategy. Because IBM India was an offshore delivery center for software, the systems could be built by the best architects, while a handful of people in the field for a short time could contribute the specifications. Some of the code producers spent three days and nights of their personal time—Friday, Saturday, and Sunday—creating software without impacting their other project schedules. Though some work was done on IBM time, volunteers added enormous capacity. The code was open source, meaning it could be given away without worrying about licenses.

IBM India could also draw on worldwide experience. When the

tsunami hit, IBM's corporate response was swift. Similar to the way IBM mobilized after the 9/11 attack on New York City, a group of about two dozen people from IBM's global Crisis Response Team (CRT) moved into place in India, Indonesia, Thailand, and Sri Lanka. But with India in the hands of local IBM experts who had developed expertise following the Gujarat earthquake, the CRT was sent onward to Sri Lanka and Thailand. Raghavan said, "We [in India] pretty much had this figured out. We said we would support the global team from the software standpoint."

IBM team members were ready to jump in, self-organizing without waiting for instructions from management. For example, while Raghavan was on his way to disaster sites, developers in Bangalore were already adapting IBM's system to track missing people, which had been used in other disasters, such as the Kosovo relief effort in eastern Europe. But then his team discovered that there were several different groups with systems tracking missing people. So the India team did not deploy the IBM system in India or the islands but instead donated it to the Indonesian government via IBM Indonesia. Indonesia wanted local modifications, some of which were done for them in India, and then the Indonesian system was available for continuing use.

Throughout IBM India, involvement in tsunami relief was widespread, well beyond the specialist teams. In vanguard companies, volunteering is almost a way of life, in and outside of formal jobs. "One of the strong points of Indians as a whole is that in adversity a lot of people will pitch in and help," a top manager said. Through the IBM Club, a voluntary association, many employees donated relief materials, from medicines to clothes and cash, made easy through signing up for payroll deductions. All the cash was consolidated and given to the Red Cross. Despite IBM's dispersion over several locations, each with several offices, there was a feeling that the entire IBM company came together, because so many people in India did what they could. A senior woman leader explained, "Bangalore is a cosmopolitan city where people come from all over to work, from smaller places. Many are young, not married. They have a lot of free time on their hands, and they want to relate to something, to belong somewhere. Volunteering makes them they feel they're doing something productive with their lives."

Shanker Annaswamy was proud of IBM's agility as well as its compassion. "You see the whole organization connecting within minutes. IBM is a very large corporation, right? It has its own advantages and disadvantages. Because it's spread out and so many people are involved, to move them all quickly at a lightning speed is a challenge. But in this effort, the moment IBM committed, it moved at a lightning speed. Some other Indian companies were surprised at IBM's speed."

Overall, the worldwide community donated more than $7 billion in humanitarian aid following the tsunami. Indian prime minister Manmohan Singh established the Indian Prime Minister's National Relief Fund; the government and NGOs (including the International Committee of the Red Cross and Red Crescent) coordinated relief efforts in India; and the Indian Ministry of External Affairs, along with the Indian defense forces and the Home Ministry, coordinated relief operations to Sri Lanka, Maldives, and Indonesia. Pfizer, Deutsche Bank, and Coca-Cola headed a long list of corporate donors. Pfizer's $35 million included $25 million in medicines, the rest in cash. Microsoft donated $3.5 million, Cisco $2.5 million, and Infosys, an Indian IT company, donated 50 million rupees, about $1.1 million. IBM was down the list as a $1 million cash donor.

About twenty-seven companies donated more cash than IBM, but IBM provided critical capabilities. IBM contributed an organization registry to allow for the rapid registration and collection of information about NGOs, government agencies, and multinational organizations; a request management system to coordinate and track relief requests; a people registry to support tracking of those missing or deceased; a camp registry to track location, numbers of individuals, and operations information; and an assistance database, damage tracking system, burial information system, health and incident management system, and logistics management system. For IBM India, the tsunami experience added new capabilities for dealing with crises in general and stimulated innovation that could be used in other Smarter Planet initiatives.

IBM received an award from the president of India, among other accolades. But Raghavan added a more personal indication of value: "I think that these opportunities are real eye-openers for many of us, because otherwise we are very sheltered humans. We work nine to five or nine to seven or whatever, and then we head out; we're used to doing a set of things in a certain environment. I think this experience has been life changing for many of our people, because you get to see the worst of how things can get, and you also get to see how people can rally around and try and help in those situations. Quite a few guys who were just a few years out of college came across and spent two or three weeks in Gujarat with me. They'd talk about their learnings out of that experience. In terms of enriching oneself as a human being, this is tremendous. No management development course is going to be a substitute."

FROM DISASTER TO SOLUTIONS

Corporate staff took note and provided vehicles for other humanitarian efforts, such as IBM's swift response to Hurricane Katrina in 2005, which destroyed much of New Orleans and the surrounding area. Under the leadership of Stanley Litow, vice president of corporate citizenship and corporate affairs, IBM codified its innovations into a set of resources for NGOs, a kind of "disaster relief in a box," featuring open-source software tools called Sahana, which means "passion." Sahana is a free disaster management system conceived during the tsunami aftermath and developed by volunteers from the technology community in Sri Lanka to compensate for the devastating consequences of a government attempt to manually manage the process of locating victims, distributing aid, and coordinating volunteers. Used in other disaster relief efforts in Asia, with funding from the Swedish International Development Agency through the Lanka Software Foundation, Sahana won the 2006 Free Software Foundation Award for Projects of Social Benefit.

With evidence that a vanguard company has capabilities and responsibility to contribute, IBM sprung into action yet again following the earthquake in China in May 2008, which took another huge toll in human lives and displacement. In this case, the government acted quickly and effectively. The main challenge became rebuilding, especially the schools that had proven to be poorly constructed and unsafe for children. Henry Chow, chairman of IBM Greater China, met with the mayor of Chengdu, in Sichuan Province, to determine options for IBM involvement. The government adopted the Sahana disaster relief software and implemented it throughout Sichuan. Chow and the mayor, with support from Litow at headquarters in Armonk, New York, agreed to expand IBM's efforts with schools, to deploy more KidSmart workstations, an early childhood teaching tool, and to increase use of Reading Companion, an innovative Web-based voice recognition system to teach English. IBM worked on databases for building safety and a system for predicting earthquakes using IBM's supercomputer, Blue Gene. These are all examples not just of onetime humanitarian aid but of innovations to make the system smarter.

IBM also committed to send Chengdu a corporate service corps team. The corporate service corps is an IBM innovation announced in 2007 to enable selected volunteers from around the world to perform a month of community service wherever needed, on company time, as global citizens and future global leaders. The formation of the IBM service corps is a fitting postscript to the tsunami story. Now, many hundreds of IBMers from anywhere in the world can take direct action on the world's most pressing problems, experiencing the satisfaction that Shanker Annaswamy and IBM India gained after the tsunami. Service corps members will take that learning back to their countries and translate it into how they do business and how they think about the world. Imagine the cumulative impact, as this ripples through and beyond IBM's 386,000 people and their work in 170 countries.

This is hardly bureaucracy or stifling conformity, as contained in images from the past, nor is it corporate greed and political manipulation. It is a whole new way of working.

who is in the vanguard?

THE STORY OF IBM's response to earthquakes, terrorist attacks, hurricanes, and the tsunami represents more than simply an example of wonderful people at a great company responding to humanitarian needs during an emergency, though they certainly did that. The story shows more than generosity; it shows that innovation can arise when people seek systemic solutions to make things run in a smarter way the next time.

While IBM is an unusual company and did extraordinary things during these crises, it is hardly alone. It reflects the paradigm for the emerging vanguard companies that pursue their everyday business opportunities in a way that reflects humanistic values and promotes the highest standards in the countries where they operate. This, in turn, helps them grow quickly and effectively, with strong profits and solid reputations. I know that this is hard for some people to believe, because they think of big companies as inherently immoral or, at best, amoral. But the proof is in their actions.

Some companies that qualify for vanguard company status are giants with household names, like IBM or Procter & Gamble (P&G). But many others are emerging from a range of countries and operate in a range of industries. Consider the following examples from around the world.

- Cemex, which began as Cementos Mexicanos in 1906, is one of the world's largest building materials companies, operating in fifty countries, with a philosophy of improving well-being through innovative industry solutions and a commitment to sustainability. Its Cemex Way methods have helped it grow successfully through significant international acquisitions, improve productivity and working conditions in cement factories in the United States and Europe, and also develop cleaner biofuels. It has raised wages and supported community development in Egypt and has created innovative solutions for affordable housing in rural Mexico. In 2002, Cemex won a World Environment Center Gold Medal for International Corporate Achievement in Sustainable Development, despite being in one of the most polluting industries, because of its commitment to alternative fuels and environmental cleanup.
- Omron, a Japanese electronics company that describes itself as "small but global" (with nearly $7 billion in revenues and thirty-five thousand employees worldwide), invokes its motto—"At work for a better life, a better world for all"—as the impetus for numerous innovations, such as the world's first online automated teller machines, the world's first automated train station, a system to increase safety and reduce deaths in industrial laundries, and a blood pressure monitor for women. The Omron Principles, first articulated in 1960, are said to be responsible for its success in acquiring outstanding smaller U.S. companies with similar values, without being the highest bidder and without the usual merger turmoil.

• Banco Real, headquartered in São Paolo, Brazil, makes social and environmental responsibility the centerpiece of its business strategy. Starting early in this decade, it grew quickly to become Brazil's third-largest and one of its most admired banks. Its strong culture and numerous examples of raising banking and societal standards have made it the survivor following the acquisition of its former Dutch parent, ABN AMRO, by Grupo Santander of Spain. Banco Real's commitment to the environment reinforced ABN AMRO's successful effort to encourage the World Bank's International Finance Corporation to write the Equator Principles, guidelines for environmentally friendly project finance, in 2003, which over sixty major international banks have signed to date.

These are not just random examples of companies doing occasional good; they are a reflection of a comprehensive set of business practices that constitute the vanguard company paradigm. For P&G, its corporate statement of purpose, values, and principles, known as the PVP, is the central tool by which it guides the activities of 140,000 people across the world to deliver excellence to customers and consumers.

In the fullest flowering of the model and its ideal, these vanguard companies strive to be global thinkers building global networks. They seek to be connected within and across countries as a kind of extended family with their partners; they draw on suppliers, distributors, venture partners, or alumni as sources of ideas. They want to raise standards by attempting to operate by one set of values and principles, taking the highest standard as their common denominator and spreading that ethos to the extended family. They try to both globalize, transcending the particularities of place, and localize, attempting to deeply understand the society around them and see where they might innovate and even change their global mind. They seek to use their business prowess to improve society and, at the same time, take social or human needs as a starting point for the business, seeking solutions that propel innovation. What they get out of all this is not only business opportunities and market position but also influence, innovation, employee motivation, company solidarity, and attractiveness to potential business partners, whether independent or acquired.

I think this is a universal model, applicable anywhere companies strive for excellence. My research has taken me and my research group to over twenty countries, where companies in this book have facilities and employees. For example, we were on the ground with IBM in Australia, Brazil, China, Egypt, India, Israel, Russia, Turkey, the United Kingdom, and the United States; with Cemex in multiple cites and towns in Egypt, Latvia, Mexico, the United Kingdom, and the United States; and with P&G in Brazil, China, Egypt, India, the United Kingdom, and the United States. Add our site visits to other companies in Canada, Finland, France, Israel, Japan, Kenya, Netherlands, Singapore, South Africa, South Korea, and Ukraine, and a sizable chunk of the world has been covered.

Differences are obvious, starting with the noise level. African drummers at a Johannesburg conference of mobile phone operator MTN's top managers from twenty-two African and Middle Eastern countries set a very different tone in terms of clatter and clutter than a quiet Japanese banquet in Kyoto with Omron in serene rooms empty of furniture and artifacts. But each company's leaders would recognize the management ideals the other company invokes. How to unite people from diverse national cultures in a common cause is a challenge that the vanguard company model tries to address.

I say "tries to address," because the companies at the vanguard are still a work in progress. They articulate the ideal while still on the journey determining what it means. They have flaws and inconsistencies. They are often the best among their peers, but not always. Most outperformed the industry in the global financial crisis year of 2008, but some did not. Some of them might use market power to muscle the competition out of the picture, which can keep prices high for local customers. Their discipline and work ethic can be hard to live with. They are likely to be apolitical and pick their causes to avoid controversy. They can disappoint some employees because they promise more, which can raise expectations faster than the ability to meet them. The globalism that gives them reach across borders can make them look disloyal in their home-base country and easy targets for populist politicians. The vanguard company model has limits for society too. One company can make a difference but not necessarily change the surrounding system, at least not without multiple collaborators and other institutions such as government driving or spreading the change. And it is not yet clear whether the vanguard companies are exceptions or the rest of the business world will follow their lead.

Vanguard companies are effective because of the combination of talents and resources that they can mobilize. That's the other meaning of the IBM India tsunami story. Ultimately, a vanguard company is only as good as leaders' ability to attract, motivate, and retain skilled people and enable them to self-organize and collaborate. It takes smart people to create a smarter planet and to do so profitably and sustainably.

THIS BOOK SHOWS why companies using the vanguard model of managing by values and principles are well positioned to master the challenges of globalization, including the backlash against it. After examining the forces for change in chapter 2, the book looks at the vanguard model first from the perspective of business strategy, showing how companies' principles provide a guidance system (chapter 3), stimulate high levels of innovation (chapter 4), and help them integrate acquisitions and make big transformations more effectively than common practice (chapter 5). The next part shifts perspective, to examine these issues from the outlook of employees and society—the people who do the work and the places that are impacted by it. The book looks inside vanguard company's workplaces around the world, exploring the dilemmas of flexibility and empowerment (chapter 6) and individual identity and workforce diversity (chapter 7)—how people get work done and who emerges as leaders in complex but flexible organizations, and how different kinds of people from many parts of the world can get along. Chapter 8 follows vanguard companies out of the office and into society, providing examples of how vanguard companies play a role in the public sphere through community contributions or gain a seat at the government policy table. The final chapters ask the related questions of whether this model answers the critics (chapter 9) and what kind of leadership is required to realize the positive aspirations (chapter 10)—the new work of leaders.

YOU DO NOT have to be a giant to act like a vanguard company. Small and midsized companies, NGOs, and nonprofit organizations can find useful guideposts in this model, because it sets forth principles for leadership and innovation that put people and social purpose first.

There is also a pragmatic reason for individuals and organizations of all sizes and types to understand this new paradigm. IBM counts thirty-three thousand companies as part of its partnership network. To join a vanguard company's extended family and to reap the benefits—recall the Internet service providers and humanitarian relief agencies working with IBM after the tsunami—potential partners or suppliers must make sure they operate by high vanguard company standards themselves.

This is a mind-set as well as a business model, and it is possible for individuals as well as companies to adopt it. It can be as simple as spending time at work thinking about what is happening in the world around you, not just the immediate task at hand. Humanistic values and attention to societal needs are a starting point for smart strategy in the global information age.

chapter two

challenges of global change: forcing a new model

THE OPENING YEARS of the twenty-first century will forever be known for turbulence, including, in the fall of 2008, a full-blown tsunami of financial disaster. But even before the crash of the capital markets that started in the United States and quickly spread elsewhere, powerful waves of global change had begun to wash over the world.

The vanguard company model provides a timely and necessary response to this turbulence. The volatility, complexity, diversity, and transparency associated with technological and geopolitical change call for a new approach to doing business, one that can open opportunities to ride the waves rather than be swept under them. After reviewing the big forces causing the turbulence, I will bring them down to earth with an example of a smaller, entrepreneurial company and its employees—a company that shows why it is important to join the vanguard.

big waves of change

A SERIES OF GEOPOLITICAL events starting around 1980 created excitement—some would say exuberance—for a theoretically borderless and peaceful world of infinite economic opportunity facilitated by information technology and led by American multinational companies. For a while, this trend seemed to be the way the world was going. Then the turbulence began.

In the 1980s, deregulation of industry and privatization of state-owned enterprises were propelled by political leaders who believed in the superiority of markets. European community deliberations toward a common currency fueled hopes for boundaryless markets. Other events reinforced this trend, and the world seemed headed toward near-universal acceptance of free-market capitalism. For example, in 1989, the fall of the Berlin Wall marked the end of Communism in eastern Europe. The same year, Asian financial markets liberalized and opened the doors to more foreign capital with fewer conditions. Some Latin American regimes democratized. In early 1990, Nelson Mandela was released from prison in South Africa, ending decades of oppression of blacks under apartheid and bringing foreign investment back to southern Africa.

The opening of the World Wide Web to public use in 1993 and the subsequent Internet business boom furthered these trends by accelerating global communications connectivity and making more information available to more people in more places more of the time. While old industries such as banking and telecommunications consolidated and sought economies of scale and scope, the "new economy" of small dot-com start-ups attracted massive amounts of capital.

At the same time, the formation of regional trade blocs enlarged market potential. The North American Free Trade Agreement was one of the largest in market size, after the European Union. Developing countries grew quickly enough to be renamed emerging markets, and many countries opened their doors to foreign direct investment. By the beginning of the twenty-first century, liberalization for the purposes of trade and foreign investment brought even formerly socialist regimes such as Egypt into the global capitalist camp.

But about a decade ago, it began to appear that zealous advocates of globalization had overshot the mark. Overall prosperity in the United States was accompanied by growing inequality, as the gap widened between the highest income earners and the lowest, and the middle class faced stagnating wages and job insecurity. In many parts of the world, financial investment ran ahead of the capacity to manage it. The 1997–98 Asian financial crisis hurt not only Asian economies but also the fortunes of U.S. multinational companies such as Gillette and Procter & Gamble, which were counting on market growth for consumer products in Asia. That regional crisis was soon followed by the end of the Internet boom in the United States in 2000. The dot-com crash in

2001 depressed stock markets everywhere and put technology spending on hold, even before the United States was shocked by terrorism on September 11, 2001.

Antiglobalization protests were already on the rise. Ironically, the 1999 demonstrations at the World Trade Organization meeting in Seattle were organized heavily via the Internet. Protests at the 2001 G8 Summit in Genoa, Italy, a meeting of the eight largest industrial nations, reflected discontent in Europe, leading organizers to move future international meetings to less accessible locations. Protests were benign compared with the terrorist attacks in the United States, Madrid, London, and around the world. Globalization was blamed for slow growth in developed countries and tightened national security. Overtly socialist regimes returned to Latin American countries such as Venezuela and Bolivia, which then nationalized industries. Peace became the exception, as the world faced skirmishes and wars in the Middle East and central Asia, an increasingly unpopular and costly U.S. war in Iraq, a growing nuclear threat from Iran, and a pugilistic regime in Russia harking back to cold-war politics. Some analysts posited a dire "clash of civilizations" between the West and the Muslim world.

Public concern about capitalism was fueled not just by populist politicians and the media but by the actions of a handful of visible companies as well. Corporate accounting scandals discredited capitalism from within. Enron's fast rise and the lionization of its executives in the 1990s, and then equally big crash, became the emblem for corporate crime. Revelations of excesses and misdeeds at Tyco and World-Com in the United States, Parmalat in Italy, Samsung in South Korea, and others around the world were followed by a tightening of regulations and accounting standards. Following the October 2008 global financial meltdown that began with the U.S. subprime mortgage lending crisis, even tighter government control returned.

Meanwhile, as America recovered from recession following the 2000–1 dot-com crash and the terrorist attacks of September 11, 2001, emerging markets became contenders, not just customers and suppliers. Countries such as Brazil, India, and China became sites for high-value-added production of goods and services, not just sources of cheap physical labor. Increasingly well-educated populations in developing countries began to compete for high-skill jobs with developed countries. Companies from the United States and Europe signed up manufacturing plants in China or outsourced data processing and call centers to India, whose business process outsourcing industry boomed.

The United States, which had been producing over half of all of the world's doctorates in science and engineering, lost global share of technology talent production. By the mid-2000s, American institutions of higher education conferred only 22 percent of these doctoral degrees, many of which were earned by foreign nationals. Technology engineering talent and management expertise were increasingly found in developing countries, and multinational companies no longer had to rely on expatriates to staff their operations outside of their home countries. Emerging champions from developing countries could beat multinational companies on their home territory, without special government protection. For example, ICICI Bank evolved from a government-sponsored development bank to a major retail banking force, holding the number-one share in branches and deposits in India, outcompeting established global banks like Citibank, HSBC, and Standard Chartered.

Companies emanating from emerging markets, including many in the vanguard, made high-profile acquisitions in mature markets of North America and western Europe. Starting in 2000, Cemex from Mexico acquired, in rapid succession, an American company, a pan-European company, and then an Australian international giant, quadrupling its size within a few years. In 2005, Lenovo, a company from China, bought IBM's worldwide personal computer business and its famous ThinkPad brand, giving engineers in North Carolina a new set of Chinese bosses. Mittal Steel bought Europe's Arcelor in 2006, becoming the world's largest steel company, even after fierce French opposition and dismissal of Mittal as "a company of Indians" by Arcelor's then CEO. South Africa Brewing bought Miller Breweries in the United States ("the beer that made Milwaukee famous"). MTN of South Africa bought regional mobile telecommunications providers to become a giant operating in twenty-two countries in Africa and the Middle East. In 2008, Tata Motors of India bought Jaguar and Land Rover, former British icons, from Ford Motor Company, the best performer among America's troubled auto companies.

* * *

THESE CHALLENGES COVER a broad range and include technological developments, economic volatility, cross-border mergers and acquisitions, global industry consolidation, the rise of emerging market countries, and public pressure for corporate responsibility. All this is just a sample of the forces, counterforces, surprises, disruptions, and role reversals that make global change both a threat and an opportunity.

The pressures can seem so far away, yet they are experienced by professionals and managers every day in companies of all kinds. Complex interdependencies link the fate of companies across the business ecosystem, as we shall see with the story of Digitas, a small, entrepreneurial, technology-centered company in my hometown of Boston, Massachusetts. Dependent for its livelihood on the fate of large-company customers who were themselves struggling with change, this small company was hit with successive mini-tsunamis, starting with the dot-com crash and continuing through the challenges of globalization. How Digitas responded and adapted is a real-time case study of how the vanguard model provides the ability for a business to adapt in a time of continuous, almost violent change.

One can read the Digitas story with anxiety about what will happen next or relief that mastering change is possible. During its early years, Digitas employees had both reactions, sometimes at the same moment.

"digital with gravitas": experiencing change

DIGITAS IS A COMMUNICATIONS company specializing in marketing through new media channels. Founded in Boston as a reinvention of a previous company in 1998, at the peak of exuberance about American-style free-market capitalism, Digitas endured even while nearly every one of the assumptions of its founding era changed.

The Digitas name was chosen to suggest "digital" with "gravitas." Its founders wanted it to be the digital marketing provider for mature corporate giants. Digitas was created from a combination of the traditional and the new. Its formation integrated Bronner Slosberg, a direct mail marketing company, and Strategic Interactive Group, an offshoot of Bronner formed by Kathy Biro in 1995 to tap the power of the Web. Biro, whom I met when she was creating SIG, was among a handful of highly respected women Internet pioneers. David Kenny joined Bronner as CEO at the end of 1996 from a management consulting firm, replacing Michael Bronner, the original entrepreneur. Kenny became integrator-in-chief, changing the company's direction as well as the name. It was an exciting, heady time. Digitas's youthful employees coaxed veterans in sluggish giants to make internal changes better suited to the digital age, including collaboration and coordination across siloed business units.

Digitas's sleek modern headquarters, on nine floors of a high-rise building across from the Boston Stock Exchange, still exudes high-tech savvy and creative energy. Signs for a Digiperks *Wheel of Fortune* show employees what their hard work might win them, such as a new car, a cruise, or tickets to their favorite sporting event. One can find Digitas in-house videos on YouTube, including a Chicken McNugget–eating competition (featuring teams of two, an eater and a sauce handler).

The Digitas culture, and leaders who watch over that culture, are about the only aspects that remain the same since 1998. The wild ride of Digitas through the ups and downs of ten years of global change personifies the challenges faced by professionals and managers across industries. Some of this was even more extreme for Digitas, putting the issues in sharp relief. But the Digitas story also shows why, in fact, culture and values are the best hope for surviving and flourishing despite business tsunamis.

TAKING OFF INTO TURBULENCE

Digitas thought big from the start, opening U.S. offices in Boston, Chicago, Miami, New York, San Francisco, and Salt Lake City and international offices in London, Brussels, and Hong Kong. Talented professionals and managers were recruited to augment the founding team, such as Laura Lang, who had been running a marketing consulting firm in Connecticut. The capital markets supported this approach, and the fledgling company took off. In March 2000, two years after its founding, Digitas had an initial public offering, opening at $30 per share, which was considered a high valuation of a small services company. Digitas stock reached a high of $40 per share.

But after a slowdown in technology investment, the powerful wave crashed in 2001, destroying almost all of that financial value. In the fourth quarter of 2001, following the dot-com downturn and the terrorist attacks in New York City, Digitas stock fell to a low of 88 cents. "That was a bad day," David Kenny deadpanned later.

The dot-com crash was then the worst financial crisis since 1987. Digitas leaders had bet on the gravitas side of its name, feeling that targeting big customers would insulate it from a downturn in pure Internet companies. But the effects were felt everywhere, even before the shocks of September 11, bringing New York and much of America to a standstill.

The culture was all Digitas had to rely on to get through the bad weeks and months. Kenny needed to summon the will to keep going despite the damage following disasters. "What was really important then," Kenny said, "was to realize that markets might be perfect over time in theory, but on any one day, they were probably wrong."

So Kenny focused on the human element. Every Saturday, Kenny recorded a five-minute "radio address" for staff that was transmitted through voice mail. In an e-mail culture, it signaled importance to use voice and made people feel connected with top leaders. He hit the highlights and made it clear that he knew what was going on. Otherwise, fear would paralyze people. He built trust and confidence. He would tell employees whether he anticipated layoffs; sometimes this made some people's lives difficult, but it also eliminated any suspicions that there were hidden decisions and second agendas. One message involved the importance of quality. People in production functions at lower levels in the organization were surprised and pleased that top leaders actually knew what they did and that it mattered, that their jobs made a difference. Employees in Chicago and London for whom Boston was a remote, impersonal headquarters stopped worrying that people in Boston were told things that they in dispersed locations did not hear. That was also a first step in moving away from the idea of a single all-powerful center.

Kenny received the most feedback from the recording he sent two weeks after the September 11 attacks, to soothe concerns about whether it was safe to travel. He spoke from his seat on an airplane as he was about to fly to London. In the background, listeners could hear the flight attendant's announcement that the door was about to be closed. Kenny's message was reassuring: that you can show up, it is not too bad, that if the leader is not afraid to go, you can take the first trip after 9/11. Many Digitas employees liked that message. One told Kenny that he played the voice mail for his wife, to reassure her that he would be safe.

Inevitably, the recession that followed required painful changes. Kenny and other Digitas leaders downsized the company. They closed two of the three international offices, reduced activities outside of Boston and New York, and cut nearly one-third of the workforce. But they knew that doing the same things with fewer people would not ensure survival, let alone success. Digitas had to master evolving technology and rethink its customer base. The company was still less than four years old, but its business model already required massive change.

TECHNOLOGY TURBULENCE: EVOLVING TOWARD SOCIAL NETWORKING AND MOBILITY

The Internet itself was evolving into what was soon dubbed Web 2.0, a more interactive and networked version of the Internet that puts much more control over generation and dissemination of content in the hands of users. Web 2.0 vastly amplifies the voices of people who want to go directly to other people to make something happen; it is a highly empowering, democratizing force that allows ideas to surface and networks to form spontaneously.

Digitas not only had to learn how to use this new technology, but it had to make a shift in mind-set from American domination of the IT industry. At the dawn of the global information age, the important new computer and software companies were largely American; Microsoft was founded in 1975, Apple in 1977, Oracle in 1977, and Cisco in 1984. The much older IBM hit troubled times at the end of the 1980s, hiring its first outside CEO in 1993, who quickly moved IBM toward software and services. Only the German enterprise software company SAP rivaled the all-American team. Well into the 2000s, American companies are disproportionately represented among successful growth companies, with Google the leading example but Facebook an echo of the 1990s Internet start-ups in college dormitories.

Digitas cultivated multiple relationships with important technology companies, which served as a significant vehicle for keeping up with technology trends and considering their implications. Rather than trying to combine services with technology, the way Digitas competitors such as Aquantive did in buying Avenue A, which means betting on particular technological directions, Digitas preferred to understand trends that would help it choose the best partners for the situation. Executives from Microsoft and Yahoo sat on the Digitas board, as did Paul Sagan, CEO of Akamai, a Boston start-up whose technology helped run the Internet faster. Digitas was a big customer for Google. In 2006, David Kenny decided to call Tim Armstrong in New York, who ran Google North America, to ask about Google's view of where technology was heading and how Google intended to support other parts of advertising. That conversation eventually led to discussions with Digitas at Google corporate headquarters in Mountain View, California. Kenny felt that the technological infrastructure was dragging down the potential for Internet communication, because there were many small pieces that did not scale well. He wondered how Google would solve that problem. Ultimately, Google sent people to work with Digitas on solutions.

The Google partnership aims to share technology and to embed talent within each other's organization. Unlike other industry executives, Kenny saw Google not as a direct competitor (called a "frenemy" or "froe" in the new parlance) but as a builder of "the New York Stock Exchange for advertising," which Digitas can serve as the most respected adviser and broker, helping direct digital marketing investments. If that example is hard to wrap one's mind around, consider it a reflection of the complex new world of the global information age, where everything is in play: Google bought DoubleClick, while Microsoft and Yahoo are buying advertising companies, and advertising companies are buying technology companies.

Other communications technology trends no longer tilt American. The exponential rise of mobile telephony has made it the world's most ubiquitous information technology, dwarfing the number of televisions, radios, and personal computers. In 2008, over half the world's population had a mobile phone, compared to one in eight in 2000. Over fifty countries had full penetration rates while China and India were home to the largest (and fastest growing) number of users, according to the International Telecommunication Union (www.itu.int). In Africa and Asia, mobile telephony is more important than the Internet, and applications outpace those in the United States. Internet usage rates are growing but are still well behind mobile telephones. Mobile phones have already begun to revolutionize banking in India, South Africa, and Kenya, a process that will continue with media convergence, as the lines among the Internet, telephones, and television increasingly blur.

As early as 2000, Digitas had felt mobile communications would be important. If information became untethered, and people could take it everywhere with them, information would flow more freely. David Kenny wrote an article for *Harvard Business Review* with John Marshall on what would happen when advertising was delivered on mobile devices. Digitas headquarters demonstrated this: A flat-screen monitor in the reception area signals that the company is on top of mobile phone trends. The on-screen message invites visitors to call a number on their cell phone. This connection turns the phone into a remote control to select from a menu of Digitas Web advertising videos, which visitors can view on the big screen or on their phone. Still, most of Digitas's work with mobile telephony occurs outside of the United States, with companies such as China Mobile.

Carrying Digitas through the technology waves is its emphasis on people—its employees and the ultimate users whom they see themselves as serving. Digitas bet not on particular technologies and not even on the right partners. Digitas was never defined as a technology company building websites, as were some of its long-gone competitors; it calls itself a services company applying technology to get messages to users. The company bets on employees' capacity to absorb new knowledge and to know what to absorb by watching closely the users of technology, not just the producers. People can be flexible and adaptive. Kenny observed, "What we really track are human beings. We are a technology company but focus on humans. If people struggle with what human beings will get from new technology, then that technology will not work. We are the interpreter of the technology. We were in the direct mail business when we started. Some of the direct mail people are still here. They learned."

MARKETPLACE TURBULENCE: GOING WHERE THE GROWTH IS

Between 2001 and 2004, Digitas derived half of its revenues from three major U.S. clients: General Motors, American Express, and

AT&T. This was a strategic choice, that it was better to have fewer, deeper customer or client relationships and do more for them than to supply a little bit to many customers. Digitas was not only reacting to global change, but it was also trying to help its clients master these changes, and that required being on top of the volatility in the global economy as well as knowing their clients' business deeply, from many vantage points. These clients were viewed by Digitas as having leaders who really believed in moving to digital marketing and had the scale to do it.

Reliance on these three big relationships was also a source of vulnerability. Their industries and the role of American companies in the world economy were changing dramatically, and Digitas's three clients were struggling themselves with industry changes. AT&T was rapidly becoming a weakened takeover target, whose name survived while the company was folded into SBC, but it was still a major advertiser. Laura Lang had originally joined Digitas to run the AT&T business. The troubled American auto industry was an even more questionable place to bet one's business as General Motors joined Chrysler in heading for losses so massive that another federal government bailout loomed.

David Kenny, Laura Lang, and the leadership team looked for other companies that could fit the model of deep Web-savvy relationships. Delta Airlines and Intercontinental Hotels became clients—both of which also had an international presence, which Digitas now deemed essential. Digitas also diversified to fit the "new" new economy, acquiring Modem Marketing in 2004, which helped broaden the client base. Digitas bought Modem for stock, and its own stock price took a hit. Although investors believed in Digitas's business model, there were concerns about whether it knew how to integrate a branding company less skilled in e-commerce. Digitas achieved cost synergies through consolidating backroom functions but otherwise integrated too slowly and did not get enough innovation out of the merger. The first time top professionals from the two companies got together was well after the acquisition, at an event at the old Ritz-Carlton Hotel in Boston at which, coincidentally, I was the lunch speaker, talking about confidence, a sweet spot between despair and arrogance. "We approached this with arrogance," Kenny recalled. "We thought that we were a better company, we'd help them. They rejected that."

The company's second, and only other, acquisition was Medical Broadcasting (MB), a health care marketing company in a growth industry, which later became Digitas Health. Kenny had long felt that health care and especially pharmaceuticals were naturals for the flexibility of the Internet, because people want information immediately when they are sick but tend not to care about it when they are well. The MB acquisition was a runaway success, in contrast to Modem, in part because Digitas treated it as almost a reverse takeover, a common phenomenon in vanguard companies. Digitas tried to understand what MB did better than Digitas—and then put all of Digitas's health-related business under the MB management team.

What kept Digitas going despite many moments of doubt and concern, at a time when other companies collapsed, was a consistent focus on creating value for its clients, which would bring in the cash. Kenny said of Laura Lang, for example, "She always believes in the vision, to create value for clients. Thick and thin, she will create value for them." The senior leadership team worked hard to say the same thing to everyone, so that investors, the board, management, and clients knew and believed the same things. Kenny said, "The companies that I saw folding had an imbalance. They spent too much time on the investors. It was more critical to get employees and customers aligned. Then investors will follow." Clients and major investors stuck with Digitas.

But Digitas was still small, still entrepreneurial, still primarily American. Kenny knew that a U.S.-dependent business was not sustainable; the firm needed a global presence quickly, especially in underserved growth markets ripe for sophisticated marketing models. Even before *New York Times* columnist Thomas Friedman declared that the world is "flat," Digitas leaders understood that they needed a presence in emerging growth markets much farther physically and culturally from Boston and New York than London. And Digitas could not compete effectively for the business of U.S. multinationals without a global presence and clout.

In 2005 and 2006, as global markets recovered from recession and digital investments were taking off again, Digitas was a market leader and was now a prize that others wanted to acquire. "If you talked to Microsoft, Yahoo, or Google, our name came up. People knew us viscerally or via their media planning groups," Kenny said.

Digitas was approached by acquisitive major advertising and marketing giants, which had been buying their way to worldwide reach and trying to reshape their mix to fit changing communications technology.

In 2007, after rejecting overtures from several communications conglomerates, Digitas agreed to be acquired by Publicis Groupe, the world's fourth-largest advertising and communications company, led by a visionary French executive, Maurice Lévy (who will be introduced more fully in chapter 5). Lévy saw advertising move from traditional media to new media and content being delivered in new ways, so he wanted Digitas as the centerpiece of Publicis's strategy for the future. That was ultimately why Kenny decided to sell Digitas—not because the board thought it needed to sell (although it was always an option to connect with a big network at the right time in order to become global and deal with media convergence) but rather because Digitas could become an even more significant shaper of change. "Honestly we didn't need to sell," Kenny said. "Other people wanted us because they wanted us in their collection, as just another arrow in their quiver. But Maurice wanted us to change his company."

WORKPLACE TURBULENCE: TOWARD GLOBAL MIND-SETS

By 2008, almost half of the senior leadership team had been with Digitas since the beginning. It is a company known for high standards—it is tough to get a foot in the door and equally tough to keep it there—and one that generates immense loyalty, even through change. The great opportunity Publicis Groupe represented to most Digitas employees—to enlarge their mission and perform on a much bigger stage—meant even more upheaval for others. The chief financial officer (CFO) and the general counsel, both of whom were essential actors in the sale to Publicis Groupe, knew that when this task was completed and the company sold, they would lose their jobs. There were tears in their eyes on the last day.

Some faces are gone, many others remain, but numerous new ones are encountered every day. For Digitas's Boston employees, the office building is the same, but work life has become more complex. Behind the front desk in Boston is a large screen with a continuous loop of photos of a diverse bunch of employees, first in formal portraits and amusing self-caricatures, including many women and people of numerous colors and ethnic facial features. Diversity inside the United States was always a Digitas concern out of a conviction that a creative mission requires people from different backgrounds to work together effectively. Sondra Sims-Williams, a sixteen-year veteran of Digitas and its predecessor company, Bronner Slosberg, has run the diversity effort since 2001, focusing on training managers to be better leaders. But encounters with global diversity present a new source of challenges.

As the result of the sale to Publicis, Digitas professionals and managers are under the direction of a French company, working alongside a dozen international agencies within the Groupe, and managing people, brands, and offices all over the world. In addition to staying ahead of constantly evolving Web technology, they must keep their eyes on more countries, more industries, and more cultural differences. They work closely with peers in France, Japan, China, India, and around the world whose companies were rebranded as Digitas shortly after the Publicis acquisition. Almost overnight, Business Interactif, which serves Europe, was rebranded Digitas France; Nihon Bi became Digitas Japan; and CCG, with offices in Beijing, Hong Kong, Shanghai, and Shenzhen, became Digitas Greater China. The new Digitas outsources digital production to "factories" in China, Ukraine, Costa Rica, Czech Republic, and India.

David Kenny has gone up a level to sit on the Publicis Groupe executive committee and oversee an evolving portfolio of digital offerings and a range of complex and continuously evolving partnerships. He is learning French by reading children's books. Laura Lang, former president of Digitas USA, is now CEO of the worldwide Digitas unit of Publicis Groupe.

Digitas senior executives are constantly on the move, flying to see clients and one another. Joe Tomasulo, the CFO, works three days in Boston and two days in New York and lives in Connecticut, where he keeps on working. Creative director Mark Beeching has his office in New York but shares a corner office when he is in Boston with chief operating officer Jim Rossman and has decided to live in London to manage international time zones more easily (and return to his native Britain). Those commutes are relatively easy compared with David

Kenny's frequent jaunts to China, India, and Europe. He and Maurice Lévy have visited nearly every Publicis location in the world.

ECOSYSTEM TURBULENCE: COMPANIES, COMMUNITIES, AND PARTNERS

The same winds of change that pushed Digitas to sell to a larger international company blew Gillette, an early Digitas client, to the altar with Procter & Gamble in 2006. Now, through their new owners and the even bigger networks to which they belong, Digitas and Publicis are even more tightly connected in many more places.

Gillette was an established century-old Boston-headquartered global company that had just completed a five-year turnaround under CEO Jim Kilts. Kilts had been a client of David Kenny's in his former post as CEO of Kraft; he enhanced Gillette's digital presence and expanded the Digitas role just as Digitas was trying to diversify beyond its big three clients of the 2001–4 period. P&G was already much larger and over 170 years old; after adding Gillette, P&G became the world's largest consumer products company and one of the world's largest advertisers. A long-standing client of Publicis Groupe agencies, P&G now became a Digitas client as well. Digitas is among the business partners credited for helping P&G win a major international award at the global marketing festival in Cannes, France, in May 2008, via a humorous mini-website, www.thankstoallouragenciesfor helpinguswinadvertiseroftheyear.com.

Even more than other businesses, Digitas is aware not only of the interconnections among the parts of company networks but also the shock waves reverberating from the backlash against global capitalism, fueled by the empowerment and voice made possible by the Internet and digital communications technology. Digital messaging can (and some say *must*) be used to create online communities that benefit real communities in many places.

In 2007, Digitas worked with American Express, one of its early big three U.S. clients, on the company's Members Project, a good example of widespread digital involvement that could be harnessed to solve global problems. The Members Project website drew 1.5 million unique visitors to submit and view seven thousand project ideas for nonprofit innovations that could receive a grand prize of up to several million dollars depending on the votes of American Express cardholders registering on the site. (I was on the advisory committee.) In a small-world coincidence with no nepotism involved, the $2 million winner was Children's Safe Drinking Water (CSDW), a nonprofit initiative started by P&G to improve health in developing countries. P&G's partners in establishing CSDW included United Nations agencies such as UNICEF; U.S. government agencies such as the Centers for Disease Control and Prevention; and nonprofit organizations such as Care, AmeriCares, and Samaritan's Purse International Relief. This mirrors the broad coalitions with which IBM was involved for disaster relief, as described in chapter 1. Coming full circle, P&G donated water purification packets after the tsunami under the CSDW umbrella. IBM is also a Digitas client; Digitas will be involved in helping form communities to further IBM's Smarter Planet initiative.

This reflects the new way companies must respond to global change. They must use their power not to bully people into buying but rather to influence them to join networks for the greater good, in which their voices can be heard. David Kenny, who has made a fast rise from local entrepreneur to global statesman, said, "I am a big believer in generosity, but if companies do things for the wrong reason, for example, just to sell products, it backfires. You cannot sell things anymore because digital empowers people to make their own choices. So we should be generous. If you are not generous with empowered people, they will not choose you. This leads you eventually to generosity to community. Generosity breeds returns." Kenny also thinks that generosity will solve the current financial crisis or, at least, that values will be rewarded. Indeed, in September 2008, while financial markets were starting to crash and fear gripped New York City, Publicis Groupe CEO Maurice Lévy met with United Nations officials to initiate pro bono work on the UN's campaign to address climate change.

THE DIGITAS LANDING after the crash was softened a bit because company leaders tried never to let arrogance into the culture; when it started to appear, they beat it back. They had genuine admiration for their large company clients, and they were willing to learn. "Better talent always wins," Kenny reflected. "We want to create an environment where people achieve their own potential. Digitas is known as a hard place to get hired into and a hard place to stay in. Good talent will adapt to the environment. We want people confident enough in themselves to deal with the changes around them. Through all of these changes, what really matters is an institution that exists to support the people."

leadership for turbulent times

THROUGHOUT THE UPS and downs of the global information age, while companies such as Digitas have faced its new realities, countless scholars and practitioners have called for a new management paradigm, a new way for leaders to lead and companies to operate. As the world becomes more globally connected, assumptions that used to guide organizations are rapidly being consigned to the trash bin of history. Boundaries that kept things simple and contained are being breeched. Organizational structures are flattening, and hierarchies are giving way to networks. Differences among people who were kept at arm's-length are now visible, vocal, and potentially contentious. Organizations can no longer be engineered from the top as impersonal machines that, once cranked up, just keep running. And a market logic of profit maximizing is starting to be joined by a social logic of good citizenship.

Vanguard companies, including Procter & Gamble, IBM, Publicis Groupe, and the others described in this book, are responding to four general forces.

- *Uncertainty and volatility.* There is frequent, rapid, unexpected change. Everything about a company is subject to change—its business model, product lines, customer base, partner network, and ownership—and that holds true for everything it touches. System effects send ripples that spread to more places faster, with innovations in one place proving disruptive in others, problems in one economy triggering problems in others. There is even uncertainty about the next source of risk, as evidenced in October 2008, when the biggest financial crisis since the Great Depression began in the United States and spread throughout the world instantaneously.

- *Complexity.* The loosening of boundaries internally and externally, including greater geographic scope for transactions and interactions, means that there are many variables in play simultaneously, and many moving parts, which connect and disconnect frequently—and that includes projects as well as alliances and mergers. There is a rapid flow of people, money, and ideas in and around organizations. There are more choices and also more competition. There is more information accessible to more people about more things.

• *Diversity.* Overall, there is greater heterogeneity, even in the midst of homogenizing forces of global interconnectedness, such as pressures for a single set of rules or the primacy of the English language. As people communicate across places and move physically among them, identities rooted in culture, community, and nation as well as gender or race become more salient as people encounter differences. With broader geographic scope comes a greater variety of people and organizations in contact and more dimensions of difference noticed among them, especially as roles are reversed, and those once called "developing" leap ahead of the "developed" with advanced applications of innovations.

• *Transparency and responsibility.* There are pressures for transparency and accountability coupled with the digital tools to achieve it. There are higher expectations for conduct combined with greater cynicism about whether high standards are met. There is comparison across places. For companies, successful globalization often means localization—that is, recognizing the differences that matter to people in particular places and contributing to accomplish the public agenda. These contributions may be for humanitarian reasons; some may be pragmatic and political, to gain the goodwill of government officials, for example; and some may stem from a desire to be part of, not apart from, the communities where employees live as well as work.

Taken together, the trends and tendencies I have outlined in this chapter represent forces that cannot be ignored or reversed by the actions of individual companies. They spread through the local ecosystem via the interactions among companies across their extended family of suppliers, distributors, customers, and investors in complex, overlapping relationships. This becomes a self-fueling dynamic. Globalization adds pressure on companies to be global—"world class"—in orientation, sourcing, and standards, if not market scope. Smaller organizations such as Digitas feel that they will thrive best by joining global networks. Professionals and managers feel the pressure in their travel schedules, work hours, time zone awareness, and knowledge requirements.

All companies must respond to uncertainty, complexity, diversity, and responsibility with new business models and new ways of working. For vanguard companies, that model starts with values and principles, which provide a guidance system that helps them make strategic choices with an eye on long-term institution building, generate high levels of innovation using a wide societal lens, and integrate acquisitions quickly and effectively. Vanguard companies also strive for flexible workplaces that reward self-organizing employees, deal with diversity by expressing differences but seeking a basis for unity, and engage in community projects and public diplomacy that raise standards and address unsolved societal problems.

Success in the face of rapidly changing technology and globalization of markets requires more than mere expertise and a good product; it requires an underlying organizational framework and leadership style enabling mastery of constant change in a world where more is expected of businesses and businesses expect more of their employees.

Some people and their companies will be distracted or paralyzed by the successive waves and occasional tsunamis that wash over them; they will find it difficult to cope, let alone survive. In contrast, the winners will find that this is exactly the time to make transformational changes—as long as they are guided by values, principles, and a humanistic approach that provide grounding and guidance in the midst of turbulence.

part two

strategy and business

chapter three

standing on principles: strategic priorities and a values-based guidance system

SOMETIMES THE TRUE test of whether a strategy will be implemented is not the big idea or the grand gesture but something as simple as the condition of the alley next door. Just one filthy, abandoned alley, adjacent to Banco Real's headquarters tower in central São Paulo, Brazil, stood between the bank's compelling strategic vision and employees' belief in whether it could be realized. The alley was the shadow between idea and execution.

The alley issue arose in 2001, nearly three years after Banco Real began its ultimately successful journey to global prominence, moving into the vanguard in Brazil and the world. In 1998, Fabio Barbosa, a Brazilian who had worked in the United States and Europe, became CEO after Banco Real's merger with the Dutch global bank, ABN AMRO. It was a year that saw many international banking investments in Brazil as the economy liberalized and the financial sector consolidated. Banco Real had been founded in 1925 as a farmers' cooperative. By 1998, it had a solid but not extensive retail presence, with 726 branches and 716 subbranches in other facilities; 17,331 employees; and over 2 million retail customers, to which ABN AMRO's 50 branches and 5,000 employees were added, but it was not among the major banks.

Barbosa had big dreams: to become the biggest and best by building a new culture and a new identity in the marketplace. Banco Real competed with banks that were much bigger and had better IT systems, lower cost funding due to the scale of their retail networks, stronger brand recognition, and longer experience with state-of-the-art practices such as customer segmentation. That was a formidable business test in a nation that also experienced severe challenges of persistent poverty and environmental degradation, including the threats to the Amazon River and rain forest. Barbosa looked into himself to see what he cared about, and he looked at Brazil's political, economic, and social climates. He saw a way to combine these. Banco Real could be differentiated by basing its business strategy on values of social and environmental responsibility.

In informal Wednesday brainstorming sessions for nearly a year, Barbosa, COO Jose Luiz Majolo, human resources executive Maria Luiza Pinto, and about five other bank leaders challenged themselves to think creatively about mission, management model, and brand, with occasional external consultants to provoke them. The discussions themselves were a sign that Barbosa, with his beard and twinkling eyes, was a different kind of leader, approachable, friendly, and open to ideas, certainly not an authoritarian paterfamilias like many CEOs in the region. Talk roamed over many topics, from the physical environment to problems of poverty to employment policies. Some executives participated in a seminar organized by a nongovernmental coalition, including Friends of the Earth and the International Finance Corporation, the World Bank's private branch. Eventually, the concept of *banco de valor* (bank of value) took shape. The leaders chose to emphasize "value creation" as the bank's distinctive theme, encapsulating it in a mission statement emphasizing clients, stockholders, employees, and communities. They were banking on sustainability.

"Behind all those sometimes incoherent ideas, we were guided by the feeling that we were creating something different," Barbosa observed. "We wanted to put aside the thought that social responsibility could only be obtained through philanthropy, which lessens difficult situations but does not overcome problems. Our focus had to be strategic, with corporate responsibility seen as doing the right thing in a systematic way. In other words, to do the right thing right."

Numerous self-assessments were conducted to determine what was strategic and "right." In 2001, a self-evaluation based on social responsibility parameters developed by the Ethos Institute helped the bank to identify environmental risks, including its sponsorship of Formula 1 races, outdoor displays in environmental protection areas, and the illegal artesian pond supplying water for its head office. In May 2001, a report was issued, "A New Bank for a New Society," which explained the bank of value concept and identified initiatives already under way that exemplified it. Maria Luiza Pinto became the first head of the new Sustainability Directorate, supported by three management committees; the directorate was meant to be a "biodegradable department," which would go out of existence when the new strategy was fully embedded in the culture and operations.

That is how the alley next door came into the picture. Abandoned alleys symbolize many social problems. Downtown São Paulo is a traffic-congested jumble of buildings sometimes surrounded by rubble and trash. At that time, less than 10 percent of Brazil's wastewater was treated and up to 40 percent of the country's solid waste (forty thousand tons a day) was not collected. In São Paulo, transportation costs consumed one-fifth of a poor person's income and more than 2.5 hours a day in commuting time, according to World Bank data. Crime plagued the 82 percent of people who lived in Brazil's cities; Rio de Janeiro reputedly had among the world's highest murder rates. In fact, on my first visit to Banco Real headquarters, I was not allowed anywhere near alleys of any kind and never touched the pavement on a street. The bank sent a helicopter and security guards to the international airport to meet me; we landed on the roof of the building, where new guards took over escort duties.

The alley in question was just beside the bank and known as a base for thugs and drug dealers. One of the bank directors pointed it out at a meeting, arguing that employees would never embrace the bank's goals if that alley remained a dangerous eyesore. This did not seem as big an issue initially as, say, major financing projects in the Amazon region. But it was important just the same. It was a test of commitment to the values and a chance for them to take concrete, tangible form. The first big decision was not to turn to the police, who would have said it is someone else's problem, but instead to take responsibility as a bank. The next was to use this opportunity to involve employees and the local community to effect change from the grassroots and ground up, literally as well as figuratively. The bank invested, and people volunteered. A garden was created, pavement and lighting were replaced, and two kiosks were installed that could employ teenagers from low-income families. The street was made safe and pleasant.

"From that point on, we knew what had to be done," a bank leader said. "If each one of us makes changes to the alley next door, we can change the world."

A second incident, widely discussed by bank managers and employees, turned the idea of values at the heart of business strategy from an abstraction on a poster to an operating reality. Culture change is a slow process. It takes time to transmit the message from high-level brainstorming sessions of eight executives to more than twenty thousand employees, and many employees did not immediately understand or embrace the values. Here is what happened: A bank employee sold to a seventy-year-old gentleman (an age not far below Brazil's life expectancy) a bond that would not mature for decades and that would incur a loss if cashed early. When the customer's family found out about this, they took to the Internet to denounce the bank's lack of ethical professionalism. Managers quickly canceled the transaction, but the harm was done. The "bond after death" became an often-repeated lesson in the bank as training to instill new values and principles got under way: It is better to lose a deal than a relationship. Responsibility means knowing about the whole system surrounding a customer and taking responsibility for consequences.

Fabio Barbosa reflected, "We could not possibly build a brand focused on customer satisfaction, social responsibility, and environmental sustainability if we did not experience the new culture—that is, if we inside the bank did not work on our own conduct first. From this point on, we knew that we would examine our own practices before associating ourselves with good causes." And, he added later, actions had to be initiated not just at the top but from anywhere in the organization and in collaboration with external stakeholders.

Banco Real's next steps show what needs to be done to become a vanguard company. Abundant training and discussion disseminated the principles widely to thousands of managers within the company and opened minds to new issues, such as climate change or the credit problems afflicting the poor, which in turn stimulated new thinking.

That paved the way for a range of new banking products to be developed, which opened new and profitable lines of business. Special loans were made available for environmental upgrades to cars or homes. Microlending in the poor favelas in São Paulo helped small business entrepreneurs, such as a video store owner and a diaper shop proprietor who had been previously ignored by banks but were reliable customers for Banco Real. The average term was seven months, and the default rate was only 4 percent, compared with a 7 percent rate for banks in general. An "ethical" mutual fund drew new investors (though it raised some managers' eyebrows—did this mean that regular funds were somehow less than ethical?). As a sign of environmental leadership, Banco Real was the first in the region to trade carbon credits.

Implementing the new strategy could not be accomplished by internal actions alone; relationships with external stakeholders had to be changed, and they also had to be educated about societal needs and challenges. To ensure societal impact and consistency with the values, the bank took end-to-end responsibility for customers' and suppliers' actions as well as its own. Managers developed new tools to assess environmental and social performance, which could be used with customers and suppliers. Loan officers screened customers on the environmental impact of the projects for which they were seeking financing and either helped them to raise standards or walked away from the transaction. Some customers began to request the help.

Suppliers became a focus when bank executives using the private parking garage at headquarters noticed a group of employees from the external cleaning service having lunch amid smoke from car exhausts. Jose Luiz Majolo, the COO, recalled, "It was unacceptable for us to think that this was the responsibility of the hired company and not of us, the contractor. How could we develop relationships with companies that degraded the environment, used child labor, or did not pay their Social Security taxes?" The bank convened suppliers of all sizes, from giant IBM to small bicycle messengers and asked for their help meeting higher standards, especially as the bank undertook its own recycling and workforce diversity programs and insisted on strong labor practices. In fact, the first time that suppliers were invited to a meeting at the bank, an atmosphere of anxiety pervaded the room because the suppliers had automatically assumed that Barbosa was going to tell them that Banco Real was cutting suppliers or lowering the prices it would pay. Instead, he told them they would work together to improve conditions in Brazil. As a result of one of those meetings, several suppliers got together on their own to help a secondary school with technology.

The bank issued reports on social and environmental responsibility, which is now standard fare for good companies. But there was one difference. The CEO, Barbosa, was accessible to critics. He talked openly with customers questioning bank practices, and the transcript was published in one of the reports.

All this helped retain current customers and attract new customers and investments. For example, in 2004, the World Bank took the unusual step (a first for Brazil) of granting U.S. $51 million to the bank to lend for socioenvironmental and corporate governance improvements. This was an enormous sign of trust in the wisdom and values of Banco Real's leaders.

Ten years after Fabio Barbosa and his team put their values-infused strategy in place, Banco Real was growing fast and profitably, increasing net profit 20 percent per annum between 2001 and 2006, outpacing all of its big-bank competitors in percentage return on equity. On surveys of the public, Banco Real scored number one in "brand awareness" and was neck and neck with a larger bank for the top slot in "brand attractiveness." In 2007, Barbosa was elected president of the Brazilian banking federation, an acknowledgment of his reputation, leadership skills, and new vision for the banking industry.

In June 2008, in recognition of how far the bank had come and how much it had accomplished on the world stage in setting world standards, Banco Real received a major global award. Edging out 129 institutions across fifty-four countries, Banco Real was named the Sustainable Bank of the Year by the *Financial Times* and the World Bank's International Finance Corporation.

Meanwhile, global industry consolidation continued in the financial sector, and Banco Real's European parent was caught in the cross fire. ABN AMRO's global assets had been sold to a consortium in April 2007, with Banco Real and its stellar financial performance considered a stand-alone prize. Banco Real's merger partner was Santander from Spain, which also had a Brazilian banking presence. But rather than subsuming Banco Real under the Santander umbrella, the opposite occurred. Fabio Barbosa was named head of Grupo Santander, and he continued to lead Banco Real as the surviving entity and brand. Banco Real absorbed Santander Brazil, adding twenty-five thousand new people to the thirty thousand Barbosa already led. The goal is to infuse Banco Real values and culture through the combined entity.

Banco Real continues to build "a new bank for a new society," reinforcing the role of banks and businesses as agents for economic and social development. But Barbosa also makes clear that Banco Real is not a "green bank" in the charitable sense. Banco Real is a profit-making enterprise that happens to be guided by societally oriented humanistic principles that are also smart business strategy, pervading every aspect of the business.

the strategic value of values: a new guidance system

ANY COMPANY can say it has values, but what Banco Real did was to embed them in business practice and make them credible to the skeptics inside and outside of their walls. Vanguard companies go beyond the lists of values posted on walls and websites by using their codified set of values and principles as a strategic guidance system. They gain business advantages from actions they take based on the societal responsibility these statements imply, as Banco Real does, both in terms of external constituencies in their extended family of partners and stakeholders and with regard to their employees.

After outlining some of the strategic uses by vanguard companies of their new or renewed values and principles, I will turn to exactly what is involved in transmitting them to people in the organization so that they internalize and use them in practice.

For vanguard companies, grounding strategy—which businesses to pursue and how—in a sense of wider societal purpose provides many significant advantages and only a few potential disadvantages. Values and principles of this sort not only speak to high standards of conduct but also stretch the enterprise beyond its own formal boundaries to include the extended family of customers, suppliers, distributors, business partners, financial stakeholders, and the rest of society. Vanguard companies gain both a moral compass and an entire guidance system.

The range of advantages for vanguard companies through their strategic use of values and principles include the following.

• *Competitive differentiation.* The Banco Real case shows how an emphasis on purpose and principles builds specific lines of business as well as building the brand. Of course, success means that competitors might start emulating particular initiatives, and that happened in Brazil too. But that merely raises the bar. The clear sense of purpose provides a wellspring that can produce the next wave of activity. Those who attempt to copy the strategy without having the underlying core principles in place will always be behind the vanguard.

• *Public accountability via end-to-end responsibility.* Societal purpose and values help meet an emerging public demand that companies know about, care about, and report about everything that goes into their products and services, from sources (e.g., labor conditions in paper plants where company stationery is manufactured) to applications and ultimate fate (e.g., how used computers are disposed of). Whether this is called acknowledgment of multiple stakeholders or ecosystem consciousness, greater contact across the value chain and especially with end users builds the company brand and triggers opportunities for innovation.

• *Rationale for thinking long-term.* Sustainability is more than a buzzword for vanguard companies, and it means more than being "green." Values and principles help them create continuity through time, from past successes and traditions to present goals to future visions and changes. They become institutions that have meaning beyond the current bundle of assets or lines of business. That is important in a world of change. Values and principles help vanguard companies avoid "short-termism" and make choices with an eye on the future. "Management is temporary; returns are cyclical," IBM CEO Sam Palmisano said, explaining to me why he puts so much emphasis on values and culture. IBM is the sole survivor among the other major computer companies prominent in 1975; it has entered and exited businesses, but it is recognizably the same institution.

• *Common vocabulary and guidance for consistent decisions.* The need for fast decisions and actions in far-flung or differentiated operations makes principles an essential decision-making guide. Clear articulation of values and principles helps employees choose among alternatives in a consistent manner. "One Cemex, we are only one Cemex," CEO Lorenzo Zambrano declared to me. The Mexican company is one of the world's top cement makers. At the time I met Zambrano, it had doubled its size by acquiring a large European company and was about to do it again by buying an Australian global company. Zambrano viewed clear core values and standards as an important element of success, particularly as Cemex expanded quickly overseas through acquisitions starting in the 1990s. Via the Cemex Way, a set of "best practice" principles and processes developed over the years to help people succeed in the Cemex family, the company disseminated its culture across its increasingly far-flung global network. "We know that high standards have to be applied everywhere."

• *Talent magnets and motivation machines.* Talented people with many options are increasingly attracted to companies and stay there because of compatible values. Banco Real became one of Brazil's most desirable employers for top college graduates; P&G and IBM also get the best in highly competitive labor markets because of their reputations and values. "At first, we thought of our reputation conceptually, as something that we needed to keep improving. Now we know it affects our ability to attract the right people. After all, businesses are a network of people working toward the same end. And everyone has to be proud of what they're doing," Zambrano said.

• *"Human" control systems—peer review and a self-control system.* In vanguard companies, belief in the purpose and embrace of the values generate self-guidance, self-policing, and peer responsibility for keeping one another aligned with the core set of principles. This kind of human control system does not work perfectly by itself, but it certainly reduces the need for rules and thus helps people feel autonomous.

Rather than feeling forced into conformity, employees feel that they are willful actors making their own choices based on principles they can support.

Not everything is good, true, and beautiful, of course. There are potential pitfalls. One is foolish choices, in which, for example, social commitments do not have an economic logic that sustains the enterprise by attracting resources. Another pitfall is the creation of heightened expectations that are difficult to fulfill, leading to disappointment when performance falls short of the ideal or cynicism about whether company leaders really believe the lofty words in their statements of values. The first issue raises the question of whether companies should have anything in mind other than immediate business considerations; the second suggests that companies cannot live up to their pronouncements anyway. Vanguard companies must be on guard against these extremes.

Moreover, obtaining strategic value from principles-based guidelines requires attention to the business itself. Values and principles may be invoked to shape approaches, but a "business case" is also important. To be strategic, an initiative must also contribute to the fundamental way the company makes money, with customers and clients in mind. That strategic use of principles based on end-to-end responsibility is illustrated by one of Cemex's international initiatives.

embracing the extended family: marrying commerce to communities at cemex

IN 2001, Cemex started Construrama, the brand name for a distribution program for small hardware stores, to counter competition from U.S. giants Home Depot and Lowes as they entered the Latin American market. This was strictly business, in response to a competitive threat. But the form of the response—a way to increase the sophistication of mom-and-pop enterprises and their communities—would not have been contemplated without the stimulus from Cemex values and principles. CEO Zambrano wanted all Cemex employees, even in the most remote outposts, to know and care about Cemex's core values—integrity ("acting with honesty, responsibility, and respect at all times"), leadership ("envisioning the future and focusing our efforts on service, excellence, and competitiveness"), and collaboration—and then behave in a way that reflected them.

When stores join the Construrama network, they get training, support, brand recognition, and easy access to business-enhancement products, such as the first computers and Internet access for these small enterprises. By mid-2004, this network in Mexico and Venezuela was the equivalent of the largest retail chain in Latin America, and it was expanding to other developing countries.

The business model for Construrama marries performance and social principles. Cemex seeks dealers with integrity who are trusted in their communities and are compatible with Cemex values. Cemex rejects high-growth/high-margin candidates whose business tactics do not meet Cemex ethical standards. Cemex owns the Construrama brand and handles promotion but does not charge distributors, operate stores, or have decision-making authority, although service standards must be met. A partnership ethos surrounds the initiative; about a third of the Construrama management team at headquarters spend six to eight months working at the stores, and partners participate in councils on a rotating basis. "We believe that if they have a professional business, they will enjoy better returns than competing stores," said Construrama director Luis Fernando Lozano. "They can get out of the agreement whenever they want. We can get out of the agreement whenever we want. But at the end, it's a matter of trust. We are giving them tools to develop their business. They are loyal to us."

Helping small businesses succeed by training them in high standards and offering infrastructure is certainly a societal contribution but a conventional one. After all, these are distributors selling Cemex products in a commercial transaction. Vanguard companies extend their values outside corporate walls, and Cemex is no exception.

Cemex helps Construrama distributors reach end users through Construcard, a construction financing initiative launched with GE Capital in 2004 for low-income, do-it-yourself consumers without other financing options or collateral. Customers get an average credit line of $1,000, enough to build a nine-square-meter room. Over eighty thousand cards were issued in 2004 alone. That meant that at least eighty thousand low-income people were suddenly able to improve their housing. For some of them, the improvements included replacing dirt floors with cement floors, which brought significant health benefits, since dirt floors breed organisms associated with diseases.

When Cemex participates in community-building endeavors (e.g., by contributing human and material resources to expand an orphanage or improve a school), its values are disseminated to its Construrama partners.

When Cemex began the Construrama program, it expected the program would help it gain understanding and knowledge of its direct customers—the distributors. What was not expected, Fernando recalled, was that Construrama would also help Cemex grow closer to its customers' customers—the consumers—and help improve communities and lives for lower-income families. The societal sensitivity behind Construrama involves, Cemex leaders say, "understanding the last link in the value chain." This is not just a principled approach; it is smart business strategy.

finding twenty-first-century values: ibm votes with its keyboards

A HUNDRED YEARS, or even a few decades ago, when founders or top leaders of many of the companies I studied first voiced the values they wanted their companies to live by, the process was top directed, guided by a kind of benign paternalism company owners felt for their people. Early industrial capitalism in the United States, for example, was populated not only by robber barons who had to be reined in by populist regulators but also by company founders who built entire towns and shaped entire communities, such as the Houghton family who built Corning the company and Corning, New York, the town. Gradually, many of these close-knit locally based family-style enterprises, some of which grew large and international, found it difficult to maintain and enrich their cultures by long immersion or oral transmission alone.

The pushes and pulls of globalization, the addition of new people through acquisitions or hiring, the search for new markets in countries whose cultures veered to the corrupt, stock market short-termism, and the decline of lifetime employment even in Japan made oral traditions too slow and too easy to misunderstand or just miss. This triggered a desire by leaders, particularly in the 1990s and early 2000s, to find a new way to identify principles that could deal with new demands, such as diversity or the environment, without changing fundamental founding values. All of the vanguard companies in my project recently rewrote or strengthened their statements of values and principles using a participative process. For IBM, this was done in a particularly dramatic way.

IBM'S 140,000-PERSON VALUESJAM

IBM CEO Sam Palmisano's process for reinventing and reinvigorating IBM's values for the twenty-first century began with a dialogue on a scale beyond anything any company had ever done.

Successful transformation of a vanguard company starts with a conviction about what should never change. Since its founding in 1911, IBM has been known for a strong culture and a commitment to fairness and social responsibility, operating under a set of principles articulated by founder Thomas Watson. As IBM entered its second century, the time was right to take a fresh look while remaining unwavering in ethics, integrity, and—to use twenty-first-century terminology—the highest standards of corporate citizenship. By 2002, IBM had outlasted others prominent in the industry twenty-five years earlier, but from a business perspective it could hardly be considered the same company. Over the years, it had downsized or sold manufacturing operations (later selling its PC business and signature ThinkPad), grown in software and services, and emphasized the Internet over mainframes; it now has nearly as many employees in India as in the United States and is investing in all the BRIC nations—the new sobriquet for the growth markets of Brazil, Russia, India, and China. IBM has given itself a new identity as a globally integrated enterprise.

One of the early leadership actions that Sam Palmisano took when he became chairman and CEO in 2002 was to refresh the IBM values through a unique participative process involving a seventy-two-hour Web chat in July 2003 about what IBM stands for, open to over 350,000 IBMers in 170 countries if they chose to participate. All of this was done with strategic use of IBM technology and innovative methodologies.

When Palmisano first presented the plan to the IBM board, one of the directors, a former CEO in a conservative industry, questioned him about whether this was "socialism." Palmisano explained that this was the only way to build an enduring institution in which IBMers embraced and owned the values. "It wouldn't do to create values from the top, like Watson did; today people are too sophisticated, global, and cynical," he told me. "We want people to connect to the entity in a way that's relevant to them." He wanted people to have pride in IBM as an institution, not merely to be following the dictates of a leader: "To have a culture that connects people's success to the success of the entity, we have to be faceless. Then they have pride in the entity's success and will do what is important to IBM. Management is temporary; returns are cyclical. The values are the connective tissue that has longevity." An IBM sector director in Latin America concurred. "When you are working for the same company for twenty years, you need to be proud of it. The reason I wake up early every day to come to IBM is because this company has values that we really believe in. This is the reason I'm here, because I really believe in this company. I know we are doing good things for society. Of course we are a business, and we have our targets, but we can give other things. And we do it."

The massive scale of Palmisano's Web chat, or ValuesJam as it was called, required innovation, and it was also a test of the culture, because people could say what they thought. But negativity on some people's part was countered by many others who jumped in to correct them, in a classic example of peer policing. Noha Saleem, who ran software support for the Middle East from her home base in Dubai, did just that: "Someone had a problem with the [lack of] openness of management, so I commented and said, 'You cannot blame it on your manager; it's a two-way thing.'" Maybe Saleem did not change that person's mind, but she was one of many voices reminding the community that they were creating the future together.

Over 140,000 people participated in IBM's ValuesJam. A team took the results and eventually boiled them down to three overarching values:

Dedication to every client's success
Innovation that matters, for our company and the world
Trust and personal responsibility in all relationships

Veteran IBMers see continuity between the new statements and long-standing principles and slogans such as "Think." They also praise the process by which the new values were drafted. "Instead of top management telling us what to do, the new values externalized and made more explicit what was already engraved in the minds and hearts of the IBM community," observed Ayman Mashoor, head of quality in the Cairo technology lab. "The values have helped people to get emotionally connected," Palmisano said. After they were announced, he received messages amounting to three feet of paper printouts, which he took to a staff meeting.

The values appear everywhere, on the Web, on ubiquitous posters on walls and cubicle counters, and in training for leaders and new hires alike. IBMers report variability in how much managers refer to the values. Some never mention them. Other managers coach people on the values. Sergio Xavier de Brito, distribution sector director for Latin America, tries to blend the values into day-to-day situations for the people in his group across the region. When he visits a country, he meets with people individually or holds roundtable discussions, asking not about sales transactions but about the job. He then matches the situations they describe to the IBM values.

IBMers say that the values are relevant everywhere. In Russia, communications executive Igor Larin ran research to see how the Russian market thought about the "innovation that matters" value and found that innovation was desirable to everyone from customers and the public, pointing also to statements by the then president Putin. He also saw the internal benefits, saying that "values help us to feel ourselves as one company, and to understand the way we should behave and cooperate."

Jennifer Trelewicz, director of the Russia Lab who had moved there from the United States, was impressed at how quickly the values were picked up, citing the case of a native Russian member of her team who joined IBM only six months previously. "On same-time message with me, he was very distressed that one of the people on his team was not displaying passion for the client's business. He was quoting the values back at me." In India, because of rapid growth and a huge influx of new hires, there is still a long way to go to completely internalize the trust and personal responsibility value as well as dedication to clients' success, but an executive there concluded, "We have started to see that the values are foundational to our business. All three IBM values together give us competitive differentiation."

Wait a minute. Can all of that really happen because of three sentences? We all know that actions count, not words. How do the statements lead to actions? Understanding the way that values and principles are used is next on the agenda.

"it's not the words; it's the conversation": transmitting purpose and principles at omron

WHILE VANGUARD COMPANIES invest heavily in their statements of values and principles, there is little variety, and many sound alike. Companies that would not be considered in the vanguard also have values statements but garner little, if any, competitive advantage from them. So the strategic value clearly cannot come just from having a statement or posting a few morally high-minded sentences—and it does not. Despite the frequency with which people in the vanguard companies point to the values and principles as guiding their choices or selling their ideas, the words themselves do not actually tell anyone what to do in any specific situation.

In short, you cannot find the answers in the actual words, and the words do not prevent contention. People have heated arguments in vanguard companies, although they tend to resemble a late-night college dormitory debate about philosophy rather than a pitched political battle. Banco Real had over two years of conversations and conferences and then put support processes in place, before leaders felt comfortable describing their principles and strategy to the external world. The process was described as both "slower than what many had hoped for and deeper than what many believed it would be."

Then what is the value of values? It is the engagement, the dialogue, the conversation. Vanguard companies breathe new life into long-standing values statements by engaging multiple levels of employees in the institutional task of identifying and communicating values. They create and reinforce principles through active recitation and search for interpretation. The statements are not hung passively on the wall; they are internalized through inquiry.

The point is not the exact words themselves but the living process: to open a dialogue that keeps the sense of social purpose in the forefront of everyone's mind and then to use that as a guidance mechanism for business decisions. For Omron, a Japanese global electronics company, a formal statement of purpose and principles is credited with Omron's endurance, its capacity to change, and its ability to open conversations with multiple stakeholders—not because the Omron Principles sat in the background but because they were constantly updated and used as conversation-starters.

The stagnant Japanese economy and the 1997–98 Asian financial crisis had hurt Omron because of its dependence on both Japanese manufacturing customers who used its sensors and other components and on the Japanese government for its systems business, which created "smart card" entry for transportation systems. Yet, through its seventy-five years, Omron had weathered numerous business crises by sticking to credos laid down by founder Kazuma Tateisi as he rebuilt the company after Japan's defeat in World War II by updating them for the times. Omron's twenty-first-century leaders turned around the company by reinforcing Omron's values and principles.

A COMPASS THROUGH CHANGE: THE OMRON PURPOSE AND PRINCIPLES

Starting in 2002, CEO Hisao Sakuta led a restructuring of Omron that brought sustained profitability, growth, and leading world market shares in most lines of business. Between 2002 and 2007, profitability grew quickly; Omron reached its 2005 goals of 10 percent return on equity one full year early, and revenues ballooned to $6.3 billion by 2006. Most Omron business domains (the company identifies over eighty of them) are the world market leaders in their fields. Sakuta-san credits the Omron Principles for its effective change, not its rearranged business portfolio or technical engineering prowess. Indeed, he found the principles so useful that he decided to engage employees in updating them in 2005.

Omron's motto and corporate core value is working for the benefit of society: "At work for a better life, a better world for all." Its management principles—"challenging ourselves to always do better, innovation driven by social needs, and respect for humanity"—are further refined into management commitments and guiding principles for action. There is also a technology guidepost: "The best matching of man to machine."

The renewed principles were translated into twenty-five languages and transmitted through a massive communication process, which could have seemed a distraction from the managerial work of restructuring but proved instead to be the glue that helped Omron through its business ups and downs. Today, groups of employees begin each workday by reciting the core slogan; salespeople start conversations with customers by talking about the Omron Principles; and representatives invoke the principles first when meeting with companies they are vetting and courting for acquisition. Mentioning the values and principles is almost religious in its ritual quality and certainly spiritual in its nod to higher purpose.

Keiichiro Akahoshi, CEO of Omron's health care subsidiary, echoes the idea of endurance through change as a key aspect of the principles. He came to Omron thirty-five years earlier and stayed because of the values. He said, "Truthfully, I had no plans to become a Japanese salary-man, but I came to really like Omron. I can honestly say that not all of Omron is excellent, but the values give us a platform to improve the areas that are broken. The principles are very important to that process. They are not just words but rather something I have always felt I am living."

Like every statement of values and principles I have seen (and most religious texts), the words point to an orientation or an aspiration ("respect for people") rather than to a specific action in a specific circumstance. Omron leaders are well aware of this, and they talk explicitly about wanting the conversation, not rote obedience.

I asked Sakuta-san—through translators, while we were seated in a lounge on the executive floor in Kyoto headquarters—about how he expected the principles to improve the business and whether he felt that people used them consistently. He replied that he fully expects that thirty-five thousand people in Omron might have different interpretations of the principles—maybe thirty-five thousand different ones. But engagement and discussion is the important thing. "Whenever I speak with employees, I tell them your answer should not be a set answer. Please tell what you understand and how you can express it using the language of the principles," he said. "I also promote discussion among peers, colleagues, and teams to share these understandings with one another."

He puts this in terms of a distant horizon, which is certainly more typical of Japanese than American leaders: "No matter how different the workplaces are in terms of race, value sets, geographical locations, et cetera, as long as we can continue this debate and discussion, we are able to maintain our attractive and strong work environment and principles with a flexible attitude to respond to any changes to come in fifty, one hundred, two hundred, three hundred years."

Fifty years seems impossibly long to American ears, let alone three hundred years. A quick glance back at Omron's first seventy-five years shows how embedded visionary thinking is in the culture. Omron was founded in May 1933 as the Tateisi Electric Manufacturing Company. It became Omlon Tateisi Corporation in 1948, named after a district in Kyoto, Japan. In 1959, the name was changed to Omron, because that was more easily pronounced in foreign languages. That year, management legend Peter Drucker met the founder, Kazuma Tateisi, and was sufficiently impressed to write in a letter to his wife, "If this man lives, Japan will become a major economic power in no time." That same year, Kazuma-san was exposed to ideas about the responsibilities of business to society, and in 1960 he set forth Omron's motto and principles.

Kazuma-san also gathered a team of engineers to study history, performing mathematical analyses of what they saw as major innovative shifts over the past hundred thousand years. The result was a theory of major societal and technology trends that they called SINIC (seed-innovation to need-impetus cycle), from which they extrapolated trends through the year 2033, a hundred years after Omron's founding. This theory, posited in 1960, predicted the end of industrial society and the rise of optimization society through biotechnology in the year 2005—a fairly accurate forty-five-year prediction, as futurism goes. But the remarkable thing is that founding legends, spiritual principles, and theories of history laid down in the past are still invoked—and that Omron employees tend to use similar words to do this. Masaki Ikeda, a supervisor of research and development (R&D) planning, said: "Our main purpose is working for the benefit of society. Before the optimization society, we were chasing productivity and efficiency gains, but now for the optimization society, our main targets for development are in the areas of safety, security, environment, and health."

COALESCING AROUND VALUES: HOW OMRON PRINCIPLES PRODUCE BUSINESS ADVANTAGES

As Omron globalizes, its principles are a tool for managing a complex network of external relationships, not because of the words themselves but because of the conversations they open. In China, where Omron is growing its manufacturing facilities, "our initial conversation with a potential Chinese supplier is not 'We need this part manufactured' but rather is 'This is the kind of company Omron is,' " an Omron executive said. In Japan, Hideo Higuchi, head of business process innovation, points to the Omron Principles and the company's "candid, 'challenge mind' culture" directed to its socially based objectives as underlying the success of a new customer-centric inventory system, while some of the best Japanese companies, such as Toyota, Canon, and Matsushita, still struggled with such an approach.

Omron's R&D increasingly involves partnerships between Omron's central research laboratory and companies and universities in the United States and China. There is a "ten-year friendship" with Stanford University, for example, that senior software architect Ryota Yamada feels is sustained by the principles.

On the sales side, in an industry where roughly half of cold calls result in immediate rejection, "first contacts almost never result in a rejection to speak to us; they are always willing to give us time and hear us out," declared Steve Yukawa, president of Omron's electronic components business, attributing this to customer knowledge of the Omron Principles. He feels that the principles motivate Omron to respond quickly to problems and that some customers choose Omron for that reason. "Customers put tremendous trust in our ambition to do what is best for them," said Kenji Kuwahara, manager of business promotions.

Is it an exaggeration that the principles are so central in multifaceted relationships? How can we tell? What matters is that the people of Omron believe that they are and talk about them regularly—and have done so in over seventy-five interviews throughout the corporate ranks in the United States, China, and Japan. And in one domain,

Omron's acquisitions, the principles have proven their strategic and economic significance.

The Omron Principles are central in every step of the acquisition process, from assessment of companies to buy to integration. During due diligence, every potential target is evaluated on both performance and corporate philosophy; companies with differing philosophies are rejected. Omron's first presentation to a Silicon Valley company, STI, involved an explanation of the principles and especially the "challenge spirit" philosophy, which resonated with STI leaders. STI's Jim Ashford, a senior manager and son-in-law of the founder, said, "We had a set of behaviors that were based on a value system that we held dear. They lined up almost identically to the Omron value system. I can remember a meeting in Chicago with Sakuta-san (Omron CEO) and Fumio Tateisi. Sakuta-san was going through the Omron Principles, and our CEO, Joe Lazarra, and I looked at each other and said, 'That's very interesting because it's almost identical to ours.'" STI accepted Omron's offer.

There are other examples of acquisition advantages for Omron. Because of similar values and principles, Omron's health care subsidiary managed to acquire Colin Medical Care from the private equity firm Carlyle Japan even though other companies had a stronger presence in the professional side of the health care market. Colin Medical was rescued from bankruptcy by the Carlyle buyout and had been plagued by exits of high-skilled professionals before the Omron purchase. Once Omron was in charge, no one left. Moreover, Colin Medical made Omron a desirable alliance partner for prestigious GE Healthcare, because the combination met high standards and appeared sustainable.

Omron gets conversation starters from its principles that build business, but that is only the opening gambit. The belief in a mission of addressing social needs makes even an internal support group like global cash management feel that it is contributing to doing something noble. The principles encourage long-term goals and the spirit of never giving up; even if short-term profits do not emerge, it is worth staying with a good cause. The principles provide a sense of history and faith in the future, with a time line well beyond employees' lifetimes. The principles also provide continuity across generations, as they are used by leaders to mentor young people entering the company and as they inform a "challenge culture" that always seeks new opportunities, which keeps the company interesting to long-term employees, like the executive who came thirty-five years ago never intending to stay.

can you believe it?: symbols, signals, and iconic stories at p&g

OKAY, SO VALUES and principles open conversations. They provide a basis for discussing philosophies and cultures. They can be noble and enduring, and they can provide comfort and guidance in times of change.

But are they credible? What does it take to make skeptics believe this is real, not just fairy dust or window dressing or lip service? Obviously, credibility requires action. Leaders must show that the company makes decisions in the name of its values and principles, that short-term gain is sacrificed for the long-term logic of the social purpose. Leaders use symbols and signals to demonstrate their commitment to the values. And out of events that reflect the values in action, such as IBM India's response to earthquakes and tsunamis described in chapter 1, emerge iconic stories that show employees and other stakeholders that the company lives by its words. Stories are important, because research evidence shows that people remember stories better than they remember facts and figures.

Procter & Gamble has many iconic stories to tell that show how values guided tough choices. But before telling two particularly revealing ones, I want first to describe the development of those values and why they can guide behavior.

THE P&G WAY TO INDUSTRY AND
MORAL LEADERSHIP

P&G leaders are convinced that its values and culture are central to its survival and, in recent years, to its profitable growth. Top leaders are conscious of the symbolic consequences of their actions and think carefully about ensuring that their own actions send signals of what the values mean in practice. Chairman and CEO A. G. Lafley and vice chairman/COO Robert McDonald spend much of their time teaching and discussing the values and principles in formal programs and in visits to locations around the world.

In 2005, with the acquisition of Gillette, P&G, headquartered in Cincinnati, Ohio, since its founding in 1837, became the world's largest consumer products company. It was already one of the world's most admired companies. P&G is among the companies lauded in the 1982 best-seller *In Search of Excellence* that is still alive and still excellent nearly three decades later. But like the other vanguard companies, P&G has had to change. It has entered and exited businesses, and it has restructured to better position itself to address global forces and challenges. It has worked to move from a rules-ridden culture so conformist that people were known as "proctoids" to one where people are outspoken and feel in charge. They still have to sell their ideas, but they are encouraged, from the bottom up, to have ideas to sell in the first place, and they can gather support from peers to move forward as long as they can demonstrate both business facts and consistency with P&G's values and principles. P&G uses so many acronyms that a glossary is needed to decode them, but that's the P&G way—which at least means that employees worldwide can talk shorthand to one another and have a common framework for communication.

In 1986, then president John Pepper led a project involving dozens of senior managers, representing hundreds more people, over a period of several months, to put in writing the key tenets of P&G's culture and approach to doing business, which had been passed through oral tradition but not codified. It was called the PVP, which is shorthand for the P&G statement of purpose, values, and principles.

The impetus was globalization. With rapid global expansion and thousands of new employees, many of them from recently acquired Richardson-Vicks, P&G's largest acquisition to date, it made sense to codify company values and principles on the eve of the company's 1987 sesquicentennial. Corporate culture had become a hot topic in the 1980s, and other companies were also writing mission statements. Unlike many others who were expressing unrealized ideals, P&G leaders tried to derive the words from experience and make them comprehensive.

Pepper's term as CEO from 1995 to 1998 led to further transmission of the PVP, including translations, but it was still not enough. After a short and troubled period under Durk Jager, A. G. Lafley was appointed CEO in June 2000 with low external expectations—the company's stock price immediately dropped. Defying expectations, Lafley has led P&G to new heights, with the PVP as one of the main tools. Lafley has opened P&G's windows and doors, embraced globalization as an opportunity for innovation from the regions as well as market growth, and empowered people using the PVP as a guidance system.

CONTENTS OF THE PVP: "IMPROVE THE LIVES OF THE WORLD'S CONSUMERS"

The PVP statement is thorough, covering a wide range of standards for how to work effectively and with integrity and responsibility, all oriented toward high performance on behalf of the world's consumers.

> Our Purpose: We will provide branded products and services of superior quality and value that improve the lives of the world's consumers, now and for generations to come. As a result, consumers will reward us with leadership sales, profit, and value creation, allowing our people, our shareholders, and the communities in which we live and work to prosper.

Next are the values. The list of values begins with praise for the employees.

> P&G is its people and the values by which we live. We attract and recruit the finest people in the world. We build our organization from within, promoting and rewarding people without regard to any difference unrelated to performance. We act on the conviction that the men and women of Procter & Gamble will always be our most important asset. We are all leaders in our area of responsibility.

The PVP ends with acknowledgment of the end-to-end responsibilities that vanguard companies undertake:

> Mutual Interdependency Is a Way of Life. We work together with confidence and trust across business units, functions, categories, and geographies. We take pride in results from reapplying others'

ideas. We build superior relationships with all the parties who contribute to fulfilling our Corporate Purpose, including our customers, suppliers, universities, and governments.

And there is more in between. The PVP is both lofty and detailed.

For the PVP to be so central, employees need to see that the company will sometimes sacrifice short-term financial interest in the service of doing the right thing for consumers, even those who can't afford P&G products, and for all of Procter's employees and their families. That is where action and tough choices come into play. Two recent iconic stories symbolize P&G's commitments and send signals throughout the company and beyond.

THE STORY OF CHILDREN'S SAFE DRINKING WATER

One major signal of P&G's commitment to the societal goals in its PVP is the fate of PuR, a water purification powder that failed as a commercial product. In 1995, P&G partnered with the U.S. Centers for Disease Control and Prevention (CDC) to research and develop water purification technologies. The CDC understood the public health benefits of clean water; P&G saw a commercial opportunity in developing markets. Although the first market tests were discouraging, P&G acquired Recovery Engineering and its PuR brand water filtration technologies for $265 million in August 1999 and, with the CDC, developed easy-to-use, low-cost sachets. In 2001, Greg Allgood, a doctor of environmental toxicology and UK citizen who joined P&G in 1991, moved to P&G's health care business to oversee the initiative, leading market tests in Guatemala, the Philippines, Morocco, and Pakistan, which were also unpromising. Although educating schoolchildren in Morocco increased usage rates for families, PuR still required consumer education or people would not bother to take the time to use the sachets.

In November 2003, the health care business unit threatened to pull the plug; P&G had spent $20 million in development and testing, with minimal financial return. Allgood and his team spoke to corporate management about the noncommercial benefits for stakeholders and employees, including in disaster relief (verified in Ethiopia) and in nongovernmental organization partnerships (e.g., Population Services International). External relations head Charlotte Otto and vice chairman Robert McDonald saw the benefits for saving lives. "The way I felt at the time was, this is so consistent with our statement of purpose. We must find it a home. The issue is the business model, not the brand or the product. We must find a way," McDonald said. After debate that still did not convince all the skeptics who saw it as an albatross, Lafley decided to extend the project. In December, PuR was moved to the corporate sustainability unit within Otto's external relations division.

Allgood tried one more time to sell PuR in Pakistan but fell short, leaving millions of sachets in warehouses. Then the Asian tsunami struck in December 2004. AmeriCares, UNICEF, and the International Red Cross called to request immediate massive shipments of PuR, which quickly emptied the warehouses. P&G sold fifteen million sachets at cost in the first forty-eight hours after the tsunami, sending them in cargo planes to Sri Lanka and Indonesia. Two weeks after the disaster, it donated thirteen million more packets. In total, P&G delivered roughly a billion glasses of safe drinking water for tsunami victims, receiving plaudits from aid partners, governments, the media, and P&G employees. Lafley became a more active sponsor.

A few months later, in April 2005, Children's Safe Drinking Water became a corporate signature program for P&G's Live, Learn, and Thrive philanthropic initiative. Allgood worked closely with Population Services International to further develop the product's social marketing model, expanding to other countries throughout the globe and reaching over fifty million children. In April 2008 in Nigeria, PuR produced its one billionth liter of clean drinking water.

THE STORY OF EVACUATING LEBANON: PEOPLE-FIRST PRINCIPLES

We heard another iconic story about the PVP in Egypt about two months after the 2006 war in Lebanon ended, because P&G leaders for the Near East region were convinced that their heroic response to disaster was the result of the PVP. The Lebanon war was a thirty-three-day conflict that began when Hezbollah paramilitary bands attacked Israeli border towns, and the Israeli Defense Forces retaliated. The conflict killed over a thousand people (most of whom were Lebanese civilians), severely damaged Lebanese civil infrastructure, and displaced approximately one million Lebanese and between three hundred thousand and five hundred thousand Israelis. A P&G warehouse was damaged, but more concerning to P&G Near East leaders was what would happen to employees and their families.

Mohammed Samir, head of P&G Near East, who had offices in both Beirut and Cairo (P&G Israel reported up a different line to Europe), worked immediately to ensure the safety of P&G employees—not just expatriates as most companies would do but also local Lebanese. This was without regard to cost, which proved to be considerable. There was a feeling among P&G Near East leaders that the PVP demanded this; to do less would violate the values. Without hesitation, and before discussion or approval from bosses in Vienna or Cincinnati, Samir and his managers offered to evacuate all employees along with members of their extended families and house them in hotels in Cairo, while also moving offices in Lebanon to new locations. They invoked the PVP as the basis for their decisions, especially the first value that I described earlier in this chapter—that P&G's people are its most valued asset. P&G's evacuation happened quickly and smoothly, ahead of practically any other entity including foreign governments moving embassy personnel. P&G Near East leaders were applauded for doing it.

Both the Lebanon evacuation and the commitment to Children's Safe Drinking Water reflect use of the PVP and reinforce its centrality. They are among many similar signals of the company's commitment to doing the right thing (one of the values) even at a financial cost. Iconic stories become symbols of what the company stands for and why standing on principles brings benefits beyond the bottom line. Yet they also become a basis for developing products and making profits that benefit the bottom line, as we will see in the next chapter.

Values and principles can inspire positive action, but that is not enough. They must also prevent negative action by setting boundaries of appropriate behavior, telling people what not to do and what lines cannot be crossed.

"not a wink-wink culture": punishing values violations and using values as a control

VANGUARD COMPANIES are not perfect. They cannot please everyone all the time. They have critics, lawsuits, stumbles, and internal violations of their standards. In any complex enterprise, some people test limits, have flaws, do not internalize the standards, or do the wrong thing intentionally or inadvertently for reasons of their own. Iconic stories of an uplifting sort provide positive symbols and signals of commitment. But credibility also requires that negative sanctions be in place. After all, a company's official values statement and code of ethics can avow all the good things it wants, but it is rendered meaningless if meanwhile in practice everyone knows that the principles aren't serious and that employees can get away with tweaking them. This is especially a danger in countries with histories of corruption, because people in those societies are generally not educated to the norms of behavior set by vanguard companies. For example, in developing countries, both IBM and Cemex managers have to exercise particular diligence because their companies' standards are higher than those prevailing in the country—a tribute to Cemex's vanguard status, since Cemex originates in Mexico, not from a developed country with long-standing ethical codes.

"It is not a wink-wink culture where we say one thing and do another. We mean what we say," Inderpeet Thukral, vice president of strategy for IBM India, declared emphatically. IBM's ethical principles are captured in its business conduct guidelines (BCGs), which are presented as part of new-hire induction and thereafter signed yearly as a condition of employment, regardless of level. In Russia, IBM's human resources manager Tatiana Khinoi said that she knows that the BCGs are followed by employees because when there are questions they call their manager or human resources, and in her seven years in the role, she had seen not one deviation. "The guidelines are translated straight, with no need for local adaptation, and the annual recertification makes them really very deep in you," she observed.

In India, IBM managers indicate that IBM has walked away from deals because they could not agree to unethical "commissions." Infractions would result in disciplinary action, including dismissal. India also has a common problem with fraudulent résumés—unacceptable to IBM. Years earlier there had been an amnesty, with salary docking, for inflated travel expense reimbursement, and those who did not come forward were let go. With a young workforce, it was important to provide a second chance, but warnings were severe enough to prevent future misconduct.

Companies show that they are serious about their values and principles when they fire people for lapses; reject high-margin, high-growth distributors because they don't meet ethical standards or lack the right values, as Cemex's Construrama does; or walk away from customers who fail to pass environmental and social screens, as Banco Real does.

Francisco Garza, Cemex president for North America, feels that employees are happy to have a guide on how to behave in certain circumstances and to be part of a common culture, although occasionally the code of conduct runs into resistance—and in some countries, such as Latvia, laborers in cement factories are not motivated by the same desire to join a company for a career that Cemex has found in other places, so the self-policing system is still challenging. But Garza can point to actions that put teeth into Cemex principles. One year, a manager in a then newly acquired South American unit was caught pilfering returned products. He justified this by saying that the materials would have ended up going to waste. He was arrested and found guilty in court, but when the time came for him to go to jail on December 20, a group from the newly acquired entity approached the president to ask for leniency, claiming that it was Christmastime and that the man's behavior did not really constitute stealing. Cemex leaders remained steadfast in their decision, sending a signal that the code of ethics was nonnegotiable. Had it happened that a talented, successful, and well-liked executive started taking favored employees on company-paid weekend getaways, charging personal dinners to the company, and allowing some employees to use company cars for personal matters, Cemex would have fired him too. Garza said: "Some people are too young or too weak; they just follow the boss's orders even though they don't want to. But when you stop a bad practice, the organization aligns very fast."

In addition to the common practice of having new hires sign a code of conduct and by providing regular training, Cemex asks prospective new executives during the hiring process about their values and how they go about achieving objectives to see whether they fit with Cemex culture. At monthly executive committee meetings, top leaders are expected to ask country managers probing questions to ferret out ethical dilemmas and help managers make the right decisions. For instance, if a country manager needed to fire a top salesman over an ethical issue and expected to have trouble meeting sales objectives for a half year as a result, the executive committee would encourage him to fire the salesman regardless of the lost revenues. Garza himself might visit the country for a few days to help with sales and show support, sending a message to employees about the importance of company values.

EXTERNAL REPUTATION AND INTERNAL SELF-CONTROL

Employees in vanguard companies learn that they are part of a company community and a wider business ecosystem in which the standards are known, so that expectations are set on everyone's part, at least theoretically, about acting with values. It is easy to exercise self-control when a community is self-policing internally and its external customers or suppliers know what the standards mean.

Throughout the world, IBMers say that adhering to high ethical standards is facilitated by the company's external reputation for high standards—which also means that a lapse would affect everyone negatively, making it even more important to behave responsibly or face peer pressure and disapproval. Noha Saleem, a manager in software in Dubai and Egypt, commented: "Customers have good respect for IBM. Even when we go into competitive situations, they know the business ethics of IBM. They know we have barriers, lines that we cannot cross. This helps you a lot that you feel there is a respect for you. They know that you're coming there for their welfare, for their business, and you care about them. We see it when we're young and go with the older client reps, and then you introduce the next generation." Dravinder Seetharam in India concurs. "We have never had a problem dealing with government officials. They do not ask for money, do not ask for any favors, always have a professional approach. They know about our ethics, they know what we stand for, and they appreciate our stand."

IBM CEO Sam Palmisano responded to my questions about enforcing principles and standards by declaring, "What would put someone over the edge—screwing up? It's simple. If they push the system on revenue recognition—channel stuffing. If they give a gift to a government official, to any official. Sexual harassment, it is OVER. And on the business, not delivering results for a couple of years, we'd put them in a place where there is a better fit." In short, fall short on revenues or profits, and you get another chance. But violate a value or principle, and you are out fast.

aspirational standards: "now, and for generations to come"

"WE HAVE TO AIM at a better future," Zambrano said about Cemex. "I've always asked, why not be the best in our industry? And then the best altogether, why not? Sometimes being the best means bringing what is done within other companies into ours. I'm very proud that I have shown in a country like Mexico that had been conquered and split apart with half its territory taken away, a country with great cultural history but not a lot of self-esteem, that you can do it." He added: "We also want to be an example to our competitors and other industries of how things are done. And in that respect, I'm not satisfied with what we have yet." A vanguard company has flaws, but it is also has mechanisms to correct them via a culture that includes high aspirations.

In 2007, Procter & Gamble added the phrase "now, and for generations to come" to its statement of purpose. Creating and disseminating values and principles provides a strategic guidance system for the present, and it also provides an aspiration to do better in the future. This is institution building, giving the company a long-term survival strategy by creating an institution that can endure even when specific business circumstances change. Globalization increases the likelihood of shorter organizational life cycles, as a result of mergers and acquisitions, industry consolidation, and intensified competition driving out weaker competitors. Yet vanguard companies are successful in the present and weather changes that help them envision continuing as successful entities well into the future. Maybe not three hundred years, the way Omron's CEO talks about the long term, but they convey a confidence that there is something strong in a values-based organizational community that will help them manage through tsunamis, physical or economic.

Recall the happy outcome for Banco Real because of its emphasis on a strong culture and strategy guided by social and environmental responsibility. In April 2008, when ownership of Banco Real shifted to Spain's Santander, Banco Real involved so much more than the bundle of countable assets. Fabio Barbosa was named CEO of the combined entity, and the Banco Real culture and values were infused throughout Santander Brazil. Banco Real is the institution that lives on.

THIS CHAPTER HAS explored a fundamental element of vanguard companies: that they stand on principles that have strategic value in terms of business choices, internal guidance and control, and external partnerships. Business strategy rests on an understanding of external markets and the company's technical capabilities, but for the vanguard, it also is inextricably linked to corporate culture. Statements of principles and codes of conduct come in many forms that are common to larger companies in major countries. Vanguard companies go beyond the conventional by living their principles actively. To do this in light of the uncertainty, complexity, and diversity brought by globalization requires the following.

- Values must be a priority for leaders, invoked often in their messages and on the agenda for management discussions.
- The entire workforce must be allowed and encouraged to enter the conversation; employees should be invited to discuss or interpret values and principles in conjunction with their peers, who help ensure alignment.
- Principles need to be codified, made explicit, transmitted in writing in many media, and reviewed regularly to make sure people understand and remember them.
- Statements about values and principles should invoke a higher purpose, a purpose beyond current tasks that indicates service to society, and this can become part of the company's brand and a source of competitive differentiation.
- The statement's words must become a basis for ongoing dialogue that guides debate when there is controversy or initial disagreement,

and decisions should be supported by reference to particular values or principles.

• Principles must guide choices, in terms of business opportunities to pursue or reject or in terms of investments with a longer time frame that might seem uneconomical in the present moment.

• As they become internalized by employees, values and principles should substitute for more impersonal or coercive rules and serve as a control system against violations, excesses, or veering off course.

• Actions reflecting values and principles, especially difficult choices, need to become the basis for iconic stories that are easy to remember and retell, reinforcing to employees and the world what the company stands for.

• Violations must be actively monitored and swiftly punished.

• Values must be aspirational, signaling long-term intentions that guide thinking about the future.

By promoting consistent high standards everywhere, vanguard companies also spread universal standards throughout their supply chains and to every community and country in which they operate. The potential for change increases outside the company. Within the company, a reliance on people to do the right thing once they buy into and internalize core principles is highly empowering. It promotes a kind of corporate humanism—through which each person becomes sensitive to the impact of his or her behavior—and unlocks creative potential.

chapter four

innovation: the values dividend

INNOVATION CAN SPRING from unexpected juxtapositions of people and ideas under challenging circumstances. Tarek Farahat and Juliana Azevedo Schahin can attest to that.

Egyptian-born Tarek Farahat visited the Procter & Gamble booth at a recruitment event for college graduates in Cairo in 1989 and was impressed by the company's thirst for excellence. He joined P&G as an assistant brand manager in Saudi Arabia, moving up the organizational ranks in Switzerland, France, and Germany—European operations that were familiar territory for the American giant. Then he was sent farther afield, arriving in Brazil in 1999 as a marketing director for the paper products business, which included diapers and feminine hygiene pads.

It did not take long for Farahat to learn how difficult the Brazilian situation was. P&G was a recent entrant, operating in Brazil only since 1988, when it bought a bar soap and personal care manufacturer and introduced Pampers diapers and Pert shampoo. It was not only new but weak, especially compared to European powerhouse Unilever. By 1992, P&G Brazil had produced the single largest yearly country loss anywhere in the company and, despite capital investments sometimes second only to the United States, remained in the red for years. Farahat was an observer in the room when then CEO Durk Jager and his global leadership team traveled from the United States to grill executives about whether some P&G brands should even stay in Brazil. The ultimate answer was "there is light at the end of the tunnel," Farahat recalled—but only if he and other managers proved it to corporate management in Cincinnati. Soon Farahat moved to Venezuela, as P&G Latin America's global business unit category head for paper products, but he continued to watch Brazil carefully, because it was the largest Latin American market, and besides, he had begun to care about the country.

Juliana Azevedo joined P&G in 1996 after being told by a college friend that the company's values aligned with hers. "There is a lot of integrity here at P&G that I value," Azevedo said. Azevedo, a warm, energetic leader who loves to hand chocolates to teammates and chew gum to calm her nerves, worked as a marketing manager. Continued losses were demoralizing. "Our first years here were not ones of glory," she commented much later, perhaps understating the difficulties as a way to forget them. Azevedo used a lot of gum in those days.

P&G's strategy has long been to produce premium products packed with features to "improve the lives of the world's consumers," as its purposes, values, and principles (PVP) states. But in Brazil, most consumers could not afford them. High federal and state taxes (half or more of shelf price) eroded P&G's margins while hyperinflation and a 1999 currency devaluation following the Asian financial crisis reduced consumer purchasing power. And Brazil had the region's worst income inequality. P&G applied its global business model in Brazil yet could not obtain economies of scale. Instead, its local strategy focused on cutting losses and staying afloat, not on serving the people of Brazil. Employees feared that P&G would leave the country altogether, eliminating their jobs and careers. The imperative was clear: Innovate or else.

In hindsight, the to-do list for Farahat, Azevedo, and their colleagues might have looked something like this: (1) Save the entire business in Brazil. (2) Increase sales and profits in struggling categories. (3) Create new methods to innovate faster. (4) Create new products. (5) Challenge corporate assumptions. (6) Influence global practices. (7) And do not forget to improve the lives of lower-income and poor families.

Amazingly, they did all of it. The PVP was among their most powerful tools at every step in a journey of innovation that opened new markets to serve the poor, saved jobs, and became a locally driven global model for a company that was accustomed to designing everything at the center.

Let me first put this in perspective by explaining what is different about innovation in vanguard companies such as P&G. Then I will show how Farahat, Azevedo, and friends conceived and drove innovation and how the values dividend produces rapid innovation in other vanguard companies.

a new twist on innovation

BY THINKING BEYOND today's customers to the wider world, a vanguard company finds new arenas for social betterment and anticipates markets. This is not altruistic, but it is also not how business self-interest is usually framed. Many people in the vanguard companies come to feel that if they do not tackle a big societal problem using their special prowess, then who will? Their very self-image involves an imperative to innovate, a responsibility to solve problems to improve the world.

Companies have always succeeded by emphasizing innovation. Today, the new wrinkle on an old and much-dissected phenomenon is the addition of key words in one of IBM's three core values: "innovation that matters for our company and the world." Putting "for the world" at the forefront urges everyone to make the connection between business and society, indeed feel the responsibility for finding new ways to solve problems. A short mental loop connects "changing the world" and "my daily job."

At each phase of the innovation process—generating ideas, selling others on those ideas, and executing the projects to turn ideas into realities—purpose-driven companies gain advantages, as I will show in the P&G case and other examples in this chapter. Certainly their technical capabilities meet high standards, but that is not all there is to it. Framing their missions in social terms and reinforcing the desire for social improvement with empowering organizational cultures give them a boost beyond the technical realm. In short, they have to be good at what they do, but they get even more power when they seek to create social value with those skills and technologies. And, as we shall see, this is even more important in emerging market countries such as India that are starting to produce significant innovation ahead of the United States or Europe because companies face challenging societal problems that force a search for creative solutions.

Organizational culture plays a critical role in the failure or success of innovation. That is so frequently said that it is almost a truism. But all too often, grand declarations about innovation are followed by mediocre execution that produces anemic results, and innovation groups are quietly disbanded in cost-cutting drives, largely because the culture is not friendly to innovation. For example, innovation is stifled when those at the top think they have all the answers, when they seem to compete internally among themselves rather than against external players, or when they measure too many nonessential things, narrowing people's focus to administrivia. Companies get caught in classic binds that reduce their innovation potential. These include strategy traps (valuing only big breakthroughs and ignoring promising smaller ideas); structure traps (assigning innovation to special units unconnected to the rest of the organization, which have no stake in supporting new ventures); process traps (measuring new things under development by the same standard used for the already tried-and-true, which means that innovations get starved or eliminated); and skills traps (undervaluing leadership skills that inspire effort).

In contrast, innovation thrives where people in every field and at every level are encouraged to look for new ideas, have access to channels for communicating them, and stay connected with colleagues across the organization who are willing to collaborate with them and support them in execution.

That is why Tarek Farahat, Juliana Azevedo, and numerous collaborators can produce high rates of innovation in vanguard companies. Let us see how they do it.

SEEING AN OBELISK IN THE KALEIDOSCOPE: CREATIVE IDEAS

In late 2001, soon after A. G. Lafley replaced short-tenured Durk Jager as CEO and set out to improve the business by leveraging P&G's PVP statement, Farahat thought about the implications of the PVP. He saw that P&G's focus on excellence for consumers meant seeing the world from consumers' and families' points of view rather than taking P&G business needs as the starting point. By opening his mind the way Lafley encouraged, Farahat shook up his thinking as though shaking a kaleidoscope (my favorite image for creativity). A new image came to him from his Egyptian childhood: an obelisk.

Obelisks are very tall, narrow, monolithic structures carved to perfection from one block of stone by workers coordinating their actions in a team so that once they were finished with their flawless piece, the whole obelisk could be raised and placed. Farahat said, "The obelisk model says: Know what the end is and then make sure all the elements work well, and once it is ready, erect it." He asked his brother, a tour guide in Egypt, to show him the opposite example—of obelisks that had failed. "The reason they failed is because they didn't examine the stone well. So they carve, carve, carve, and then there was a crack in the middle. That's it, you're gone." So Farahat invented a method, a kind of backward design, that started with the outcome and worked through all the elements that needed to be created or adjusted to get to that outcome. That was in itself a major innovation in methodology for P&G. Lafley later described this obelisk methodology in a memo to his direct reports and asked Farahat to present it to Wall Street analysts, who were so astonished at the financial payoff that they asked, "What's the catch?"

In 2001, the emphasis for Brazil was on turning around feminine care, baby care, and fabric care, and all three were struggling. Feminine care included paper products in Farahat's portfolio from his regional post in Venezuela, so the first application of obelisk methodology was to Always, P&G Brazil's feminine hygiene pad brand, for which Juliana Azevedo handled the marketing and Julio Nemeth the local operations. As hard as it is to imagine a connection between feminine hygiene in Brazil and carvings from ancient Egypt, creativity stems from going far afield, outside conventional concepts.

The Always line generated the smallest revenues among P&G Brazil's three major categories and was third in the market behind Kimberly-Clark and Johnson & Johnson. The declining business created tensions between local marketing and sales teams, which became apparent in weekly price meetings. Adilson Marqués, who as trade marketer worked closely with both groups, recalled that marketing believed weak results stemmed from low inventory while sales cited design and affordability—a classic shift-the-blame game characteristic of losing streaks.

Farahat flew from Caracas to São Paulo to teach Azevedo and Nemeth the obelisk methodology. They convened a joint team for a crisis brainstorming session and presented the obelisk-guided desired end point—a product that could be purchased for less than two *reais* (about 70 cents) with high quality. All knew of prior attempts (and failures) to fix the category, and they understood that the first challenge was to achieve scale. Scale was necessary because paper product manufacturing was capital intensive; machines needed to run 24/7. Advertising costs were also high, since Brazil was one of the world's most expensive media markets.

They tried out many ideas, such as a special product for high-frequency stores (HFS), which were small stores selling in small volume, typical in Brazil's neighborhoods. They thought about reducing the pack size or eliminating part of the absorbency safeguard. None of these was particularly innovative or necessarily appealing to lower-income women, and they were told to keep trying.

Eventually, the brainstorm: the *básico* idea. In Portuguese, *básico* does not mean basic as in cheaper or poorer; it means basic as in essential. Azevedo wanted the product to be "an Armani," referring to a high-end Italian designer dress, for an "H&M price," referring to a discount retail clothing chain. *Básico* would be communicated through wardrobe images: the basic black dress or basic jeans and white T-shirt, an image attractive to young women, plus orange, the fashion color of the season. Now there was a vision to move toward.

BUY-IN AND EXECUTION: LINING UP SUPPORT FOR OPEN INNOVATION

Farahat sponsored the project from Caracas. In classic change master fashion, he sought buy-in by first planting seeds. Farahat sent periodic notes to his boss, the global category head, saying such things as "we have a cost issue, and we have a volume slowdown. We're working on a different SKU [stock keeping unit] that can solve the problem. I'll keep you posted." Farahat did not mention *básico* until the concept had developed far enough and the organization was primed—a good strategy for innovators. He wanted facts in hand before seeking agreement. That was the P&G way.

Pushback was appropriate. Global brand guardians were concerned about diluting the image and about cannibalizing P&G's high-end product. But Azevedo felt empowered by what the PVP said about consumer knowledge; no one knew their local consumers as well as the Brazil team did. And the premium product would be supported with an upgrade a few months following the Básico product launch.

In São Paulo, Azevedo worked with coleader Nemeth, who was also the plant manager, to support and expand the team. She mended a tense working relationship with the HFS sales group, and when the HFS head unexpectedly left the company, Azevedo seized the opportunity to bring both groups together. "Let's stop pointing fingers, we've got to make this work, we are winners, you are winners," she said. Azevedo's internal team sought collaboration externally with suppliers, the plant manager, an advertising agency, and trade customers. Customers were asked for input as "coowners," even though time was very tight, and the project was in expedite mode; this was a first for Brazil but considered critical by the team. Azevedo's strategy was to "contaminate" partners with passion for the idea, she said, to get the powerful support of true believers.

Belief in the concept, Azevedo claimed, held team members together, nurtured their collaborative work, and brought forth their best ideas—more so than the chocolates she handed out. She attributed all this to the culture of the PVP. Innovations blossomed to support the main idea. To minimize costs and speed time to market, Nemeth recommended using an old technology that was already familiar. Creative new packaging was designed, with an orange inner wrap and a transparent outer wrap, another P&G first, which was not only creative but saved money by using less ink. But because orange ink was novel, it was not yet "P&G qualified." Suppliers were asked for help, and many rounds of calls among São Paolo, Caracas, and Cincinnati discussed the ink question alone.

The night that production began, the core office team and the regional R&D person, who flew in from Caracas, went to the factory in Louveria, outside of São Paulo. "We were all waiting on the line for the product to come. Everybody was holding hands," Azevedo said, "helping and cheering and praying that everything would work well." When the first product came off the line, "it was a big celebration," she added, laughing. The first week of the launch, Azevedo's team went to the field to support sales and distribution.

Even the launch was innovative. Always Básico was introduced at Brazil's largest trade fair, also a first, in a mysterious locked room painted orange with admission by invitation and long lines to get in. "Marqués made two hundred presentations in one day and I'm not exaggerating. He ran out of voice," Azevedo said. It worked. Many customers who placed orders felt that they had helped design the product. They received orange display blocks to place at the entrance to their stores. Some of the neighborhood shops were so small that the blocks spilled out onto public sidewalks. High awareness compensated for a low advertising budget.

Demand exceeded expectations. In fact, P&G had to dole out products to customers in smaller batches while ramping up production. Always Básico was profitable within a year and became the category leader within two years, and its market share kept rising—and sales of P&G's higher-end products increased too. Meanwhile, the obelisk method was used to redesign other products, resulting in a 29 percent increase in overall revenues in one year despite unfavorable economic conditions.

MULTIPLYING INNOVATION: CONTINUING TO SENSE, CREATE, COLLABORATE, EXECUTE

Baby care, the second struggling category in Brazil, provided another opportunity for a Básico innovation. Farahat had moved to head baby care from the Venezuelan regional office, and Azevedo had moved to the commercial side of baby care in Brazil. Obelisk reverse engineering was applied to Pampers, disposable diapers with even higher brand equity than Always but a similar struggle with affordability issues.

To sense the consumer environment, Azevedo lived for a week in a low-income home with two babies—an example of P&G's encouragement to go out into the world to get a feel for real lives. For security reasons, she did not sleep in the house, but she spent the whole day there, sometimes waking up and arriving at five in the morning to join the family for breakfast, other times staying until dinner, helping change the babies, bathe the babies, and take them to the doctors. What she learned helped shape product design and packaging. One result was a bargain pack grouping Básico with an expensive night-time extended-use diaper, because, she said, "in the low-income houses, the baby is sleeping in the same bed as the couple. So if there is a leak-age, it's a leakage on the parents. They can save money by using just enough product during the day, but at night, they need to rest to go to work the next day." Pampers Básico eliminated built-in antirash cream but retained an antileak barrier and added attractive drawings on the diaper, to provide a product low-income people would be proud to use. As with Always Básico, demand quickly outpaced pro-duction forecasts.

Laundry, P&G Brazil's biggest category, was the next challenge. Ace laundry detergent was a struggling money loser caught in com-petitive detergent price wars with Unilever and local brands. Juan Fernando Posada and Hermann Schwarz were infected by Farahat and Azevedo's enthusiasm and success and sought to create similar in-novations for detergent. In Brazil, only 40 percent of urban and 10 percent of rural households had washing machines. Marketers report-ing to Posada and Schwarz visited poor areas frequently and observed the time-consuming process by which low-income families washed clothes by hand. Moreover, they saw P&G lose market share in Peru to a local company offering soap flakes that felt soothing during the hours hand washers spent dipping into soap-filled water.

Support from higher management was hard to generate at first, de-spite the Brazil team's invoking the PVP and pointing to a Básico-like product in China, and even though manufacturing changeover time was faster for a chemical process than for paper products. Action was stalled until a crisis changed minds. Several national distributors delisted Ace laundry soap for low sales, certainly an attention-getting event that made the skeptics willing to let the team try anything. The regional product head decided to give the go-ahead for Ace Básico, and innovation accelerated. The regional R&D group added soap flakes and foam to give the detergent a mild feel; a perfumed scent was devel-oped with a local fragrance firm as part of P&G's open innovation pro-gram, Connect and Develop; and costs were lowered by removing cleaning agents not needed for the typical scrubbing of hand washing.

PVP-driven solidarity and support for colleagues helped regional and local teams work together to get the product to market in only six months under the name Ace Básico Naturals, a name that highlighted the detergent's sensory components. The laundry team not only learned from the first two Básicos but also improved upon them. More so than Always and Pampers, Ace Básico customized the product to consumer needs and created a superior product to save time for lower-income people who needed to work outside the home.

A BUSINESS SAVED AND A NEW WORLD OF OPPORTUNITY

As the three Básicos spread from Brazil throughout the region, they turned out to be the biggest initiatives of Latin America of the decade. Tarek Farahat returned to São Paulo from Caracas in July 2006 as the new country general manager just as P&G began to absorb its Gillette acquisition and Ace Básico was being readied for the market. Its March 2006 launch was an immediate success. In the first month, the sales force sold over twice their objective. After three months, P&G sought to replicate this success by launching a similar product under other names in Latin America and other geographies. P&G Brazil ended the first year selling twice the expected volume, then grew more than 10 percent the next year with the help of a new marketing director, Paulo Koelle. Ace Básico helped make up for problems in the other laundry offerings. Laundry had its best run since P&G entered the category ten years earlier. The Brazilian unit overall reached global P&G profit levels on $1 billion in sales in the 2006–7 period—and the curve continued to trend upward. Adilson Marqués, a veteran of the Always Básico team, led an internal sales tournament, with tables of scores modeled after the soccer World Cup. Tallies of sales victories were displayed on a color monitor in the second-floor employees' lounge, hanging alongside a large version of P&G's PVP statement in Portuguese.

A few crises and personnel changes helped soften resistance to innovation, but the real success factors were those common to innovation in vanguard companies: deep understanding of the world outside the business, creative thinking, great teamwork, and the power of persistence.

Belief in Básico was infused with the team's conviction that they were guided to this by P&G's global values as expressed in the PVP statement. Of course, a great deal depended on interpretations of the word *superior* in the PVP, and each new idea required arguing with initially skeptical managers in the region and Cincinnati. But basing arguments on facts generated by tuning into the environment and grounding them in sacred texts took the politics out of discussions and focused everyone on a common goal. "What guides us is the PVP, not one person's point of view, irrespective of his or her level in the organization," Tarek Farahat said. The vice chairman and COO Bob McDonald emphasized the same point. "P&G is a democracy of ideas, and 99.9 percent of the time if all managers have the same data, they all make the same decisions due to the strength of our values."

Two other innovation advantages of vanguard companies also kicked in: open innovation, in which customers as well as outside suppliers develop ideas; and faster execution, because leaders and team members have passion for their mission.

Ultimately, the teams in Brazil created change not just in the product mix but also in some global frameworks—an example of local innovations producing global ripples and provoking further change. Memories are hazy, but Andre Felicíssimo and Paulo Koelle also suspected that a phrase in the PVP was changed to emphasize superior value as well as quality.

The feedback loops were short and multidirectional. Global principles helped guide local action, but local innovations—the obelisk method as well as the *básico* concept—changed global frameworks. That is another characteristic of vanguard companies and a demonstration of the openness and empowerment fostered by their leaders. P&G CEO A. G. Lafley visits regional and local offices to preach the PVP and to listen to ideas bubbling up from the ground. McDonald thinks of global frameworks as a "menu of best practice capabilities" rather than a set of dogmatic commands, thereby leaving flexibility for regional and local innovation.

Básico knowledge of how to serve "bottom of the pyramid" lower-income families diffused outside of Brazil through peer connections, including short-term global projects, a flow of people back and forth among locations, and a few longer-term international postings. Juliana

Azevedo was invited to participate in a global project out of Cincinnati on finding the value sweet spot, including for lower-income consumers. Básico was a model for how P&G sought to use the PVP and global strategy to permit local innovation empowered by knowledge-based decision-making criteria.

Lafley and McDonald set the tone at the top, teaching the PVP and preaching open innovation to get the job done for the consumer without pride of ownership or not-invented-here turf barriers. Despite initial skepticism, global and regional leaders for products and functions moved the innovations along in Brazil and, later, the world. On the ground, people felt like a team, collaborating to shape the ultimate ideas and execute them.

The classic seven skills that help innovators master change were easier to use because of P&G's vanguard culture. Each skill was used in the *básico* experience. Check off the actions from my list.

- Tuning into the broader context: seeing needs and opportunities through firsthand experience with the wider world
- "Kaleidoscope thinking": turning conventional wisdom on its head and finding creative approaches that let a new pattern form
- Articulating a compelling vision: formulating an idea people can believe in and selling it effectively
- Building a coalition of committed backers and supporters: engaging stakeholders whose support is necessary to move forward
- Developing and supporting the working team: motivating people to work hard for a common goal
- Persisting and persevering through the difficult middle stages when the innovation is still fragile
- Celebrating success by making everyone a hero

P&G reclaimed its place among the world's top innovators just before Lafley took over, launching big new global products, such as Swiffer for mopping and dusting and Febreze, a fabric refreshener and odor eliminator. Lafley brought the Connect and Develop program to push open innovation. But the company's stellar results are not due to blockbusters alone; they are also a function of ground-up innovations from many parts of the world that provoke new thinking about serving the world. Diapers and detergents definitely do not end poverty, but by extending conveniences to the poor, they can improve lives.

sensing society: how principles and purpose propel innovation

IN OTHER VANGUARD COMPANIES, innovation also stems from remaining true to values and principles and using them to both find opportunities and act on them, some with enormous potential for social and environmental progress.

Omron thrives on a "challenge culture" of offering solutions to challenging problems of social well-being. Omron leaders see a direct line between the Omron Principles and the company's multiple engineering firsts, including the first commercial blood pressure monitor specifically for women.

Omron makes electronic sensors, but its human sensors drive its innovation. Omron's values and principles encourage its people to find opportunities to serve society through technological innovations. From the beginning, Omron founder Kazuma Tateisi saw the identification and resolution of social needs as Omron's core competence. Today's executives quote his frequent exhortation: "Selling products is not enough. I want representatives to bring back needs from the customers—as many as possible, as quickly as possible. That is the other half of a salesperson's job." They say Kazuma-san felt that the more Omron contributed to society, the more problems society would bring to Omron to solve.

Seventy-five years later, the society that Omron serves has broadened beyond Japan to the world. Only one-third of Omron's thirty-five thousand employees reside in Japan, with another third in China alone, although senior management remains mostly Japanese. Yet the same sense of societal purpose is invoked by the people we interviewed from the United States, Japan, China, and Europe as the reason Omron shines in innovation.

History feels alive in Japan even when one is surrounded by futuristic devices. Our visit to Omron's sleekly modern Kyoto headquarters included dinner with the CEO at a historic mansion up a mountain overlooking a garden of ancient stones. Thus, it is not surprising that Kazuma-san is spoken of as though still very much present, and Omron leaders consistently retell stories from decades past. They especially like stories that show Omron's contributions to its own home country. Among the multiple engineering firsts they mention (such as the world's first online ATM) is one that still benefits fellow Japanese companies. In the 1990s, when Japanese color copiers began being sold globally, it was discovered in Europe that the technology was advanced enough to allow counterfeiting of certain European currencies. The European authorities asked the Japanese Ministries of Economy, Trade, and Industry and International Trade and Industry to correct this situation or risk facing European import barriers. Omron rose to the challenge and six months later had developed technology that could be attached to all color copying machines to prevent counterfeiting. Every major Japanese color copier manufacturer, including Fuji-Xerox, Canon, and Ricoh, adopted Omron's solution.

"Although it has been eighteen years since we introduced that technology, it is still produced and used in many of those copying machines. That could not have been done by any other manufacturer on a global scale. And we eliminated economic frictions between Japan and Europe as a result," said Masaki Arao, president of Omron's software business.

To accelerate "proactive innovation," Omron has shortened the loop between theory and practice by more closely connecting R&D to its businesses and vice versa, and opening the innovation process to collaboration with partners. "Now there are few 'professors' in R&D. Instead, there are many entrepreneurs," executive vice president Shingo Akechi declared. Omron Principles provide a global guidance system for use by those potential entrepreneurs in identifying Omron-like opportunities. Omron seeks to create "the best matching of man to machine" to fulfill its corporate philosophy: "To the machine, the work of the machine; to man the thrill of further creation."

THE THRILL OF FURTHER CREATION: ACCELERATING INNOVATION

Omron employees search for ideas in several ways. They engage customers or potential customers in conversations about problems, which are then brought to engineers and the R&D lab to find solutions. Omron focuses its research on technology streams with the potential for multiple applications, often in collaboration with university research centers, as Omron has moved to an open innovation model. Omron is unusual, even among vanguard companies, in steadily devoting 8 percent of revenues to R&D in lean as well as good times. For example, when other capital investment nearly stopped in Japan between 1995 and 2004, executive vice president Shingo Akechi touted Omron's "policy for a long time and into the future." Business partners are another source of valuable ideas. And Omron leaders pick up global social cues—what are the unmet needs of society that could be addressed by sensors or software. Throughout the ranks and in offices around the world, Omron employees consistently claim that opportunities for innovation are always screened in terms of the potential societal benefits and not just market size.

Some innovations are conventional practice for an industrial supplier: behind-the-scenes ways to increase efficiency for a customer. For example, an Asian manufacturer of printed circuit boards asked Omron for a solution to a small but costly problem: a sensor to determine if solder paste was too old and would result in defective boards, since human inspectors using intuition resulted in costly false negatives. Omron's Silicon Valley team took that idea to partners in Connecticut and San Diego. Prior to their relationship with Omron, they had never thought of making products related to solder paste.

Other opportunities brought by customers have more socially significant lifesaving implications. In 2008, OSTI (Omron STI, a division of Omron's industrial automation business from an acquisition in California) was on the cusp of revolutionizing the safety of industrial laundries and preventing deaths. Explained Jim Ashford, president and COO of OSTI, "Imagine a lineup of washers and dryers with a set of railroad tracks between them. A couple of large carts move up and down the railroad tracks, remove the laundry from the washers, go look for an open dryer, and dump in the laundry. This thing moves when it is queued to move, and there's nothing that's going to stop it. If you happen to be in the operation envelope working on something and this cart leans over . . . well, they've had a few deaths. OSHA— the U.S. Occupational Safety and Health Administration—has made a big issue about it and is actively looking for solutions to stop it . . . Something like this moves it right to the top of the CEO agenda." Omron engineers worked first with a customer in Dallas, building on its knowledge of how to increase the safety of subway door openings, among other things. Their hope was that OSHA would adopt Omron's solution as a standard.

Still other ideas emanate from new capabilities. For the past decade, Omron had been working to apply "fuzzy logic" (a form of artificial intelligence permitting machines to automate decisions based on imprecise, ambiguous, vague, or uncertain information) to various social needs around the world. One recent application is digital cameras capable of automatically identifying the subject's face and focusing on it, a technology based on the Print Club machines Omron had helped manufacture in Japan in the 1990s. Another was for auto safety; instead of relying on the human ear to listen to sounds to identify automobile problems, an Omron microphone in the car can pick up sounds and produce a more accurate diagnosis. Omron's footprint is also on the latest wireless communications technologies. Pairing ultra-wideband antenna technology developed internally with technology of its global partners, Omron released the first WiMAX antenna for notebook computers in December 2007. This can replace the five antennas required for various protocols (WiFi, WiMAX, etc.) with three smaller ones, all capable of fitting behind a laptop's LCD display. Similar technology can also allow mobile phones to operate on more voice and data bands, including WiFi and WiMAX broadband access.

Omron businesses target significant societal needs of the future, such as clean energy, food safety, and women's health. With such priorities in mind, employees around the world conduct a broad search for opportunities. For example, in Spain, representatives visited a solar power company and discovered that the company was in need of controllers for their power generation system. Recognizing a fit with both Omron's knowledge base and the Omron Principles, team members reported the opportunity not only to their managers in Spain but also to the European head office in Amsterdam and ultimately to a product line manager in Japan. Omron's solar power generation system is now sold globally. Omron biosensors, newly developed by researchers at Omron Japan in 2007, are being applied by Omron Silicon Valley to improve food safety—to automatically detect when food has expired or is diseased or tainted.

It all seems straightforward, but in practice innovation at Omron can be just as contentious and controversial as it is in any company, because innovation often requires departures from tradition that managers hold dear. But Omron, like P&G and other vanguard companies, has its ace in the hole: the ability to transcend narrow interests or territorial politics by invoking the Omron Principles. That advantage made a difference in the development of a new blood pressure monitor for women.

Omron holds approximately half the global market share in blood pressure monitors, but until the spring of 2008 Omron offered no machine specifically for women. On a routine visit to Omron's manufacturing plant in China hosted by executives from Omron's U.S. health care subsidiary, a manager from a major American retailer expressed interest in a blood pressure monitor designed and marketed especially to women. While women are the most common buyers of blood pressure monitors, they generally purchase them for a husband, father, or mother under their care. But shouldn't the caretakers be taking care of themselves? Heart disease is the number-one killer of women over age twenty-five. The Americans saw an immediate opportunity to serve society. But for a device to be suited to women, something different from Omron's usual approach was necessary. For one thing, the arm cuffs needed to expand in diameter for use during pregnancy (one of the most important times for women to be monitoring their blood pressure). The device also had to be small enough to fit in a woman's purse.

It took a great deal of discussion to convince managers in Japan to support and expedite an innovation led entirely by the American subsidiary. For one thing, the headquarters group has an entire book of guidelines and regulations on packaging alone. Ranndy Kellogg, head of product development and marketing in Chicago, knew that making blood pressure monitors for American women required a different kind of design and package. He commissioned a specialist market research firm to do a detailed study, to have the facts to present. But ultimately, the Omron Principles saved the day.

Both Kellogg and finance head Paul Lipka had worked at other Japanese-owned companies. They see Omron as special, as more partnership oriented. Kellogg feels this is encouraged by "people who jointly believe that our job is to work for the benefit of society. To do that for the women's monitor, we needed to talk. We said, 'Let's talk every week, every month, we'll come to Japan and see you.' We changed the way we operate to more closely follow the principles, and it helped us better communicate. Without the principles, there would have been less interest or desire in understanding what is good for society in the U.S."

In the spring of 2008, Omron introduced its Women's Advanced Blood Pressure Monitor through retail outlets such as Walgreens. Today the United States, tomorrow the world. Omron's U.S. version was destined for Europe and Asia. A manual blood pressure monitor with a digital display that could be sold at an even lower price was designed first for the Russian market and then launched in Latin America.

Omron has a distance to travel to meet all of its aspirations. It is still learning how to think globally rather than Japan first. Its next challenge is to apply the same innovation thrust in China, which surely has many societal needs for which Omron can find a solution.

big societal problems as the next innovation frontier

THERE IS A THEME that runs through all the company examples: Challenging circumstances can trigger significant innovation, including tsunamis or everyday family needs. People more readily stretch to solve problems that have never been tackled before because they care about serving society and also because they believe in social progress. They see business as a vehicle for improving the world. They create new markets by offering people more of what they need to improve daily lives. They believe change is possible, and they believe that their company can help. The least-advantaged places can thus become the best beta sites for innovation. This is already happening in emerging vanguard companies from developing countries that have leaped from obscurity to global prominence by adapting existing products and then discovering even better innovations. That's how ICICI

Bank, through innovations to serve the visually impaired, remote farmers, and the poor, has become both a profitable giant and a learning laboratory for the world.

ICICI Bank, headquartered in Mumbai, India, began life in 1955 as the Industrial Credit and Investment Corporation of India, an economic development agency, deploying funds from the World Bank, the Indian government, and Indian industry representatives to lend to development projects. It was not yet called a bank because it could not accept individual deposits. That changed in the early 1990s, in the wake of economic reforms that also brought IBM back to India in a joint venture in 1992. In 1994, ICICI Group set up ICICI banking corporation as a banking subsidiary, phasing out the development side by 2002—moves reflecting dramatic change in India and ICICI's world-class aspirations. In 1999, ICICI became the first Indian company and the first Asian financial institution outside of Japan to list on the New York Stock Exchange.

In January 2008, K. V. Kamath, CEO of ICICI Group, was honored as a chair of the World Economic Forum's annual meeting in Davos, Switzerland, where I sat on a panel with him and listened to the innovative thinking that came from finding solutions to difficult social conditions of a developing country. Kamath, who began at ICICI in 1977, left for stints at the Asian Development Bank and as CEO of an Indonesian company. When he returned in March 1996 as ICICI CEO, he shook things up, investing in technology and changing organizational culture (e.g., by implementing a performance review system and emphasizing innovation). By 2008, ICICI Bank had market share leadership in all lines of consumer retail banking business in India, with over 950 branches, 3,680 ATMs, and 25 million customers. In terms of assets, it became the largest private sector bank in India and the second-largest financial institution overall.

In the late 1990s, Kamath made technology a centerpiece of ICICI strategy not only to emulate the best global banks in efficiency but also as a way to reach an underserved population. Why shouldn't farmers, or lower-income urban residents for that matter, have access to banking services? While many foreign bank competitors had retail branches, they were not fully targeting the Indian consumer (yet); for example, Citibank, an example ICICI leaders liked to cite, was not deploying in India technology used successfully in other countries. The answer for ICICI: Go virtual first, and then expand physically. ICICI aggressively pushed ATMs to leapfrog a lack of physical branches, then built branches where ATM traffic was high. When ICICI started, India had only forty ATMs in the nation, and 60 percent of the population did not have bank accounts. ICICI moved quickly, installing three ATMs a day, catapulting past state banks that had large physical infrastructure. ICICI innovators improved on ATM models to make them fit India's population. Its ATMs use local languages and include Braille and voice guides (talking ATMs) for the visually impaired, reflecting India's diverse and too-often physically challenged population.

ATM capabilities took ICICI to Internet banking, and it became the leader in this channel too, offering full services over the Web, with the Internet now accounting for about 40 percent of transactions. ICICI has successfully tapped Indian diaspora communities in the United Kingdom, Canada, and the United States, including large numbers who study or live abroad while maintaining an Indian bank account (which is often used to send remittances back to their families). ICICI is also the industry leader in e-commerce, with a 70 percent share. For example, ICICI has been helping airlines to sell tickets online through robust services, including the design of fraud guards and checks. This cannot be soon enough for international travelers; in the e-ticket age, security guards at the entrance to India's major international airports still insist on seeing paper tickets.

In short, ICICI followed the path of other great innovators, by first creating a market and then benefiting from it. When the economy expanded and retail banking demand grew around the year 2000, ICICI was already there.

Today, ICICI seems to be everywhere. On a recent trip to Mumbai and Hyderabad, whenever traffic slowed to a standstill, I had time to memorize the ubiquitous ICICI signs. Consumers come from every walk of life. Sonjoy Chatterjee, who heads international banking and corporate banking, likes to repeat a story often told around the bank about how even CEOs use ICICI ATMs, including the founder of Infosys, one of India's software and business processing giants, who was spotted standing in line with his employees waiting patiently for his turn at the ATM. (Chatterjee was part of the strategy group with

Kamath that charted the bank's course in the late 1990s to 2000, when things took off; in 2003, he went to London to set up ICICI's first overseas subsidiary. The London subsidiary was later joined by subsidiaries in Canada and Russia.)

So far, so good. This success is the result of innovation. The innovation comes from imaginative applications of technology and from tapping the technological prowess from India's renowned software industry to use data to understand customer needs. But ICICI's market penetration is still a drop in the bucket compared with India's population size and potential. To fill the bucket, ICICI is producing innovation well ahead of some of the supposedly most advanced places in the world, such as the United States.

Even as it emerges as one of the world's most attractive growth markets for the future, India remains full of challenges. It has six hundred million farmers, perhaps two-thirds of them subsistence farmers, scattered in three hundred thousand rural villages, most of them remote, with no electricity, no local sanitation or health care, poor roads, and high rates of illiteracy. Only 28 percent of India's 1.1. billion population lives in urban areas, and according to United Nations figures, that will rise to only 41 percent urban by 2030. For a vanguard company, determining how to reach that population with cost-efficient products and services can be a major stimulus to innovation.

That really big innovation is mobile banking—that is, banking through a cell phone. Mulling over possibilities and hearing buzz about mobile phone growth, ICICI made the connection first and fast. While only twenty million Indians had Internet service, over two hundred million had mobile phone connections, second only to China; moreover, India's number of cell phone users is growing faster than China's.

ICICI began with another hallmark of great innovators: pilot projects to provide proof of concept. Linking mobile phones with ATMs could provide cardless but safe ATM withdrawals as well as safe payments to those without a bank account. In 2005, ICICI started customer-to-noncustomer money transfers. Imagine the possibilities, say, for people working in cities to be able to send money to their parents in a remote village who do not have an account. Through their mobile phones, the parents can receive an alert and a personal identification number (PIN) to access any ICICI ATM to withdraw a specified amount from the child's account. This procedure can also be used by small business owners to send a safe payment to someone without an account, or by urban dwellers to pay domestic employees a monthly or weekly amount, with an alert notifying the workers when to get their money. A year or so later, ICICI added mobile text alerts to its voice system.

By 2008, ICICI was ready to launch iMobile, full Internet banking services (e.g., making transfers, paying bills, checking balance status, and receiving alerts) via mobile phones. The service is free of charge to all existing customers (e.g., holders of savings accounts, checking accounts, credit cards, or loans), and the program can be downloaded directly onto their phone.

iMobile is still in the "improvisational theater" phase of rapid prototyping (i.e., setting a theme, testing variations with customers, refining another prototype, and checking use again). Meanwhile, ICICI is venturing into other advanced technologies to reach the hardest-to-get consumers, that is, those with little education who are often illiterate. Talking ATMs are one solution. Another is biometric sensing, and ICICI is working to create a biometric industry standard. Instead of signatures, people can be identified by fingerprints. In rural banking, biometric handheld devices can be used for collecting payments. A consumer swipes a card, enters a PIN on a pad, and a fingerprint matching system is used to verify identity. This system eliminates intermediaries, increases collection while decreasing cost, and reduces frauds and losses.

This technology developed for the poorest people in the most remote corners of the world will someday become the standard for transactions everywhere and is an example of bottom-up innovation in action. The best models for ICICI came not from the United States or the United Kingdom but from South Africa. African banks are ahead of the pack because cell phone penetration there, as in India, has far outpaced nearly every other kind of infrastructure. Tough conditions force innovation on the companies that emerge as winners. A culture for innovation helps companies anywhere in the world leapfrog the competition.

For vanguard companies, a desire to address unmet societal needs with the latest technology, not with charity or hand-me-downs, is the best guarantee of continuing innovation. Cemex's attention to social needs and local conditions has generated ideas that have led to significant innovations: antibacterial concrete, which is particularly important for hospitals and farms; water-resistant concrete that is helpful in flood-prone areas; and used tires converted to road surface for countries with rapid growth in road construction. An idea from Egypt for salt water–resistant concrete, helpful for harbor and marine applications, became a product launched in the Philippines.

For IBM, a commitment to improve K–12 public education, which started in the United States, has produced innovations that can go directly to schools but with benefits that accrue elsewhere.

speaking of innovation: ibm's voice recognition technology and the schools

THE IDEA CAME from the first round of IBM's Reinventing Education partnerships, launched in 1994. The concept behind Reinventing Education was innovative in and of itself: to partner with K–12 public school systems to develop new solutions to problems the schools themselves identified. The schools needed to be risk takers and collaborators. IBM wanted to make a big difference for schools and to push its technology frontiers to do so.

In Philadelphia, school superintendent David Hornbeck hoped technology could make it possible for teachers to teach reading to special-needs children in their regular classrooms, without pulling them out for remedial treatment, and to do it more effectively. Literacy was emerging as a huge issue in the United States, as it was in many parts of the world, and an IBM project team from IBM's famed Watson Research Lab set out to develop a new tool. That was a challenge. Existing IBM voice recognition technology was based on a simple adult norm. It did not work with young children's high-pitched voices, their hesitant speech patterns and pronunciation variations, or the accents of those for whom English was a second language. (In U.S. urban school districts, there could be many dozens of native languages, each with their own accents.)

To expand the technology, IBM researchers collected over forty thousand utterances from eight hundred children around the United

States. A team member from Watson worked in the Barton Elementary School, observing a fourth-grade classroom and utilizing its mock TV studio, learning and adjusting as students used various prototypes. The daily presence of an IBMer helped overcome educator stereotypes about businesspeople and educated IBMers about schools.

The result was a software product called Watch-me!-Read. A child could look at written words on the screen and speak into a microphone, and the software would then compare the acoustic stream with the phonemes stored in the database, making a match that is accurate 97 percent of the time. Watch-me!-Read was piloted in grades 4 and 5 at Barton and with learning-disabled students at Olney High School.

The Philadephia team encountered the usual bugs in pilot projects, such as delays owing to unexpected events or overly optimistic expectations for getting everything right quickly. When innovating, initial plans are just best guesses rather than firm forecasts. Teachers were highly enthusiastic (although IT departments at the schools were a bit resistant to outsiders), but it still took time to learn to deploy new tools, and the press of daily work sometimes got in the way of trying new things. However, IBM's clear communication and documentation helped transcend staff turnover, a frequent occurrence in schools. IBM agreed to spend two years in the school district to create a solution, but results for children and literacy would depend on what the schools did to deploy and use the tool. Reinventing Education leaders had to invent a few pieces to add to IBM's usual work process, such as creating a formal completion document, signed by the school superintendent, that indicated what IBM committed to continue to provide as a gift and what the school would now have to acquire itself, such as training or equipment.

After the pilot period, IBM had proven the concept that the new voice recognition tool could work on a small scale to teach reading and improve pronunciation. Could it work on a larger scale? In the next round of Reinventing Education partnerships, which began in 1996, Houston came on board. IBM refined a CD-based version of Watch-me!-Read in the Houston Independent School District for a districtwide implementation, with strong positive results when the technology was used as a component part of a comprehensive literacy program.

Applications expanded after that. Working with several non-governmental organizations (NGOs), IBM developed an adult version of the user interface for its adult literacy and workforce training programs. In 2005, IBM began work on a Web-based version, Reading Companion (http://www.readingcompanion.org), phasing out the CD. Reading Companion incorporates both the children's and adults' voice models and interfaces. The Web-based version means that users have immediate access to the latest versions with all updates whenever they log on, they have immediate access to new books that are added, they receive online training, the system remembers users and what they've read, and the system collects information for teachers. The site features an online "book builder" that makes it very easy to develop new e-books to post on the site. Older kids have written for younger students, creating schoolwide literacy activities.

Reading Companion is free for schools and NGOs. While this is an example of a society-serving innovation, the benefits to IBM are also invaluable. The IBM researchers and software group working on the literacy tool are the same people who develop technology for the commercial side of the business. The impetus to innovate in new technology to meet the demanding needs of schools took voice recognition capabilities to a whole new level, resulting in numerous business applications with better products coming from a research team more skilled in innovation.

ideas from the ground up to the clouds . . . and back down to earth

I have shown that vanguard companies attempt to shorten the loop between society and solutions, but they also face the issue of deploying solutions widely—the diffusion of innovations. Close connections from the outset between developers and users are one clear facilitator. IBM researchers develop prototypes and improve on them through frequent communication with users or even location in customer facilities, as happened in the Philadelphia schools. P&G brings customers into the development process to ensure faster and more enthusiastic product adoption, as evidenced with Always Básico in Brazil.

A second way to facilitate diffusion is to pick a demonstration site carefully and offer proof of concept by showing the innovation in use. For example, Omron designed industrial laundry safety devices for a Texas company and then demonstrated them at an industrial laundry convention (which fortunately happened to be in Dallas) to create the market. A first demonstration site for mobile banking or voice recognition technology becomes the place to bring future users to educate them about what's possible. Otherwise, a great idea and a perfect solution can languish because no one understands it well enough or sees its virtues clearly enough to want to make all the other changes necessary to put a single innovation in place.

To help customers envision innovations and thus decrease lag time between technology innovation and customer orders, IBM Innovation Centers demonstrate the potential for innovation to provide new solutions. These strategically located showrooms offer futuristic prototypes for the major industries that IBM serves. I saw exciting retail space planning tools using virtual worlds and avatars at the new Innovation Center on the first floor of the China Technology Lab in suburban Beijing. An Innovation Center in Barcelona, Spain, focuses on banks of the future, and another in Brazil features banking solutions, including payment through cell phones (one piece of ICICI's mobile banking system) and a digital camera system that manages large queues so that a bank could attend to a customer in fifteen minutes, as required by a new Brazilian banking law. This is, so far, pretty conventional marketing, targeted at business customers.

What IBM adds to the mix comes from its societal contributions, offering demonstrations of innovations that are potentially more persuasive and have greater impact than the business applications in the Innovation Centers. IBM's public-facing projects, including Reinventing Education and World Community Grid (WCG), are also showcases for the power of IBM innovations, demonstrating the latest solutions applied to big, vexing problems that broad groups of people care about. Reinventing Education shows how social issues can stimulate innovation. WCG goes further in showing off the power of technology fresh from the lab, giving it away for good causes not as an afterthought but even before there are commercial customers. Society first, then the marketplace.

With the launch of WorldCommunityGrid.org in November 2004, IBM made powerful grid technology available to address the most critical health and environmental issues facing society. It is a powerful demonstration of what is now known as cloud computing. This was a launch on a fast track, starting almost when Stanley Litow, vice president of corporate citizenship, who keeps in close communication with IBM research labs, learned of a breakthrough at Watson Labs. Grid computing links distributed computers in a network as powerful as a massive supercomputer. Litow thought that this technology could best be demonstrated by doing something really big. He went to CEO Sam Palmisano and proposed using the technology immediately in a societal application. He believed it would be more powerful for customers than a commercial application and would have the added benefit of engaging hundreds of thousands of IBMers and business partners—another win-win-win-win. (Litow's understanding of the close connection between society and technology innovation is one reason his group reported for three years to the executive vice president for technology and innovation.)

The vision was for IBMers, along with people in other organizations who joined with IBM in the nonprofit venture, to donate unused time when their PCs were on but idle. The unused power would aggregate to create the equivalent of a supercomputer that could be donated, in turn, to researchers trying to find a cure for AIDS or Alzheimer's—or any major scientific project requiring massive amounts of data processing. "You can change the world," the homepage proclaims, giving people simple instructions for downloading secure software to link to the grid. "Making a difference has never been easier!"

The real-world relationships are impressive. A distinguished scientific advisory board is represented by heads of major laboratories around the world, including leaders in Asia and Latin America. Linda Sanford, IBM's senior vice president of enterprise on demand transformation and IT, is also on the board. The first projects to use WCG were the Institute for Systems Biology's Human Proteome Folding project and Scripps Institute's Fighting AIDS at Home initiative. WCG has added a cancer research project sponsored by the New Jersey Cancer Institute and Rutgers and projects on drought predictions in Africa sponsored by the University of Cape Town in South Africa and global hunger via a rice DNA project sponsored by the University of Washington.

Partners include 378 organizations ranging from an Italian oil company to U.S. public high schools; in March 2008, the latest partners to join were the Urban League of Greater North Dallas, Texas, and Amoeba Music. In Russia, where IBMer Tatiana Kipchatova promoted WCG use, the first two Russian organizations to join were a charity AIDS foundation and an Internet hosting company contributing the resources of its servers. IBM itself appears discreetly on the website, as the earliest partner and the sponsor donating hardware, software, and hosting services; a "Powered by IBM" logo appears on each page. IBM does not have to shout because its societal contributions, whether WCG, Reading Companion, or the rest, generate massive publicity, even more than routine product announcements.

This is a noteworthy way to move innovation into the world quickly with a big bang and huge potential for good. Perhaps the really big global projects could be accomplished only by a giant like IBM, but I think that the opportunities for impact are all around us, if serving society is put at the heart of an enterprise.

investing the values dividend

THERE IS AN OLD INNOVATION adage: When the climate is right, a thousand flowers can bloom. From the bougainvilleas in Brazil to the cherry blossoms in Japan, vanguard companies add new growth to classic innovation wisdom. They show that values and social purpose can produce more innovation enablers and suppress more innovation stiflers. When social purpose is at the forefront, five advantages accrue.

> • *A bigger idea pool: a wider search for broader ideas with bigger potential.* People search more broadly, see more opportunities, and generate more ideas if they are encouraged to think about the world and dream beyond their own individual function. If they look closely at society not just as a market abstraction but as a collection of fellow humans with needs worthy of attention, they see that there is always room for improvement, that "better" is always a moving

target. Having more ideas enter the innovation funnel provides more options and more improvements.

• *Greater solutions orientation: motivation to serve customers and users.* When people feel their ideas will contribute to a social purpose, and not just to revenues and profits, there is an additional motivational boost to focus on new solutions, not just pushing more of what they already know. They care about solving the problem because it is connected with their values, and they are willing to keep working until the problem is solved, not just until they have a product to throw over the transom. They want to engage those who have the problem in defining whether the solution works for them. This puts passion and heart into user-directed innovation.

• *Open innovation: a greater willingness to draw on resources outside the organization, to work with partners, and to share ideas.* With a transcendent goal in mind, it is more likely that people will embrace "open innovation"—the sharing of ideas among partners and willingness to draw on other people's technology in the service of a higher end. There is less pride of ownership; the important thing is getting the job done.

• *Less politics, less controversy, greater cooperation.* Values and principles provide a basis for cordial internal conversation that elicits cooperation. This makes it possible for innovators to assemble the right team quickly, because others in the organization share a common goal despite the different positions they occupy. Invoking shared values can also wear down opponents and critics, surfacing the underlying interests that negotiation scholars find make "yes" a likely answer. Tying projects to enduring principles helps people rise above politics. Putting the good of the wider external community first helps get backing in the internal company community.

• *Faster execution: shorter communication and feedback loops.* The very articulation of societal purpose as a driver of innovation helps shorten mental and organizational loops. Greater awareness on everyone's part of their role in an end-to-end chain of impact can help bridge the gap between theory and practice. The research lab can come closer to the world of users and those working with the wider society closer to the developers of new technology.

When you bring society inside the organization, the possibilities increase for success at every point in the innovation process. Focusing the company on solutions for the world inspires people to work hard to find them, because the quest is more meaningful than seeking financial returns alone. This culture makes it more likely that people will generate important ideas, sell change to sometimes-reluctant stakeholders, motivate a team to work collaboratively, and diffuse innovation rapidly and effectively. That is a big dividend from leading with purpose, values, and principles.

chapter five

good to grow: mergers, acquisitions, and transformations

THE WHOLE THING got off to a very bad start. Almost immediately after the announcement of a takeover bid for their company in June 2003, thirty-five hundred male employees of Chohung Bank shaved their heads and deposited the hair in front of the skyscraper that housed the headquarters of Shinhan Bank, the competitor that wanted to buy them. That amounted to a huge pile of straight black hair in the historic center of downtown Seoul, South Korea. This was hardly expected behavior for bankers. And as protests go, this instance of resistance to change was highly visible, intensely embarrassing, and a strong signal of what could lie ahead if the merger went through.

It was a hairy situation, so to speak. But it was only an extreme (and extremely visible) version of the turmoil and discontent that can lurk in the shadows of major change. Resistance to change is always a danger even in small projects and promising innovations. But when a whole company is about to change its shape, to transform itself into something entirely different through a merger, emotions can run rampant.

Mergers are a business practice that nearly everyone loves to hate. Employee anxieties rise in the uncertainties surrounding who will go and who will stay as the acquirer "consolidates" (cuts jobs), or in the disruption caused by new rules or roles. Old-fashioned company loyalty tugs the heartstrings, when people have formed important parts of their identities around being part of particular companies. For example, when Procter & Gamble and Gillette announced their agreement that P&G would acquire Gillette, there were undoubtedly many long-term Gillette employees who would have gladly supplied Gillette razors for Chohung Bank employees to shave their heads, in solidarity with all those who hate mergers. And not only employees but just about everyone else seems to hate mergers too, except the bankers and lawyers who live off them or competitors who use the confusion to poach business. Concerned investors often drive down acquiring companies' share price. Customers fear changeover problems that disrupt service. Politicians in the neighborhood of a takeover target rally populist sentiment against a change that threatens to remove a local headquarters or cost jobs.

Despite all the potential difficulties, mergers and acquisitions continue to burgeon, within countries and across borders, except in tough times when the capital spigot that fuels deals is temporarily shut off. Companies use mergers and acquisitions to fill gaps in product portfolios, enter new geographic markets or gain scale in existing ones, and, most important, add new capabilities that help them get out ahead of major external changes. Although many companies suffer losses before realizing the economic value of their changes and a high proportion of mergers fail to live up to expectations (sometimes even destroying financial value), vanguard companies tend to buck the trend.

One marker of vanguard companies is their ability to integrate new people, products, ideas, and capabilities quickly and effectively, while still remaining true to their purpose and values. Indeed, strong values encourage leaders to pay attention to culture and human emotions as they add new parts and shed others. This helps vanguard companies take giant strategic steps. Their approach to mergers and other huge but potentially threatening changes combines discipline and humanism. They stress high standards and provide tools to meet them, and they also have leaders who invest in creating a welcoming, inclusive culture. Vanguard companies provide a very different model of how companies can grow through acquisitions without making people miserable and, under the best circumstances, perhaps making employees and communities a little happier.

This chapter goes deeply inside a few vanguard companies to show how they do it. Four themes are central.

- People must feel integrated emotionally as well as operationally.
- Grouping activities into three buckets aids smooth transitions: running existing (legacy) units in parallel for a while; building unity and commitment to the overall enterprise; and creating something entirely new, not previously owned by anyone.
- Stealth integration, which people accomplish voluntarily, can occur if roles are reversed and those taken over are made to feel in control.
- Spreading high standards quickly involves a great deal of human cross-fertilization, moving people around to mentor and educate.

Shinhan used these approaches in the Chohung merger to accomplish a significant transformation. The Shinhan story is dramatic but simple. Later in the chapter, we will see these themes at work in a variety of other situations.

when the emotional is rational: the benefits of emotional integration

As THE PILE of hair in front of Shinhan's headquarters got higher and higher, so did the worries. Shinhan Bank leaders paused momentarily to consider their plans to buy troubled Chohung Bank. Chohung was a venerable 107-year-old Korean icon that had served the Korean conglomerates known as *chaebols* but had faltered during the 1997–98 Asian financial crisis and had fallen behind the times in other respects. It had to be bailed out by the government. Chohung was a little larger and much older than acquisitive upstart Shinhan and had enormous pride that had already taken several blows. Two years earlier, Chohung had tried to acquire Shinhan before succumbing to its own weakened finances. Emotional bonds were so strong at Chohung that union members (in Korea, a category reaching well into lower management) shed their hair readily and held their bald heads high as a sign of their loyalty.

Shinhan, founded in 1982, was different from Chohung in numerous respects. As a young entrepreneurial bank, Shinhan had grown by serving the new edge of South Korea's emergence as a developed country: a middle class and midsized enterprises. More open to learning from global experience and less dependent than Chohung on either iron-fisted government or equally closed *chaebols*, Shinhan had come through the Asian financial meltdown with a strong balance sheet and leaders determined to be among the best in the world. Knowing that liberalization and globalization meant stronger competition from international banks (Citigroup was especially feared), Shinhan leaders wanted to scale up quickly and then tackle the region. They looked for an acquisition and found Chohung, still with hair on its collective head representing growth potential.

By June 2003, Asia was back on track as the region of the future. Global competition was coming, and so Shinhan leaders went ahead with the bid for Chohung with an unusual strategy in mind. First they spent four days negotiating with the union. They gave away a great deal, it seemed on a superficial glance at the contract, before handing out caps to Chohung's protesters to cover their bare heads when they went back to work. Shinhan agreed to raise the compensation of Chohung employees to match Shinhan standards. They agreed to equal representation on the boards of a new holding company, Shinhan Financial Group, and on all key committees. They agreed not to formally integrate for three years. Meanwhile, some bank customers, seeing all the turmoil and the hair, took their business elsewhere. It seemed like everything was stacked against this merger.

In little over a year later, after a series of creative events designed by joint task forces under the banner of "emotional integration," the two banks were virtually integrated in all but name.

The first and most radical emotional integration idea was a big retreat, the Serabol Summit. Shinhan convened fifteen hundred top managers of legacy Chohung and Shinhan banks for several days of symbol-laden meetings, including climbing a mountain together near a historic shrine, performing rituals in concert, and shedding former roles to meet new people performing new jobs.

This event was proposed and implemented by a task force of younger professionals, including some like Cheol Park from strategic planning who had studied in the United States and spoke fluent English. Team members examined the reasons most mergers fail and decided it was the human factor. They wanted to tap into deep emotions that would make people feel united as part of something big and important. They saw that the standstill agreement with the Chohung union that prohibited formal bank integration did not ban shared experiences. They wanted the Serabol Summit to invoke feelings of solidarity, pull on heartstrings, and forge a common identity as one company while business formalities remained separate. Park's group knew that what they were proposing was a big risk. They knew of no event on this scale in the region—and certainly none where emotional themes claimed more time on the agenda than discussions of business strategy and change management. Fortunately, members of the top management committee supported them and were willing to invest.

Unlike their management elders, the younger Shinhan group came of age in the Internet era and saw the power of human connections. They had no memory of the emotional manipulation that had taken place in North Korean prisoner-of-war camps during the 1950s Korean War (the American War to them) that put north and south on separate paths, making North Korea one of the world's danger spots and one known for attempts at pernicious brainwashing in prisoner-of-war camps.

Shinhan's emotional integration was nothing like brainwashing; it was more like a meeting of the minds. The Shinhan task force's intention was benign and not coercive: to offer a setting conducive to employee empowerment—encouragement to speak up and share ideas—and for making friends with people who had once been competitors, to learn to work as partners. They were sensitive to every signal of inclusion or exclusion and tilted the scales toward inclusion. (When I rode with Cheol Park in a private car across South Korea following the Serabol Summit, where I was a speaker, and he pointed out that we were ten miles from the line dividing south from north, I speculated about how quickly the oppressed population of the nuclear arms bearing, dictator-led North Korea could be integrated into a healthy society if governments operated under leadership principles like those guiding Shinhan.)

THE INTEGRATION PAYOFF

As it turned out, Shinhan had given nothing away and had gained everything. In a short time, the new Shinhan Financial Group presided over well-functioning legacy banks operating in parallel but actively exchanging ideas with one another, displaying one another's banners in their own branch banks, and strategizing together about a new model for the bank-of-the-future. Relationships became so strong that the Chohung union of the shaved-head protest was pretty much neutralized and acquired more cooperative new leadership. At the three-year mark, when official integration could take place, the Chohung name disappeared.

Within three years, Shinhan Financial Group grew to become the largest financial group in Korea. It is listed on the New York Stock Exchange and is one of the *Wall Street Journal*'s twenty-five Asian bellwether stocks. Shinhan's financial performance and customer satisfaction shot well ahead of the competition. Its growth in stock valuation has far outpaced the Korean market as a whole. That performance is remarkable anywhere.

The managers who formed the new Shinhan Financial Groups are smart bankers, incorporating global best practices and rising to the stringent standards of Sarbanes-Oxley for Shinhan's New York Stock Exchange listing. They planned the merger carefully using advanced management systems, complete with detailed flow charts and dozens of task forces involving hundreds of people directly and thousands indirectly. But neither banking intelligence nor managerial systems would have been enough without the human touches that put egos in check and helped new identities to form. Shinhan leaders were willing to venture into the realm of emotional understanding, tying humanism to management in order to execute a growth strategy.

As in other vanguard companies, Shinhan leaders are smart enough to organize and categorize the work of change in clear ways that enable people to move from where they are step by step while envisioning a long-term future, and they pay as much attention to integrating people emotionally as they do to work processes. Shinhan made this three-part model explicit in its postacquisition activities.

the three-part merger formula: dual, one, and new

BIG TRANSFORMATIONS stand or fall on human commitment to change. In addition to the formal plans that map the direction of change, people need to be moved from protesters trying to prevent change to active participants shaping the future.

In the Shinhan-Chohung bank merger, the integration structure consisted of three streams of activity, each with a governance body and task forces responsible for specific pieces, and with equal representation from each of the legacy banks. Shinhan called these activity sets "dual bank," "one bank," and "new bank."

- "Dual bank" was the name for continuing to run legacy Shinhan and Chohung banks as distinct entities while encouraging their managers to communicate. While formally separate, they came together in dozens of joint task forces to share best practices and learn about each other's operations and methods. This separation was required by the agreement with the union, but it turned out to be good practice anyway. It helped anchor people in a home base group, prevented confusion, and permitted overlap to ease the transition to new ways step by step. As people began to learn new ways of doing things, they could gradually drop the old ways. Without coercion, managers saw the wisdom of adopting a practice that worked elsewhere, sometimes from legacy Shinhan, sometimes from Chohung. The two banks soon started to resemble each other.
- "One bank" was the umbrella for an extensive set of conferences and events to provide training, understanding of the strategy, common values, and "emotional integration," Shinhan's term for human bonding. The events were both informative and fun, so people had positive stories to tell. They involved ways for people to come to know one another outside of their jobs, which opened up many new connections. The emphasis was tilted toward togetherness, toward the emotional side, not the task side. The planners wanted people to forge relationships and feel emotionally connected to one another and to the institution.
- "New bank" task forces developed the designs for innovative financial services of the future. This was new territory for both legacy banks, and it encouraged people to look beyond concerns of the moment to envision something totally different. This was a highly empowering mandate, but one that was also challenging and required members from each legacy bank to depend on one another.

All of these three streams represent de facto integration, even stealth integration, going around the letter of the union agreement to let people see the value of integrating on their own. In short, Shinhan leaders convened people and let human nature take its course. Once people showed up and had goals to achieve, they started to want to be together and took responsibility for change.

This way of clarifying the tasks and uniting people sends important reassuring messages:. *We come from different places, and our separate individual identities are acknowledged and valued* (dual bank). *We are joined as one enterprise, one community, where we can communicate with one another and feel part of the same entity* (one bank). *Together, we are building a promising future that we share equally* (new bank).

MIX, MATCH, AND LEARN

This integration formula can move change onto a fast track, as was seen after P&G's takeover of Gillette in 2006. A P&G-Gillette global integration team had laid the groundwork, mapping processes from the two companies in order to achieve what they called (without much originality) a "one plus one equals three" merger. Differences were allowed to surface, but P&G made a point of sending messages of welcome and inclusion whenever possible and letting people know that a great new company could arise from the merger. Out of dual companies can come one company striving to become a new company.

Headquarters in Cincinnati had the road map, but it was the human touches by managers on the ground that made the real difference. Brazil was the last country in Latin America to integrate Gillette into the P&G family. Tarek Farahat, P&G's country general manager, whom we met in chapter 4, led the human integration. On the Monday of the actual merger, when Gillette people were to move out of their previous offices into P&G's high-rise building in a new section of downtown São Paulo, Farahat put everyone on an equal footing by shuffling the office space. When P&G and Gillette employees arrived at work that day, most of them, including legacy P&G people, were in new offices on a new floor. Soon they had new assignments too. He mixed middle-level employees so they could learn the other side's business. Gillette marketing people worked on P&G brands and vice versa but with minimal business risk and much potential gain from cross-fertilization. Farahat's tactics worked; employees from the two companies reported that they integrated seamlessly. "I was very lucky," Farahat said. "Hermann, my predecessor, and Eduardo Cello, the previous Gillette general manager, built a wonderful pool of talent. All I had to do was mix them."

In the first year after the Gillette integration, legacy P&G and Gillette units retained business and improved their top and bottom line growth, exceeding even their own targets. The story was similar all over the world. Each country worked out the right combination of practices and procedures, but everywhere the emotional foundation was laid for Gillette to embrace P&G's purpose, values, and principles and for P&G to incorporate Gillette's faster go-to-market processes.

That is the next major lesson. Transformational enterprises and their leaders not only change others; they allow themselves to be changed.

from wooing to winning: leadership, human values, and the strategic use of "reverse takeovers"

IN THE MOST strategically important situations, acquisitions are not conquests; they are opportunities for learning. In the vanguard, when everything works well, purpose and values guide the acquisition process at every step. Leaders might even check their egos at the door in order to let those that they acquire help their own company become stronger and stay ahead of change. This is a smart tactic for wooing the most desirable marriage partners and an effective way to create economic and social value following acquisitions.

"Who acquired whom?" Banco Real CEO Fabio Barbosa mused ten years ago when his Dutch parent ABN AMRO bought Banco Real and let its own Brazilian operations disappear into it; and then ten years later, when Santander acquired Banco Real, once again the buyer folded itself into the bank it bought. This is a role reversal I see in vanguard companies that lead with their values. Leaders of vanguard companies seek values compatibility before marriage, but they are also willing to be influenced by the practices of companies they buy. They respect the people and want to learn from them.

The growth of Publicis Groupe over a decade of highly strategic acquisitions provides a revealing story. Long-term CEO Maurice Lévy transformed a back-of-the-pack French-dominated advertising company into the world's fourth-largest global communications group. Publicis is not only a triumphant survivor in a consolidating industry faced with technological change, but it is now positioned as a leader in the wave-of-the-future digital space—through integrating another important acquisition, Digitas, introduced in chapter 2.

A VISION IN SEARCH OF PARTNERS

Tall, charismatic, and charming, Maurice Lévy is an acquisition do-it-yourselfer who builds personal emotional bonds first, before getting down to business. He says he is a mere vehicle for furthering the values of founder Marcel Bleustein-Blanchet—respect for individuals and a spirit of collaboration.

Some might argue that sensitivity to human feelings is a business necessity in a creative industry, where egos run rampant and autonomy rules. But not every management group or holding company has Lévy's touch or his dedication to making his organization mean something more than just another business. Bleustein-Blanchet spotted Lévy's feelings of responsibility early and asked him to be CEO while Lévy was still in his thirties. When a fire threatened to destroy Publicis headquarters in 1972, Lévy, who had joined the company a year earlier following university, dashed into the building to save files and keep the client work going. Fortunately, the building was preserved; it is a Paris tourist landmark on the Champs-Élysées because it holds Le Drugstore, started by Bleustein-Blanchet after World War II in admiration for American-style shops. But Bleustein-Blanchet was intensely French, and his agency was intensely national in focus and style.

In the late 1980s, Lévy saw that globalization was changing the game. Clients such as Nestlé, L'Oréal, and Colgate-Palmolive wanted fewer suppliers that could serve them worldwide, and that definitely included advertising agencies, as companies like Gillette started to launch global products, such as its Sensor Excel razor, with the same advertising message everywhere. Publicis beefed up its European network and added a small presence in the United States, but Lévy and his colleagues knew that Publicis needed to grow faster globally or risk shrinking into oblivion. Publicis eyed Chicago-based Foote, Cone & Belding (FCB), which was also on the prowl. Each was willing to buy but neither wanted to sell. Instead they formed a strategic alliance, one that was considered a model at the time.

Lévy formed a strong bond with FCB CEO Norman Brown, based on similar values and personal rapport. The alliance deal was a sensible one, and both sides benefited. But there was a snake in the grass that eventually bit Lévy. Brown's successor wanted complete control and had voted against the alliance in the first place, as Lévy discovered much later and too late, after it all unraveled. Lévy told me that his first mistake was not asking about that vote—trust without verification can be dangerous. Then when Publicis extended its presence in the United States, FCB's newly formed holding company, True North, used that change to try to wiggle out of the deal. Lawsuits ultimately ended the alliance acrimoniously, with ugly personal attacks on Lévy. At one point, according to Lévy, True North hired private detectives to shadow him, assuming that because Lévy was French, they could find a mistress or a scandal to embarrass him. They found nothing. In fact, Maurice Lévy was already one of the most respected private sector leaders in France, an irony in a country with socialist leanings manifested, among other things, in anticapitalist protesters picketing outside Le Drugstore with advertising as a target.

If this seems written only from the Publicis perspective, consider why: the divergent fate of the two entities. True North is long gone, and Publicis is a top-four global giant. What happened next confirms why Publicis emerged as the winner and shows how Lévy put Publicis in the vanguard.

CHECKING EGO AT THE DOOR

Ego management is a must-have skill for leaders of the future, especially in creative industries filled with prima donnas. In this case, the first ego that Lévy had to manage was his own. The failed alliance was a truly humbling experience. It also provided him with valuable lessons and redoubled his determination while enabling him to do something that endears CEOs to ordinary people: admit he was wrong. Lévy has said that to my students, and he has said that on a panel with other CEOs in front of a thousand of his peers at the World Economic

Forum in Davos, Switzerland. He also said that, as a Frenchman approaching American and British companies to combine forces, he understands he has something additional to prove.

After the failed alliance, Lévy knew that Publicis still needed to grow to survive and serve its clients. He felt he was the steward of an institution that meant more to its people than just another job, as it did to him. Before Lévy could think globally, he had to think American. Publicis needed a bigger U.S. presence, and it needed to overcome any tinge of damaged goods.

Lévy's first choice target was the founder-led Hal Riney agency in San Francisco, highly respected for creativity. Riney was fiercely independent, and no one had been able to buy his baby. Riney had already dismissed courtship proposals from WPP, Omnicom, and Interpublic, Publicis's main rivals. Lévy went alone to talk with him, dine with him, and get acquainted. They talked about values and vision, about the creative process. Lévy was a frequent flier on the Paris–San Francisco flight, so he could repeatedly exercise face-to-face personal diplomacy, without staff, investment bankers, or lawyers. They talked long enough for Riney to feel heard, understood, and safe. Was it his age and the knowledge that he had to put his agency in other hands to ensure his legacy? Was it Lévy's belief in creative independence? Was it the sly feeling that a corporate headquarters far away across the Atlantic in France would not manage a small Pacific Coast operation too closely? Or perhaps it was the quick emotional bonding. To the surprise of the industry and its observers, Publicis bought the Hal Riney agency in 1998.

For values-oriented, purpose-driven companies, deals are not measured in monetary terms alone, although getting a fair deal is important. The trick to forging an agreement is to have no tricks, just an ability to understand underlying interests and address them. Buyers are sometimes willing to pay a small premium to show respect and to ensure that the seller is motivated to help them. Sellers are sometimes willing to take a tad bit less to get the right buyer who will protect the thing that they have nurtured and want to see thrive. It might not seem entirely rational in the short term, but emotions have their own rationality, since they propel what will happen later. Starting with the human bond makes the business deal easier to work out and motivates smoother integration of operations.

Lévy had approached Riney because he believed the acquisition would signal Publicis's intentions to move forward after FCB/True North and demonstrate commitment to creativity. "We decided to buy the impossible buy, the agency that everyone wanted and that no one had succeeded in buying. I thought that if I could do it I would gain credibility in the marketplace," Lévy declared.

It worked. This American acquisition put Publicis on the radar screen as a credible acquirer in the world's largest market. There was an amusing moment when Young & Rubicam (Y&R) was for sale, and Publicis was approached. In characteristic style, Lévy went by himself to a first meeting in a New York boardroom where he sat alone on his side of a long table facing over a dozen executives, lawyers, and investment bankers on the Y&R side. (Publicis declined to make an offer.)

EMPATHY AS STRATEGY

Lévy's next major acquisition made headlines in the British press that were bigger than the size of the deal warranted because national pride was at stake—a French company was taking over a British company. Though no one tried to stop the deal, the press bemoaned it anyway when Publicis bought Saatchi & Saatchi. If the press felt a blow to pride, imagine how the people at Saatchi felt. Lévy imagined it and through empathy was able to deal with it.

Saatchi & Saatchi had been founded by art collector brothers and became a creative icon. It had grown big, extended into other professional services, declined precipitously, was shoved into a holding company under another name, and then rescued. Although it was still a creative shop serving some of the world's giants, it was also bleeding cash. Saatchi executives knew they needed capital but didn't really want to sell. But Bob Seelert, the chairman of Saatchi & Saatchi's board, happened to sit with Lévy at a dinner event in London, and they decided to talk over breakfast the next morning. Was it just serendipity?

Lévy next had a series of private meetings in hotel suites with Saatchi CEO Kevin Roberts, and here is where emotional skills made all the difference. Roberts was known as flamboyant, creative, and very energetic. He once ran a contest for employees in which the prize was his own portrait, and his name for the Saatchi top management committee was K-7, standing for Kevin's 7. Quite the free thinker. Among the first things Roberts said to Lévy was that he did not want a boss. Lévy nodded with understanding (while knowing full well that he was of course the boss). For his part, Lévy talked values. He talked about personal beliefs and about his origins. He recounted stories about some early childhood memories and his boyhood in North Africa. Roberts reported later that he was powerfully drawn to Lévy. That probably understates the attraction.

ROLE REVERSALS AND THE ART OF
STEALTH INTEGRATION

Lévy proceeded to treat the whole thing like a reverse takeover. It was not just because Roberts said he did not want a boss that Lévy decided to try some role reversal. Making the target feel in charge cuts off resistance before it surfaces and forges emotional bonds that make the whole thing seem voluntary. This is "stealth integration," in that people feel connected and are easily influenced even before they realize that they are being moved to change behavior. Stealth integration, we have seen, is how Shinhan worked around potential resistance and integrated before the union noticed.

Publicis paid a premium for Saatchi and insured Saatchi executives against any downside in stock price. The trick was to retain the talent that could cash out on favorable terms, and that meant underscoring Saatchi's—and Kevin Roberts's—importance. Publicis Worldwide, the original agency, became just another part of Publicis Groupe, in which Saatchi was a major part under its own name. Roberts joined the Groupe operating committee, renamed P-12, for Publicis 12 (not M-12 for Maurice's 12, still another sign that Lévy, though the CEO, knew when to put ego aside). Saatchi people made the major Power-Point presentation when Lévy convened the top group for a retreat in Fontainebleau. Lévy told Roberts he would adopt the Saatchi operating system, gave everyone a copy of a management book Roberts had written, and invited Roberts and his colleagues to offer training sessions for Publicis managers.

Lévy did not need to act like Roberts's boss because Roberts now trusted Lévy so much that all Lévy had to do was hint, and Roberts did it. That is how Lévy got Roberts to fire two Saatchi executives whose foot dragging and other acts of passive aggression were undermining merger integration. A mere mention by Lévy of some difficulties, and the deed was done. The resistors were gone. *Voila!*

Like other vanguard companies, Publicis can afford autonomy and self-direction because the values and principles are so clear and the relationships of respect are so strong. Saatchi employees found themselves drawn to Publicis despite having been proud of their previous independence. Roberts rose to Publicis top ranks as a team player.

Lévy used a similar approach to acquire another icon. That one was a messy recent Chicago-based holding company called BCom3 that had grown out of Leo Burnett, the main jewel. Burnett's culture was incredibly strong, and Burnett leaders too did not want to sell. Lévy showed the utmost respect for the culture. He was patient. He visited. They sold.

With three major international advertising agency networks—Publicis Worldwide (the original agency), Saatchi & Saatchi, and Leo Burnett—kept deliberately autonomous so that they could serve clients who were competitors, plus an alliance with Dentsu in Japan, numerous smaller acquisitions, and some central groups focused on media placements and new media, Publicis Groupe was ready for greater global integration. Consolidating back-office functions trimmed expenses and produced profit margins above that of industry competitors. The presence of newcomers from acquired companies meant making Publicis values more explicit and social contributions more explicit, such as pro bono advertising campaigns, including one on climate change with the United Nations. Profitability and size meant that the Publicis Groupe could acquire in big emerging markets such as China and India. That was all a foundation for the next major change.

SMALL GESTURES AND A VERY BIG PRIZE

Strategically, Lévy knew that digital was the wave of the future. It was already threatening old media and challenging advertising and communications dramatically. The best player in digital marketing and the biggest prize around was Digitas, the dot-com boom survivor firm founded in Boston that was described in chapter 2. All the industry heavyweights seemed to covet Digitas, the same ones that Lévy had beaten by smooth courting of Hal Riney. Could he do it again?

In March 2006, Maurice Lévy visited my class at Harvard. I wanted to take him to dinner afterward, but he opted for drinks at his hotel because he had dinner plans. Later I learned that his dinner was with Digitas CEO David Kenny, whom he had come to understand deeply and value as a leader. Lévy said:

> We had a very good dinner, and that day I understood that if you wanted to have Digitas and David Kenny, it could not be part of a division; it should be a division by itself. I started the discussion, we had a few flirting meetings to see if we could or could not get together, then something happened. They had a terrible second quarter, the stock collapsed, there were lots of problems. And when I saw that, instead of sending an e-mail saying, "Maybe it's time to speak," I sent an e-mail saying, "I'm sorry. It's so unfair that you are hurt this way because the parameters remain very good."
>
> I learned that the same day they received two e-mails, one from one of my dearest competitors saying, "Now you are at a price which is affordable, so we should start speaking." And one from me, which was very different. And until they recovered, I did not push, but I stayed close to David. When I saw that they were recovering partially their price, we started a conversation with them, and we tried and we tried. And when we felt that we could be on a good par, negotiations went pretty quickly. I said it should be done, and he agreed. My board agreed, his board agreed. We met, and in two weeks time we did everything. It was quick. And we launched and took everyone by surprise. Including the market, the competition, and even my executives who were not part of the talks.

Lévy and Kenny hatched plans walking up and down Lexington Avenue in New York on a warm evening late at night. Kenny wanted the right solution for his stockholders and clients and the right home for his people, "So we had to make sure the three components—the right price, the right strategy fit, the culture—that everything was working completely together," Lévy said. After consummation in early 2007, everything happened fast. Publicis and Digitas fixed key margin issues, protected growth by retaining people and making introductions to a range of new Publicis clients, and began to build an international effort. The Digitas network extended globally through bases in the United States, United Kingdom, France, China, and India. Digitas included Prodigious, a digital programming production facility in Costa Rica, Ukraine, and China. Acquisitions in France gave Digitas a stronghold in Europe; other acquisitions beefed up Digitas operations in China, Hong Kong, and India. David Kenny joined the P-12 operating committee and the Directoire, the ultimate board, and later relinquished the role of Digitas CEO to its U.S. head, Laura Lang, in order to take on bigger digital duties for Publicis Groupe as coleader of VivaKi, a bold new venture launched in June 2008.

Digitas is a unifying force across countries and agency streams for Publicis. The Digitas team makes presentations to Publicis Groupe offices and clients all over the world, getting them to embrace the creation of a new future for advertising. In June 2008, Publicis Groupe announced a coup that keeps it in the vanguard: a new digital advertising system that links together technologies from Google, AOL, Microsoft, and Yahoo. It is nonexclusive but pioneering. The system connects Publicis's media-buying agencies with the ad space sold by the Web giants through VivaKi Nerve Center, which focuses on creating ad technologies for use by all Publicis agencies. By working with the four big Internet competitors around the same table, Publicis can drive down prices for its clients.

Publicis Groupe has been transformed by its acquisitions, particularly by Digitas. There is still a French tilt to Publicis Groupe. At the top, there are frequent invocations of Marcel Bleustein-Blanchet. Corporate messages come in French first and then English. But that is changing fast. As a vanguard company, Publicis must now routinize and make visible values that were once a matter of informal communication in offices overlooking the Champs-Élysées in Paris. And Lévy sees a big cultural clash still to be bridged between the speedy, impatient world of the Internet—the future that Digitas represents—and the sleepier world of advertising agencies. Lévy said, "I believe they will help us to be even more attractive by helping us to think differently. This is the first time we see an aspect which is much better than what we had at the core of Publicis. That is good, not for our egos, but as an eye opener."

The best acquisitions, like the best partnerships, are eye openers and mind extenders made possible when people can suppress their egos and let a new relationship, even one they bought, influence them to change.

spreading high standards: cross-fertilization

THE LAST MAJOR ELEMENT involves the direction of change. Vanguard companies seek high standards and want to ensure that they are consistently applied everywhere. There is enormous variety in the kinds of changes that mergers require. In some cases, both companies are strong, and the marriage is indeed one of equals in competence if not in size—for example, Procter & Gamble and Gillette. In other cases, there are repairs and improvements that come up in the integration process. Even while approaching merger partners with respect, and even when integration happens by stealth rather than by command, leaders are aware of whether merger integration requires a turnaround. In the Shinhan case, Chohung was failing; pride aside, the bank had needed a government bailout, and that is why it could be bought. Publicis could get Saatchi & Saatchi because Saatchi had a cash shortfall and needed a capital infusion to survive. Digitas needed a global presence to serve customers and could not get there quickly without joining someone else's network, and its expenses were too high, squeezing profits.

For Cemex, whose rapid rise to global prominence in the twenty-first century is based on very large, well-executed acquisitions (albeit with accompanying debt), growth has depended on turning around failing operations in desirable markets and raising standards. To become global quickly as one of the top two in the cement industry and to soar ahead in countries whose natives held negative stereotypes of Mexicans has required focused attention on values, principles, consistent operating standards, and the ability to transmit them quickly. Integration involves a great deal of time by a large group of people motivating others to use tools that help them change behaviors.

Cemex's experience could be a how-to manual for global growth through mergers, from an unlikely beginning to competition with European giants.

• *Get really good at what you do.* Lorenzo Zambrano, a grandson of the founder, became CEO in 1985 and aspired to create today's global Cemex out of a local company, Cementos de Mexicanos. He received his undergraduate degree from well-respected engineering school Tecnológico de Monterrey and his MBA from Stanford

Business School, a formative experience that other Cemex leaders repeated at Stanford, Harvard, and other top schools at company expense. Guided by global best practices, Cemex leaders mastered and
codified effective processes. Zambrano and a close team of long-term
colleagues invested in people with the best education and tried to provide the best facilities. They revolutionized the low-tech cement business with high technology. Zambrano, who now serves on IBM's board
of directors, even grew a software company to provide Cemex with the
best and latest tools for running the business, then spun it off.

• *Move first to familiar places.* Cemex expanded first in its neighborhood. It moved to adjacent geographies, buying companies in
Guatemala, Venezuela, and the like. Next was an acquisition in Spain,
a foothold in Europe with no language barriers. The strategy was to
find companies that could benefit from Cemex's management expertise. Even with this limited diversity, some potential clashes of methods and cultures impelled Zambrano to seek "one Cemex"—one set of
values, one code of conduct, one set of comparable metrics, one set
of excellent methods. That became a platform for growth outside of
the familiar markets and a basis for competing with European industry leaders such as France's LaFarge. Arguably, one of Zambrano's
most significant acts of leadership is his stress on One Cemex.

• *Prove yourself in the biggest demanding market, and solidify your
methods.* In 2000, Cemex bought Southdown, headquartered in
Houston, Texas ("not without a great deal of soul-searching," Zambrano told me), and only when the price fell within range. By that
time, Cemex had begun to codify its postmerger integration (PMI)
practices and Cemex Way suite of business process tools. They were
applied, further refined, and standardized in this big U.S. acquisition
so that they would be ready for use in future acquisitions. Southdown was a big test, especially because the "Mex" part of the "Tex-
Mex" fusion food label was often denigrated across the border in the
United States. Success was not foreordained. Cemex and Southdown
had a troubled history as past joint venture partners, leaving some
Southdown people bitter, and Southdown was much more decentral-
ized than Cemex, meaning that people resisted standardization under

Cemex. Many people at Southdown saw no reason to change, and a few resisted out of disdain, but the relentless professionalism of the Cemex PMI teams and the demonstrated effectiveness of Cemex methods eventually won them over. Success is motivating.

• *Acquire big multinational companies in strategically important places.* After Southdown, Cemex was ready to go to places that had more diversity and included many countries at once. It doubled its size to $15 billion in revenues with the 2005 acquisition of RMC, a troubled ready-mix cement company headquartered in the United Kingdom, whose operations stretched to the edges of Europe, northeast to Latvia and southeast to Croatia. Cemex chose to go to non-Spanish Europe rather than India or China to make a point—that its main competitors are European, and Cemex can beat them on their turf. (Of course RMC was a good business deal too.) National diversity made this challenging, but that would prove a point as well—that Cemex had enough people power to deploy PMI teams everywhere at once, to transmit the Cemex Way. Having made RMC people happy to be part of the success of Cemex, Cemex later went after Australian giant Rinker in 2007, which has a big U.S. presence and foothold in Asia. (The acquisition was handled well, although the timing was unfortunate, because Cemex faced a heavy debt load in the construction industry downturn and worsening economy of 2008.)

INTEGRATION NUTS AND BOLTS: THE PROCESS OF ADDING BUSINESS AND SOCIAL VALUE

Cemex could have been just another middle-of-the-road company without its attention to the factors that help Shinhan, Publicis, Procter & Gamble, and other vanguard companies create a culture responsive to all stakeholders. Instead, Cemex repeatedly defied expectations as it swelled into a global powerhouse. It is not the deal making that distinguishes Cemex as a vanguard company; it is what leaders do after the deal and how new business and social value is created. We can see Cemex principles in action as we zoom in on the RMC integration.

Investors did not initially like Cemex's decision to buy RMC. When Cemex announced its bid on September 24, 2004, the price of its USA ADR slid 7 percent. If that weren't enough, some Cemex leaders felt that there were negative perceptions that a "company from the third world" was reversing history by taking over a major British company that owned facilities all over Europe, in some of the most advanced developed markets. Many Europeans, Cemex managers later reported, tended to lump all Cemex staff from diverse Spanish-speaking countries into a generic category called "the Mexicans," whom many equated with big sombreros and procrastination until *mañana*, an indefinite time in the future. But the culturally biased were shocked out of their stereotypes in short order by Cemex's professionalism and speed.

There were many others who could find misery in this merger. Country differences brought trade unions and regulators into the picture, and cement factories had to contend with community concerns about air quality. Moreover, for the acquisition to be deemed a success, whether by RMC employees or capital markets in London, Cemex would first have to turn around a major trouble spot in England. This was one test of how well Cemex values, principles, and standards would translate. But if a Mexican company could raise social and environmental standards in England, that was proof that global companies can be a force for good.

The Rugby cement plant in the West Midlands region of England was relatively new but had never worked properly. One indicator of its serious losing streak was the hiring and firing of six plant managers in six years. Housekeeping and environmental problems were obvious just walking around the plant. The town of Rugby was constantly in an uproar about the factory building, which loomed large on the western outskirts of town near homes and residential areas, visible for miles. During construction of the new plant in 1998, large cranes interfered with the townspeople's television reception of the World Cup match in France that year. Some of Rugby's eighty thousand inhabitants believed that RMC misled them about the actual size of the new plant. They were angry about increased road traffic and dust emissions, with some complaining that emissions from the plant were causing health problems.

The plant was so unpopular that a UK television series called *Demolition* named it in 2005 as one of the top ten buildings people in the United Kingdom would like to see torn down. Many employees were ashamed to admit they worked at the plant. "It was painful for people working there," an insider remembered. "They were constantly knocked down one way or another, by the plant failing, by local community antagonism."

With so many strikes against it, Rugby was challenging, but Cemex was ready with standards and resources. Within just one quarter, Cemex was already on a fast track toward a successful turnaround.

Cemex created change by investing and giving rather than taking things away. In less than three months, Cemex's PMI team identified seventy-five improvements that cut costs, saved time, or enhanced workplace safety and worker satisfaction. Cemex invested many millions of pounds in the plant almost immediately, spending £6.5 million on a new air filtration system alone. It was not cheap, and it was not strictly necessary, but Cemex leaders felt it was the right thing, the environmentally correct thing, to do.

Cemex sent quality control and maintenance experts to help fix the problems and to train their Rugby colleagues. To allay fears that the PMI team members had arrived to supplant Rugby employees, PMI team members worked next to their Rugby counterparts, emphasized their own transitional status, and recommended keeping all local managers willing to stay. More than twenty Rugby employees were sent to Cemex plants in Mexico, the United States, and Germany to experience the Cemex Way and to become change champions upon their return.

A new bonus plan spread the fruits of success to workers. A new sustainability department was put in place to focus on environmental issues. Cemex started a foundation in Rugby and increased community support by backing the town of Rugby's launch of a business improvement district.

Productivity increased dramatically. The plant halved the number of injuries resulting in lost time, which was good for people as well as the business. The plant reduced gas and dust emissions significantly, which was good for the community, and environmental complaints from the public dropped 45 percent in the first year, although a small group continued to press for still more improvements. Some plant floor workers and trade union activists remained aloof, but gradually, resisters came around. Human touches, including improvements to the community inside and outside of the facility, won people's hearts and minds.

THE PARADOX OF HIGH STANDARDS: WORKING HARDER AND LOVING IT MORE

Christine Newman was a beneficiary of the new culture of open communication, empowerment, and high standards. Newman, an accountant turned sales manager for RMC in Norwich, England, accepted Cemex's offer to join the Rugby Cemex Way team. She said yes even though Rugby was a hundred miles from her home, and she would have to live in a hotel and commute on weekends to be with her husband and five-year-old daughter. Her husband, who ran a business from home and could cover family duty during the week, encouraged her to seize the opportunity as a career boost. Perhaps, in this particular deal, Cemex didn't score high on its work-life balance commitment, but it scored very high on challenging work and the chance to succeed.

"I think they are fantastic!" Newman exclaimed about Cemex. "At RMC, I always felt I could not get my voice heard by management. I have never, ever felt as much a part of the team as I do with this crowd. They actually listen and seek your advice, and it doesn't matter if it is not necessarily what they want to hear. They are open to your ideas. I have never seen their level of motivation in a big group of people so consistently. They look as if they really do want to be there and want to confer. I look forward to coming here on Monday morning and doing a week's work with them."

Newman's fourteen-person team included people from Mexico, Brazil, Uruguay, Spain, and Hungary. She was impressed with team members' efforts to understand British culture. They took cultural classes and kept folders of advice, including things they should and should not say or do. Moreover, the legacy Cemex managers were flexible about business differences, and to help the RMC people make the transition, they kept the old running side by side with the new. Meetings started off in English but sometimes switched to Spanish. "And then they look up and say, wait a minute, we've got Christine here. And they'll bring me back in," Newman explained. "They're very inclusive. They want people to be involved. They're extraordinarily polite and well mannered." Team members set up their laptops around a long office table in a big conference room, which made it easy to overhear conversations and add comments. Newman liked that the project leader was more of a facilitator than a boss, and she even liked the rigor of Cemex's clearly defined performance management system.

CROSS-FERTILIZATION AND COMMUNICATION

Globally, Cemex had to integrate twenty-five thousand former RMC employees, raise performance standards, demonstrate its values and principles to other stakeholders, and get a return on its investment through higher productivity and sales—and do it all pretty fast. Cemex relied on another secret of vanguard companies: a flexible pool of talent willing and able to travel to listen, observe, and teach other people. Cemex engaged in massive human cross-fertilization.

In the United States, starting in Arizona and Florida and then spreading around the country, a traveling PMI team of forty people brought Cemex Way tools and culture to each facility. At numerous forums, Cemex old hands and former RMC employees fresh off their first Cemex Way implementation were expected to share ideas and best practices. Cemex team members taught RMC colleagues while learning from them. For example, Cemex adopted RMC's Ready Slump system, which is a software system on each Ready Mix truck that controls the consistency of concrete as it travels to a construction site, so that neither truck drivers nor the site's workers have to add water to the mixture.

The Cemex Way tools are widely credited with creating a common language that made the integration happen "at almost light speed," enthused Steven Wise, a former Southdown employee and current Cemex USA executive vice president. Even more effective than formal presentations was informal communication, self-organized like the voluntary integration at other vanguard companies. Americans who had felt well treated and well informed when Cemex bought Texas's Southdown now mentored RMC people about "little nuances" to help them feel part of the Cemex family, reported Ray Schorsch, a legacy Cemex USA executive vice president.

Cemex sent some four hundred experienced employees from around the world to join the PMI team in Europe, which ultimately totaled about eight hundred people serving six to eight months, fanning out across countries to identify differences among countries and to find quick wins. Fifteen coordination groups looked at opportunities for business synergies and strategic expansion and managing the synergy capture process. Experienced senior Cemex executives were sent to Europe to lead functions for at most three years; their job descriptions demanded that each identify and train a local employee to succeed him—part of Cemex's mentoring process to ensure a ready pool of talent. At the same time, RMC people who looked good were sent on the road, including to headquarters in Mexico, to gain Cemex knowledge.

Throughout the world, the three buckets of activity produced results for Cemex. Although Cemex leaders did not articulate it as Shinhan did, there is an echo of the same tripartite structure: a *dual company* element of running two overlapping systems while people learned new methods; a *one company* element of human bonding and process standardization; and a *new company* aspect of looking for future opportunities.

FROM HUMAN TOUCHES TO SOCIETAL IMPACT: DEMONSTRATING VALUES AND PRINCIPLES

In October 2005, Cemex convened about 300 of its most senior management worldwide, now including 120 senior legacy RMC executives, in Cancún, a glamorous resort on the east coast of Mexico, for a big dose of emotional integration. Tim Stokes, a witty Brit who came to Cemex from RMC, served as moderator of the all-English-language program; I was among the external speakers. But everyone said that the high point was not the hotel-based conference. It was the chance to act on Cemex values by working together, Cemex materials in hand, to build a school in a poor rural area. The school project was a bonding experience and a symbol of the progressive Cemex culture.

A defining feature of a vanguard company is to make decisions with societal impact in mind, in accordance with values and principles. Throughout its process of entering new markets and integrating acquisitions, Cemex makes decisions that take people and communities into account. Consider the following examples:

- In Latvia, workers had been underpaid even by local standards and were constantly quitting. Only about fifteen out of two thousand people spoke English, and the prospect of careers outside of Latvia was not a motivator. But workers liked Cemex's rapid approval of requests for new machinery, which made their jobs easier. Managers liked Cemex's business plan for Latvia, because there had never been one. Cemex became a community hero by spending a hefty $160 million to build a new cement plant next to the old one—then the biggest industrial investment in post-Soviet Latvia.

• In Croatia, instead of dropping an RMC supplier that failed to meet Cemex's minimum criteria, Cemex decided to work to raise the supplier's standards, in order to save a significant number of local jobs dependent on the Cemex contract. This also resulted in a better-educated small-business base ready to adopt world-class standards.

• In France, Cemex modeled business discipline for local managers, closing the books on the fourth day of each month, even when that fell on "le weekend."

• In Egypt, Cemex changed the town of Assuit when it took over a government cement works. The company cut jobs but raised wages, improved schooling, and invested in small business opportunities to create jobs and develop the city.

• In England, by turning around the Rugby plant in short order, Cemex saved rather than destroyed jobs and enhanced environmental responsibility.

Cemex's discipline could seem coercive without the humanism of its values and the large numbers of people who teach their new colleagues how to succeed and also listen to their ideas. This was why Cemex could double in size twice in four years (before the construction industry downturn due to global real estate woes) and why Christine Newman in England could work harder than ever before, juggle a challenging commute, and love her job.

leadership lessons: how to be good and growing

WHETHER INTEGRATING GIANT enterprises in many countries or putting two small offices together in one location, vanguard companies point the way to the marriage of business success with positive impact on the world.

Positive change with minimum resistance is possible when leaders adhere to humanistic values and are willing to make investments to support their application. Leaders pay attention to emotions and culture, knowing the importance of symbols and signals to show people whether change is good for them or not. They invest in the future, adding more than they take away and letting people share in the fruits of success. They try to be fixers rather than destroyers, finding more to give to all stakeholders, especially when they must overcome national stereotypes or heal wounded pride.

One consequence is that employees might end up wanting to embrace changes before they are told what to do. In mergers, they might self-integrate, as we saw at Shinhan and Publicis. They might even engage in "anticipatory integration," taking on the behaviors or symbols of the company they are about to join well before the official handover. This happened at Omron, the Japanese company described in earlier chapters. Like Publicis, Omron leaders look for values compatibility, in terms of broad principles, along with strategic fit when they screen possible acquisitions. They emphasize values in conversations during the negotiation process before discussing business or engineering details. On the other side of the table, representatives of companies Omron is trying to buy are often delighted to find commonalities between their culture and Omron's, especially gratifying when they are speaking through translators, which can make rapport hard to establish. The founder of Silicon Valley–based STI, a maker of electronic components, made a diagram to show the similarities of purpose and values. On the day that Omron's acquisition became final, Japanese managers arriving at the California site were surprised to see that STI leaders had already adopted the Omron logo, the Omron Principles were posted everywhere, and STI employees recited the Omron motto.

Leaders of purpose-driven companies have high standards, wanting to do the most good they can, even if they cannot remove all the misery from mergers. So they see their mission as seeking a highest common denominator (i.e., raising standards to whatever are the best) for the companies they acquire and the places they enter, which sometimes means changing themselves, another theme that runs through the vanguard companies.

If there is a formula across companies as different as cement and advertising, it consists of these simple principles, which we have seen in play repeatedly in the stories in this chapter.

• *Run the old and the new side by side.* Shinhan's "dual bank" of running two banks in parallel at the beginning of the merger is like Publicis's multiple-agency networks. Although the latter are meant to be permanent to avoid customer conflicts, and the former was compelled by the union, both are ways of acknowledging that the acquirer is not automatically better than the target, and that each can learn better ways from the other.

• *Find common human bonds; encourage relationships beyond tasks.* Shinhan's "one bank" reflects the values and bonds that unite a company as a community. Publicis Groupe disseminates a culture and values that create meaning beyond its separate agencies and subsidiaries. People feel connected to something larger than the current work or their particular piece of the company. They have a common language; they can move freely to other places and feel included and understood.

• *Quickly start building a new future.* Shinhan mounted its "new bank" effort to create a different and better model for the future not identified with any of the legacy companies. Publicis has added a digital direction that will soon pervade everything, and that cannot be claimed as belonging to one or another of the advertising agency networks. Pointing people toward the new helps vanguard companies stay ahead of change rather than bogging them down in divisive conflicts. Doing all three simultaneously is a triple whammy that gives vanguard companies acquisition and transformation advantages.

But effectiveness at integration and building the future is not merely a mechanical process of good change management; it is a human process of concern for people and respect for their feelings and situations. When values and principles are at the forefront, leaders are better able to forge relationships and find common ground, even across acquired companies with seemingly different cultures, and they can make changes some would find threatening with a foundation of goodwill stemming from a broader sense of shared purpose. When leaders are concerned for what is inside people's heads, fewer people (at least in Korea) will find it necessary to shave their heads.

Being able to grow quickly and effectively by adding new parts to the mix can turn organizations of all sizes into giants of their field. Business strategy is a starting point. Paying attention to humanistic values and organizing human effort with those values in mind also help improve the state of workplaces and the world—and, ultimately, produce the high performance that characterizes the vanguard.

part three

people and society

chapter six

connecting talent: virtues of the dynamic workplace

A<small>LMOST EVERY AFTERNOON</small> in Moscow, Jennifer Trelewicz received a Sametime message from a colleague in San Jose, eleven time zones away, sent before he went to the gym for his early morning workout. They chatted about issues that arose during Trelewicz's workday in Russia that he should consider during his workday in California.

Trelewicz is an electrical and computer engineer with a Ph.D. from Arizona State University who holds thirty-two patents. At the time of our first meeting, she was director of IBM's Systems and Technology Laboratory in the Russian Federation. Connected 24/7 to every part of the world, she exemplifies the new way of working in the vanguard.

To begin with, she invented her own job. During a stint at IBM headquarters in Armonk, New York, following her success as the manager of a big project in the San Jose, California, research lab, she mounted the arguments that convinced IBM to open the Moscow lab. Then she moved to Russia to head it. She was accountable in many directions—locally to the general manager for the Russian region, worldwide to a VP of development in the systems and technology group in the United States, and then less permanently on a "dotted line" to the product lines for which the lab is working. The fact that she is a woman—she said—merely shows IBM's strong long-term commitment to develop female talent in science and engineering. Alexander Klimov, one of the Russians she supervised, endorsed her on the Naymz website, a social networking site for professionals: "Jennifer is a true proactive leader and supportive manager [with an] ability to manage an incredible number of complex and challenging tasks."

Complex, indeed. The organization structure and work culture surrounding Trelewicz stems from three related priorities that put IBM in the vanguard, all of them pushed hard by CEO Sam Palmisano. First, IBM should be a "globally integrated enterprise [GIE]," a step beyond a multinational company in working across borders and boundaries. In a GIE, functions can be located anywhere that the talent to perform them exists and can work on behalf of the whole IBM world, yet without losing deep connections to communities. Second, IBM should have a "lower center of gravity." Lowering the center of organizational gravity means moving decision-making authority away from Armonk headquarters, corporate officials, and vertical chains of command and instead empowering people to work with peers across the organization, sell ideas and make decisions at lower levels, and act with greater speed. Third, IBM values of "dedication to every client's success" and "innovation that matters, for our company and the world" must show up in use of people's time. They must keep clients in mind even if not working directly with them and contribute to improving the world.

Trelewicz's work reflected these priorities. To support global integration and the ability to draw on the best IBM resources anywhere, she communicated regularly with peers worldwide to coordinate activities—participating by phone or in person in bimonthly lab directors meetings or working with labs in Poughkeepsie (New York), Mainz (Germany), and Beijing (China) on joint efforts. She was part of many policy-making teams and a leader of some; for example, as a member of the IBM Academy of Technology, which consisted of three hundred of the most capable technology professionals, she was a team leader on globalization, and as a member of a thirty-six-person global Technology Council, she helped set technology strategy for the whole company. In addition, she participated in self-organizing networks on emerging issues, connecting with people in strategy, sales, services, and research via digital workspaces.

In Russia, she modeled IBM values. She regularly joined sales teams to present to customers and took her researchers to visit client sites alongside IBM consultants, to keep technology experts connected to issues that customers face. And she was one of the enthusiastic IBMers who volunteers for the company's EXITE (Exploring Interests in Technology and Engineering) camps around the world, a program IBM launched in 1999 in the United States and worldwide to get middle-school girls interested in science and technology. EXITE has grown to fifty one-week camps in more than twenty countries, each run by local IBMers, primarily but not entirely women who also serve campers as e-mentors for a year, thereby addressing several things at once: a diversity goal, a talent pipeline goal, and a local employee volunteering goal. To cap it all, Trelewicz represented IBM at conferences on women and technology.

EXHAUSTED YET? OR exhilarated by the idea that there are jobs like this? Why pick one or the other? Both feelings are reported by employees in vanguard companies, especially senior professionals and managers. Opportunity and overload come in the same package.

This chapter examines the implications of the new professional workplace: how work experience is shaped by the twenty-first-century forces of technology and globalization; how vanguard companies draw on their values, principles, and humanistic emphasis to increase the positive opportunities and deal with the dilemmas of workplace change; and what it takes to be a leader and succeed in this kind of organization.

The complexity of globalization tends to induce and favor distributed rather than concentrated leadership. That is, fewer people act as power holders monopolizing information or decision making, and more people serve as connectors and integrators using relationships and persuasion to get things done. This is a hallmark of a flatter, more innovative organization, consistent with vanguard companies' humanistic values.

There are three major tendencies to consider in turn.

- *The rise of a new view of work.* People *choose* to do their jobs rather than feel *compelled* to, and they can be trusted to determine when, where, and at what they work. This is where company values intersect with the pragmatic need to attract and motivate the best people.
- *The desire for circles of influence to replace chains of command.* As is appropriate in a networked world, the structure of a vanguard organization involves multidirectional responsibilities and a portfolio of projects.

To focus people on serving customers and society, horizontal relationships across the organization are the center of action that shapes daily tasks rather than vertical reporting up a chain of command.

• *The growing importance of "connectors."* Connectors are those people who serve as bridges between and among groups, assembling resources and mobilizing action. Personal contacts are often as important as technical talent. In essence, "She who has the best network wins."

work as personal choice: any time, any place

PEOPLE NOW BELIEVE, in many countries, that paid work should be meaningful and reflect their personal values. It is a reflection of the expectations that employees, especially those of younger generations with the best technical skills, bring to the workplace. Building on the importance of meaning, a newer idea is that how one works is a matter of individual choice.

For much of the industrial age of the last century, the popular concept of work (the paid variety) involved images of toil, drudgery, and exploitation—an unfair economic bargain in which management holds the advantage over laborers and employees are compelled to suspend their individual desires and interests while they are confined to their workstations. If not, they will lose their jobs, joining a reserve army of the unemployed whose existence serves to keep wages down. In this view, there is no such thing as a benign or enlightened employer; only organized labor and government regulation protect against abuses. There are large numbers of white- and blue-collar workers around the world, including many in the United States and other developed countries, who still work under one or more of these conditions. Even in the absence of labor abuses, there is still a drudgery and confinement component to some jobs, including in vanguard companies. Cemex runs cement factories, Publicis Groupe has mass production software programming shops, and every company has office support staff who must sit in place for certain hours no matter what.

But leaders in vanguard companies want people at *all* levels to feel motivated, not controlled. In keeping with the expectations of a high-talent workforce and with their own commitment to have a positive impact on society, managers boost the voluntary component of paid work by entrusting employees with choices, including where, when, and with whom they work.

CHOOSING WHEN AND WHERE TO WORK: THE DYNAMIC WORKPLACE AT IBM

On any given day, about 40 percent of IBMers do not go to an IBM office and instead work at home or at customer sites. Perhaps they are on the move, en route to another location. Or perhaps they are on vacation, since IBMers can set their own schedules and take as much time as they can negotiate with managers. "Giving people more control over how, when, and where they do their work is the core of flexibility," Ted Childs, former vice president for diversity said at a meeting in my Harvard office reviewing evidence of the changes at IBM. Pointing to the 35 percent of participants in an IBM global survey who report some work-life difficulty, he went on, "I'm not saying we solved anything, but people feel we are responding." IBM's work-at-home programs, such as the one started in Japan in 2001, have caught the attention of government officials interested in keeping women with technical degrees in the workforce. In some cases, IBM offers allowances to support infrastructure in the home.

That whopping number of mobile employees enjoy IBM's "dynamic workplace." It reflects the trust and personal responsibility part of IBM's value statement. Remote work is not just a matter of working from home or switching offices, though that possibility exists too (one corporate executive whose main office is in Armonk often prefers to work from an IBM office in Manhattan, where he lives). It also reflects longer-term lifestyle choices. Even knowing IBM's flexibility, I was surprised to meet a woman on the beach on the resort island of Martha's Vineyard during my vacation who was just taking a short break during her IBM workday. She lives full-time on the island, working virtually and occasionally traveling to her current assignment at the IBM plant in Rochester, Minnesota, where she manages several projects.

"At the end of the day, IBM is more worried about the work being done and how well you do it than did you work for eight hours or did you work for twenty hours to do your job," declared a manager in Bangalore, India. He claimed that even if a person in Bangalore turned down a temporary assignment with a client in Mumbai, the manager would work it out with someone else or offer flexibility, but under no circumstances would "that person, because he or she didn't go for the project . . . be relegated or ignored. We understand the reasons why he or she is not able to go for the project." It is this kind of flexibility that permitted IBMers the latitude to work on the tsunami relief efforts, as discussed in chapter 1.

This experience is repeated around the world. From China, Moira Zheng, a relatively new IBMer who is project director for a high-profile initiative to digitize the treasures of Beijing's Forbidden City, praises the choices. She says, "Our boss never asks us to work overtime. He never mentions you had to do something. He just gives you the deadline—we might need to have these by a certain day. Then he will never say one more word. Then you know when you need to work overtime, and when you can sleep. I like this very much. I hate people telling me to work overtime. But if people don't ask me to work overtime, I might be working overtime anyway."

Remote work helps IBM's dual-career families. Magda Mourad, an executive IT software architect with a Ph.D. from France, received an "accommodation assignment" when her IBMer husband, Ahmed Tantawy, moved from New York to Egypt to head the Cairo Technology Development Center. This allows her to continue to work on U.S. IBM research, but remotely. Tantawy returned the favor when he offered a similar opportunity to a young woman who married an Egyptian working in Europe. For two years, she continued to work for the Cairo TDC full time, remotely, delivering every project on time.

It is not just women who work from home. Larry Hirst, IBM's chairman for Europe, Middle East, and Africa (EMEA), lives in the United Kingdom, where he formerly served as IBM country general manager. He gave up his London office because the space was needed, visits EMEA headquarters in Paris periodically, and travels constantly, so his home has become his office. This is not unlike the male executives at Digitas, who often prefer the quiet of home to the chaos of the office.

Fixed offices could become an endangered species. Many IBMers plug in wherever there's a station and hold meetings in conference rooms. The important issue is not the physical place of work; it is staying connected with the immediate team, peers or managers, and customers, especially in the matrix organization, where people in local functions are part of bigger global groups. Those needing to connect across time zones have to be available, erasing boundaries between work and nonwork hours. Patricia Menezes, an executive in charge of corporate citizenship and corporate affairs for Latin America, reported, "I'm always connected to the cell phone, to Sametime messages on the computer. If I don't connect, I start to feel pain. I spend a lot of time talking with my colleagues and with executives here. There is lots of interchange."

To work remotely, Menezes, who lived in Rio de Janeiro and had a team in ten nations in Latin America, had to learn to be highly disciplined, sometimes waking in the middle of the night to talk with someone in another country. So she had to be able to organize her day. "There is a lot of freedom. And freedom is the fuel to being alive and to creating things and being happy with what you are doing. So I love the freedom that technology brings." She acknowledges that not everyone could handle that freedom. "Some people need to be inside IBM to have a routine. Other people can manage working from anywhere. But it's a fact that everybody wants to have face-to-face moments." That is one reason she offers incentives for her country-based team to spend an occasional week working physically in another country.

For people who prefer to work in the office, other kinds of accommodations are possible. In Cairo, I had a sandwich lunch with a group of six young female IBMers considered "top talents" who lauded the benefits of flexibility. They especially wanted me to hear Mona Arishi's story, because she was there when IBM changed a policy to respond to working mothers. Arishi was the first IBMer in Egypt to bring a baby to the office to breast-feed. It was her second child. With her first child, she was entitled to only forty days off, and after she returned to work, she would go home during the day to breast-feed, which broke up the workday and interfered with peak performance. By the birth of her daughter, the period of leave had been expanded to three months. This time when she returned to work, her manager gave her permission to have a driver bring the baby to the office for a half hour each day. "And everybody knew. They wanted to see the baby," Arishi said.

The risk is that being able to work anytime means working all the time. But evidence shows that people are more engaged and satisfied, even when faced with big work pressures, if they feel in control, if it is their choice. Personal control is the key factor.

VOLUNTEERING AND SELF-ORGANIZING

One striking feature of the ways people work in vanguard companies is how much of their time is spent volunteering. By this I do not simply mean working as volunteers in their communities, although that is certainly encouraged in vanguard companies, and it can contribute to the workplace experience, especially for people in production or sit-at-desk jobs for whom participating in company clubs and volunteering in the community can add excitement to otherwise routine and monotonous jobs. I mean being a volunteer on projects at work. With the large number of tasks people can potentially take on, with the opportunities to hatch ideas and initiate innovations, individuals have choices about the allocation of their time. They are volunteers when they join someone else's project team. They are volunteers when they sit on an advisory board or policy council. They are volunteers when they go with colleagues to visit customers even though that is not in their job description. They might feel occasional pressure to say yes or disapproval if they say no, but it is still a matter of choice.

Job descriptions do not document what people actually do every day, nor do official performance reviews and salary bands capture the activities through which people might add the most value for the company, because sometimes those "side" efforts are not even itemized in any official database or system. In some cases, professionals are formally encouraged to spend 15 or 20 percent of their time on projects of their own choosing, as a stimulus to innovation.

Dina Galal is one of many who ignores titles to work across functions and projects. She calls herself a volunteer on many projects, because they are not part of her formal performance appraisal. She serves as government relations manager of IBM Egypt, having also served simultaneously as local communications manager, regional manager for diversity for the Middle East (Arab countries and Pakistan), and liaison for corporate citizenship and corporate affairs reporting to the United Kingdom. But that hardly begins to depict her work. She has volunteered her time for a variety of public-facing projects, such as Building Bridges to the Arab World, a portal started at the request of Egypt's first lady, and Eternal Egypt, which digitized historic treasures and involved getting to know technical team members as well as government officials. "I don't have a line item for how many initiatives [I] contribute[d]. It is my time. This is something I learn from, I'm so proud to participate in it, and I feel like I can add value to the team, having the overall picture so I can always link things together. So that's why they always feel that Dina should be there," she said.

Some of the most important volunteering occurs outside of any formal responsibility, when people come together to share information. Communities of practice link people with a similar technical expertise. Communities of kind link people from particular groups, such as women or minorities. Communities of interest connect people who want to explore particular ideas. Technology enables them to cut across wide swaths of the organization, to grow virally, to cull the best ideas, to build support for action, and to become powerful forces for change. The driving force for self-organized groups is curiosity and interest on the part of the people themselves. The company can try to facilitate them, but they flourish when they involve volunteers.

Self-organizing communities give their members voice. They are also a potent force for change, propelling companies in directions they might not have taken without the unanticipated voluntary actions of people with no formal mandate to contribute. Without such self-forming networks, IBM might have lagged or missed out on two very big business ideas. One is a virtual worlds community that got IBM involved in this new technology area, which burst on the scene in 2003 with Second Life and has grown exponentially since. The other is "green computing," which helps IBM meet environmental commitments for the company and clients. Both of these are among IBM's top strategic priorities that were crystallized following an Innovation Jam in July 2006, modeled after the ValuesJam of a few years earlier. The Innovation Jam was IBM's second global Web-based chat open to everyone in the IBM world. Over 150,000 people contributed ideas, confirming what self-organizing communities were already doing.

"It was one of the most exciting years I've spent in IBM, to watch this group come together outside of every structure IBM has," said

John Tolva, a program manager in Chicago and a leading participant in the virtual worlds community. "We acted bottom up like a corporation of freelancers. People used their free time." Nearly two hundred interested people experimenting in virtual worlds found one another through company chat spaces and created an ad hoc community. They started informally and then found an IBM executive to support them as a more official activity. Dozens of people chatted via their avatars on Second Life, and later, other platforms. There were weekly calls, with the phone line open when in the virtual world, and dozens of people would participate, though mostly not by phone. Eventually, virtual worlds was designated an emerging business opportunity with official funding for three years. IBMers could add the name of their avatars to a social networking site.

A different kind of self-organizing group, focused on the environment, drew on worldwide virtual discussions about environmental sustainability but also had a more local face-to-face dimension. Before soaring energy costs put this issue high on the U.S. agenda, people at IBM in the United Kingdom were already moving to turn it into a mainstream initiative. At IBM's South Bank facility in London, people began "talking around the watercooler," Steve Bowden said, about how to make IBM more environmentally friendly. Personal values coincided with corporate responsibility and a perception of a big business opportunity. It ballooned through word of mouth (or word of screen), and soon there were regular meetings of several dozen people drawn from different business areas, many of whom had not previously met one another despite sharing the building. The group created a five-person steering committee with representation from every business unit, setting guidelines and identifying tasks. People reached out to their own networks locally and around the world. Nothing was authorized from above yet. "We wind-tailed ourselves," Bowden, a steering committee member, said. "Once we'd got together as a leadership team, we declared that we would work together for these values, and bring the ideas to senior management for inclusion in the rest of the business." Then UK general manager Larry Hirst got on board, assigning a project manager.

What started spontaneously, organized by volunteers, has become serious business, central to IBM's signature Smarter Planet campaign.

IBM is devising ways to use IT to make companies more energy efficient (e.g., consolidating server power and measuring and reducing heat in data centers). Solutions are as simple as turning computer terminals and PCs off at night or as complex as switching from distributed to centralized but thin client server environments. In South Bank itself, green images are everywhere. Near the cafeteria is a green "house of carbon" built like a large dollhouse against the wall where people can contribute carbon-saving suggestions. On upper floors, green and blue footprints on the carpet lead to recycle bins.

Green computing quickly joined virtual worlds on IBM's top ten strategic priorities list, and Sam Palmisano got his own avatar. When Palmisano announced the results of the Innovation Jam in Beijing in November 2006, he also announced a partnership with the Chinese Ministry of Culture to digitize Chinese treasures. A large screen showed Palmisano's avatar entering the Forbidden City. In November 2008, he introduced the Smarter Planet campaign to major client CEOs at the IBM Business Leaders Forum in Istanbul, Turkey.

open and direct: horizontal structures

FORMAL STRUCTURES OFTEN seem to fade into the background at the most innovative of the vanguard companies. Titles are less important to some of the volunteers than the chance to be involved in important tasks. And leaders want to ensure that structure—job locations and reporting lines—do not get in the way of the actual work. So they grapple with how to organize to stress the horizontal direction—across boundaries of silos—rather than the old-fashioned vertical command hierarchy in which a fortunate few get to tell the rest what to do.

Managers and professionals tend to have multidimensional jobs with a portfolio of projects, which can be linked to other people and projects facing different parts of the company. The work lives of those in the middle increasingly include responsibilities once only in the hands of top managers, such as making decisions about customers, representing the company to external audiences, and shaping policy directions. Of course, those who formerly felt on top do not always let go easily, but they are pressed to change by new structures as well as the expectations of those below.

A MATRIX ON STEROIDS: MORE BOSSES, LESS BOSSINESS

The matrix organization, an organizational invention dating from the dawn of the global information age several decades ago, is hard to describe to people who have never worked in a large organization, but it is well known to those who have.

Imagine that jobs are connected not by a chart of little boxes, with one box on top representing the boss, but by a spreadsheet with one set of categories down one side representing one way to sort the jobs and another set across the top representing another way to sort the jobs. You find yourself occupying one of the slots in the middle of the spreadsheet. You are responsible for both aspects and at least two managers will expect you to satisfy both of them. In a matrix organization, people at middle levels have more than one boss, each one reflecting one dimension of the work. For example, in a company with multiple product lines being sold in multiple places, the manager for widget production in Florida might report both to the brand manager for widgets and to a director of manufacturing. It would be up to the Florida widget production manager to figure out how to satisfy both bosses and negotiate any conflicting instructions, such as those that might arise from the brand head who wants to maximize features and the production head who wants to minimize costs.

Vanguard companies put the matrix on steroids, bulking it up in terms of the number of people with matrixed jobs and the dimensions reflected in responsibilities that extend in many directions—the technical input or function, the product or service line, and the geography. Managers and professionals tend to have a home base in one group but then are responsible all over the map in terms of the projects on which they are deployed, as in the story opening this chapter. Multiple accountabilities to many so-called bosses are particularly true in customer-facing groups, such as the marketing and distribution organization at Procter & Gamble or the business consulting services groups at IBM. One manager might handle their official performance appraisal and salary review, but their work orders might come from many other managers to whom they are accountable for results. It is hard to know who is the boss. And that confusion is actually intentional.

In the new model, the goal is to think externally about serving customers rather than internally about pleasing bosses. The goal is to look horizontally for peers with whom to collaborate on external impact rather than vertically for orders to get (or give). Upper managers who insist on control find it harder to get things done when they are not the only one in charge and have only some of the carrots and sticks. In the worst-case scenario, a matrix organization is a nightmare of ambiguity pulling people in too many directions and constraining their ability to act. In the best case, a matrix liberates people to think more creatively about ultimate impact, as is consistent with the purpose at the heart of vanguard companies. If upper managers let go (or are let go), then the company needs fewer management layers.

Further complicating the formal charting of jobs is the number of overlays that vanguard companies add that expand and blur the boundaries of jobs and get many more people at more levels looking across the organization: high-level councils, advisory committees, teams, and task forces. The goal is not "death by committee," which puts issues on the sideline or denies new initiatives, but instead giving more people a chance to contribute to decisions.

RELYING ON THE MIDDLE, REDEFINING THE TOP

The restructurings of companies such as Omron and P&G in the past decade have been aimed at not only reducing layers but empowering the people at the interface with customers. For IBM, a solutions orientation means those dealing with customers should be the ones to integrate IBM with customers, taking innovation from any part of the company to apply to customer needs with a minimum of organizational or operational barriers, by requesting and negotiating for resources directly, without going up one hierarchy and down another.

Letting go of control begins at the top. Banco Real CEO Fabio Barbosa says that he succeeded at implementing the bank's strategy of differentiation by social and environmental responsibility only when he lost control of the effort. In the beginning, projects started with top managers identifying priorities. But a few years after the new direction was established, middle managers started contacting one another to create and execute initiatives that he knew nothing about. That's when Barbosa felt good—when he was least involved. Similarly, in P&G's

open innovation approach, leaders find they must permit people more autonomy and encourage them to talk directly to colleagues in any part of the company, even if their ostensible bosses are not yet informed.

That shift is not easy when people still think in linear, vertical ways and when career systems still stress management rank over professional accomplishment, paying accordingly. IBMers traditionally saw opportunities as involving moves upward, and people measured themselves by distance from the top, with the top meaning regional and global headquarters. Although facing resistance to locating decision making lower in the organization, CEO Sam Palmisano has made some radical symbolic changes. In Europe, he moved about five thousand people and two hundred executives above the country level out of European headquarters and back into country organizations. He also elevated the role of account manager to high status, signaling its importance, by asking a few key executives to move from top positions to become executives for big accounts. The example he gave me is a division president whose team had won the technology side of the 2008 Olympics for IBM: "I said to him that this is the biggest job for you: running an account with four thousand IBMers worth $1 billion a year. I said I need you as an example of what I'm tying to do, to demonstrate that this is every bit as important for the highest level below me, to show that we are serious about our strategy." Good citizen that he was, the president became a former president, and his role became account manager.

Other managers get it. Marcelo Spain, VP for the financial services sector in Latin America, applauds Palmisano's vision from his office in São Paulo. He manages the relationship between IBM and customers— presales, postsales, and continuing customer satisfaction. "It's difficult, but I like it because I believe that this is the most important position inside the company. We have to integrate the other organizations and put the customer interest in front." For example, his group would determine the best platform for a customer and then persuade the hardware organization to supply it.

DIRECT ACCESS

Position in a vertical hierarchy once determined who spoke to whom, which people got informed first (the next up the chain), and who determined where communication could be directed. Today, open access and direct communication irrespective of levels increasingly prevail in vanguard companies. Younger generations in America and elsewhere are even more informal than their predecessors. They send e-mails directly to top leaders, whom they freely address by their first names, include people at all levels on their e-mail distribution lists, and feel free to make irreverent comments. The Internet is a great leveler.

Even in countries with more authoritarian traditions, people are emboldened to go directly across the organization rather than up a chain of command. I heard many before-and-after contrasts from employees whose memories extended to the 1990s and back. In the old days, they say, they had to go through their vertical boss first for everything. Beyond the immediate boss was "a ceiling you cannot see through," a middle manager recalled. Going to a higher level was called escalating, and it set off alarm bells as a violation of protocol. Going outside the vertical structure was not even considered. One manager sighed with relief at the change: "Now I can exchange e-mails with any corporate director. This is the beauty of the matrix organization—you find the know-how anywhere, anytime," he said. In Brazil, Banco Real's open forums seeking ideas for environmental and social strategy caused skeptics to scoff that people in Brazil are accustomed to being told what to do and would not respond well to invitations to participate in decisions. So much for the skeptics. The company is flooded with applications from the best college graduates.

It is striking how quickly people embrace this work style everywhere. Noha Saleem, an Egyptian based in Dubai who had built the first software sales team in Egypt and was later responsible for software support services for the Arab nations, spoke for numerous women in countries in which women were taught to be seen and not heard when she said, "One good thing about IBM is that you don't feel that there are layers. We're open with our management. We don't say 'sir' to our managers. When you first join as a young person, you feel strange that you're talking to your manager and using his direct name. Once you get over this barrier, it makes you feel closer." In China, Moira Zheng praised her boss as a "very good boss" but felt no need to check with him about going directly to her peers in other departments to invite them to join her project. In Russia, Jennifer

Trelewicz heard similar appreciation for "democracy" from Russian workers accustomed to respecting hierarchy: "People in the laboratory have told me that they like working here because they know I'm the director—my position is respected—but they also know that if they have a problem, they can come knock on my door, and they can ask me, and they know that if I have a question, I'll come to them and ask them."

Younger employees, or those from newer fields, expect direct access and sometimes express impatience with slow responses or ideas that get stuck somewhere in transmission. At Publicis Groupe, there is a culture clash between the fast-moving, empowered digital entrepreneurs of Digitas and the advertising agency managers accustomed to a slower and more formal mode. But like other vanguard CEOs, Maurice Lévy wants the directness and decision-making speed of Digitas, not the drag of formality and protocol, to infuse the entire company with a new approach.

power to the connectors

ACCESS ACROSS BOUNDARIES frees people from constraints, such as waiting to be told what to do, while adding to their responsibilities for taking initiative. A distributed organization has more ears to the ground and more people who have to do something with what they hear. Success requires spotting opportunities, generating ideas, and getting them circulating. Thus, many people serve as idea scouts, transfer agents, and integrators, to ensure that ideas flow and resources move to where they are needed. The most powerful people do not always have the biggest titles but rather the best networks.

CONNECTOR ROLES

Connect and Develop is Procter & Gamble's name for its open innovation emphasis. That phrase captures the essence of how vanguard companies want professionals and managers to work: look broadly for ideas, make connections, and put ideas in motion.

As we have seen, a large number of people juggle multiple responsibilities and work with an expansive set of peers drawn quite broadly throughout the organization and with external partners in the extended family. They sometimes lead initiatives and sometimes lead the flow of ideas that keep other initiatives moving. Many people in vanguard companies perform integrative work, serving as direct bridges between one specialized team and another or among groups that function separately but must coordinate. Connector roles are sometimes part time and temporary, for example, for an extraordinary event such as an acquisition, where the need for integration is clear. Shinhan Financial Group's success is due in part to mass deployment of large numbers of people, sometimes reaching the lowest ranks, serving as temporary connectors on dozens of task forces following the Chohung Bank acquisition, even during the standstill period when no formal integration could take place. Cemex pulls people out of their regular jobs to serve on postmerger integration teams at Cemex and sends them to acquisition sites to link the sites and the new employees to Cemex structures and practices. The company takes its best people out of their jobs for integration tasks. To make this flexibility possible, managers are expected to train replacements who can stand in for them while they are gone.

Some jobs are explicitly devised to connect activities taking place in otherwise separate silos, to stand on the boundaries of domains and provide human bridges that represent each to the other. Other jobs involve assembling temporary teams to accomplish something specific. Project managers, for example, draw people from disparate areas for a particular goal, such as the launch of P&G's Básico products in Brazil, for as long as needed.

New connector roles are constantly being invented as managers see the need for better bridges across areas. John Turek moved from a senior research director position in the United States to the China Development Lab in Beijing to create and head a team bridging research and development, to ensure that what was coming out of research could match customer needs. Turek, a Canadian affectionately known as "Moose," had worked as a team member on a similar effort initiated in New York by Josephine Chang. When I met him at the lab, he was still learning Chinese, because the whole thing had happened so fast. He had visited China as a member of the software group architecture board steering committee, and the next day, on his way back to New York, he stopped in Japan, where he received a Sametime message from Chang offering him the job. (His wife, an IBM engineer, moved with him to the China lab.) But what was the job? It was hard to figure out from his title what he does; it took the first fifteen minutes of our conversation in Beijing for him to explain.

The imperative to connect is a sensibility that extends to many jobs and makes people in vanguard companies look more broadly outside of the particular responsibility they are given. Inderpeet Thukral, strategy VP for India, defined his work not simply as developing plans for India but as connecting business units in India with the rest of IBM and finding ways that other parts of IBM can take advantage of India. Liu Bo, strategic partner executive for China, said, "In a job like mine, I have to touch almost every business unit. Because I have to know what they are thinking about, right? At the same time, I have to understand the role of headquarters, their strategy, and the current situation of China, and then combine them."

MANAGEMENT BY FLYING AROUND

The tools of the global information age help people stay connected, from e-mail to workspaces on the Web to the more traditional weekly telephone conference call. But for those who integrate and connect across areas, there is no substitute for periodic face-to-face interaction. In fact, the ubiquity and ease of electronic communications make "face time" a status symbol—who gets to see and be seen in person.

With so many people out of the office and mobile so much of the time in vanguard companies, convening them becomes even more important. Marcelo Spaziani, a Brazilian IBMer who likes to say that he learned leadership from soccer, persuaded people from sales, hardware, software, services, and consulting to move out of their function to be on his integrated financial services industry team colocated on one floor. He is convinced that the move was responsible for business growth of about 120 percent over four years. When he was promoted to a similar integrative job for the whole Latin American region, he could not move people from ten countries to São Paulo permanently, even if had wanted to, so he convened them often. He visited people to build trust and for direct observation to aid in difficult decisions (e.g., in cases of poor job performance). Spaziani could have been talking about counterparts in other companies across São Paulo, such as Tarek Farahat at P&G or Maria Luiza Pinto at Banco Real, when he said, "The leaders, they have to like people. They have to have a strong relationship with people, a face-to-face relationship."

Good managers and project team leaders have always practiced MBWA—management by walking around (a catchphrase borrowed from Hewlett-Packard). But if few people are in the office, and there are a large number of people working elsewhere to connect with, what is a vanguard leader to do? Walking around is a good form of exercise, but hopping a plane is a leadership necessity. MBFA—management by flying around—should be the new slogan. (You heard it here first.)

Distributing leadership responsibilities to many people and dispersing activities to many centers of excellence make travel a necessity even for U.S. domestic companies. Add to that a variety of global connections—international operations, new opportunities in growth markets, work with suppliers, or approaches to investors—and people take to the air. Lorenzo Zambrano, Cemex CEO, has his main office in Monterrey, Mexico, headquarters, and another one to which staff accompany him in New York. Maurice Lévy and David Kenny of Publicis Groupe make regular tours to major cities to meet with people from the various agency networks within each country.

Connecting by air can also involve connecting in the air. With only his ThinkPad for an entourage, IBM CEO Palmisano circumnavigates the globe six or seven times a year, picking up key regional executives for particular legs and holding meetings in the air. Many others in the senior executive ranks are also frequent fliers, though generally flying by themselves. They speak at universities, meet with government officials and major clients, coordinate activities across geographies, and mentor and coach people in distant locations.

Managers and professionals below the top who are fully wired and always available by Sametime messages still fly frequently for training, client meetings, or in-depth project meetings. Project teams whose members work virtually from dispersed locations (e.g., a technical expert in Chicago working on an Atlanta-based project) travel to exchange periodic visits. An Australian manager responsible for an activity across the Asia-Pacific region might have back-to-back trips to Shanghai for regional meetings and to the United States to learn from initiatives there. Learning on the ground is considered essential. A regional executive commented, "To achieve delivery excellence, we must have a team, not a group of people, and draw on best strengths working virtually. But client knowledge and cultural fit come from the 'geos' [geographies], so we must make sure to be there."

MBFA would not be noteworthy except for one thing: Vanguard companies are big users of technology for connection and integration, yet they still fly around. Cemex even grew its own software company before spinning it out and uses numerous online tools and templates (the Cemex Way) to ease communication and ensure consistency, but the company relies on hundreds of people moving to newly acquired sites to connect the sites to the Cemex Way, face-to-face. IBM tools and technology are increasingly globally integrated and can support not only routine work but also problem solving remotely (e.g., a test engineering system can diagnose and solve problems in any plant from any location). Yet for problem solving, or in a crisis (such as the Asian tsunami), many people grab their passports and head for airports. Troubleshooting still involves MBFA. A senior executive said, "If there's a problem or a critical situation, we fill the skies."

POLITICS AND PERSUASION

When people acting as connectors lead projects or initiatives that require cross-cutting groups, they do not control any of the people, and they cannot order them to participate. Broad priorities are generally set by high-level leaders, but within those agendas there is often freedom to negotiate the work itself with the team and the managers. This adds a "political" dimension to projects, not in the negative sense of backroom deal making but in the positive sense of campaigning, lobbying, bargaining, negotiating, caucusing, collaborating, and winning votes. That is, an idea must be sold, resources must be acquired or rearranged, and other people must agree to changes in their own areas. There is a constant dance of adjustment that is akin to self-organizing, like a line dance in which one performer shifts directions and others start turning to follow, but the direction setter is never the same person.

Leaders below the top who guide integrative groups or try to make connections between areas must attract both financial and human resources. Their set of colleague and direct reports enlarge and shrink like an accordion, depending on the particular project. The financial resources often come from multiple budgets and the people from many different groups, recruited person by person or subteam by subteam. Leaders must be beggars and borrowers. Project managers even at senior levels "door knock" for support, stopping in to see many people and arguing for how their efforts fit priorities, "tin-cupping" for spare resources.

The bigger the idea, the faster a group can suddenly balloon in size as people from other areas come on board. One particularly effective senior executive has a small full-time staff (many of them matrixed into other areas) but creates very large initiatives by persuading other executives to collaborate, which means that the others provide both money from their budgets and some key people. So he always keeps an eye on the interests of other areas, and he always frames his initiatives in terms of their agendas. The leaders of those groups end up looking good while his reputation grows, which helps him pursue ever-bigger dreams.

Generally, projects get support not because someone at the very top wants to do it (although that helps bump it up on the review list) but because an initiative meets two tests: strategic to the business (which attracts capital) and motivational to the individual (which attracts talent). Consistency with values and principles is also important. Vanguard companies have many community projects because of that motivational aspect, which tends to encourage more people to dream up such projects.

Time is the scarcest resource and the most coveted. The use of people is more controversial than the question of money. There are always issues of whether people can leave one assignment to join a new project or move to a sudden high-priority task. It is challenging to get the right people to the right tasks, especially as technology changes, and in regions experiencing rapid growth. For a manager, it comes down to, "Can you find the talent fast enough, and if you do, will they let you move it, and how many fights do you have to have before it finally moves?" An executive in another company told the story of an initiative in which he persuaded people to join an exciting new business effort but had to ignore critics at regional headquarters: "I present this to the corporate crowd, and I get people shouting at me, 'You can't move people around. You're taking my resources.' Because what I did was I took two from one group, two from another. Just two from each! So anyway, we got criticized, I was told we couldn't do it, and we did what we always do—smiled, nodded, and came home and did it anyway. We put it together, and now it is celebrated as a model." It helped that this executive already had a committed team, so criticism did not bother him or stop him.

Negotiations are sometimes drawn out and contentious, slowing down commitment and thus project delivery, which can be especially frustrating to the Internet-speed generation. But it is striking how little negative politics I saw throughout vanguard companies. When the shouting dies down, people accept the outcome and move on. Invoking company values and principles makes decisions less personal and discussions more respectful, as was the case for P&G Brazil's Básico initiatives described in chapter 4. And the sense that work has a voluntary component means that if people want to do something in keeping with those principles, and if a manager can be a leader who attracts people to his or her efforts, then critics need to get on board or get left behind.

"SHE WHO HAS THE BIGGEST NETWORK WINS"

Finding the resources to beg for in the first place is often a function of leaders' social capital—their stockpile of personal relationships with many people. Though technology tools are increasingly common to help people find one another, I find that even the most technology-savvy leaders still rely on their own personal networks to find the best resources quickly. Personal networks of people whom managers have met or worked with are often better sources for key assignments than databases of résumés. One manager called this "the old-fashioned way, the knowing people type thing: I know a person who might know a person . . ."

It is striking how much personal knowledge of other people matters. It is almost a paradox: The larger and more global the company, the more human connections it must foster. Social capital is often, but not entirely, correlated with length of organizational experience; the other factor is whether the nature of the job encourages getting to know large numbers of people, that is, whether the job involves mobility, a portfolio of varied projects, and participation in initiatives that require connecting across many areas. In short, giving people integrative work and encouraging them to be connectors is a way to grow the potential for more connectors at ever higher levels, in a nice multiplier effect.

Vanguard companies seek to retain employees and keep in touch with "alumni," because that is the best way to ensure that people will know a person who knows a person. The companies in my project do not necessarily pay the most, although they are certainly competitive, but they invest a great deal in personalized treatment to help people get what they need and also find inspiring special opportunities such as community service. Values and principles are powerful means for institution building, making the company feel like a source of meaning and more than just a job. All of this aids retention. But still, people leave (even Jennifer Trelewicz, who just moved from IBM to head research for Google in Russia). So the next best thing is to maintain warm relationships with alumni. Vanguard companies that were traditionally more like closed cults than open systems got religion in the twenty-first century of a new kind: "Once an X Company member, always an X Company member." There is now active outreach to former employees and retirees, and they can stay in the networks.

Turnover is costly in terms of recruitment and start-up costs, but more important, turnover disrupts networks. Technical skills are transferable across companies, but relationships are not. Companies can train people on the technical side. Companies can provide tools, templates, and models in handy Web-based forms to use on the job. Buddy systems can pair more experienced with less experienced employees. But relationships take a different kind of effort. Gillette employees being integrated into P&G report finding it challenging to learn how P&G makes decisions but even more challenging to learn which people to go to for which matters and how to find people to invite onto teams.

This kind of organization-specific knowledge of the most human kind facilitates success. When Shinhan brought fifteen hundred managers from Shinhan and Chohung banks to climb a mountain together at a conference shortly after the acquisition, they called it emotional integration, as I reported in chapter 5, but it was also a rapid way to create social capital and start the networks forming across both banks.

Mentoring is an important way to transmit organization-specific knowledge and make connections. It is also good for the mentors, enlarging their networks and their stock of social capital. Mentoring at Cemex ensures that managers have backups, which makes it easier for them to be chosen for plum international assignments. At IBM, the best leaders coach large numbers of people. Henry Chow, chairman of IBM Greater China, has been named one of the top IT executives and best CEOs in China. He personally mentors about one hundred people at a time, he says as he counts them off: twenty-five formal and active mentees, twenty-five informal mentees and around fifty "graduates"—former mentees with whom he maintains a close personal relationship. Chow seems to know everyone, and everyone knows him.

To be known is to be in the know. This is why connectors with big networks have so much power. They don't need to be the boss if they have the connections. Nick Donofrio, who recently stepped down as IBM executive vice president, encouraged ninety thousand technical people to think of themselves as working for him, even though they did not work directly for him in any formal or official way. He tried to answer hundreds of daily e-mails personally, counting on this as a major bottom-up source of information about issues, opportunities, and developments.

rewards and dilemmas: "rubik's cube moments" and their price

WHEN THE NEW WAY of working is done effectively, one reward is what I call "Rubik's Cube moments." Suddenly all the moving parts click into place for an effective and highly satisfying response. All the work of seeking resources, spending social capital, motivating volunteers, maintaining commitment when people are pulled in other directions, and persuading people to stick with it pay off in a significant event.

Sometimes there is one big memorable moment. In Brazil, P&G's Juliana Azevedo and Tarek Farahat had one of those moments, as I described in chapter 4, when the first of the innovative Always Básico products she had championed and he had sponsored rolled off the line, the result of highly effective cross-functional and cross-boundary integrative leadership by Azevedo with employees, peers, and customers, and equally effective cross-organizational integrative work by Farahat regionally and with corporate headquarters. Everyone on the team stood in the factory holding hands, smiling broadly.

Sometimes there are a series of moments under more difficult circumstances. For many people at IBM India and IBM United States, the response to the Asian tsunami (see chapter 1) and Hurricane Katrina in Louisiana were Rubik's Cube moments. The best of the company lined up—all the values, desire to serve society, passion for innovation, flexibility to go anywhere and do anything, networks of partners and government officials, a tradition of volunteering, and supportive managers who would rearrange project staffing to enable some people to work on disaster relief full-time.

It is human nature to find such moments satisfying. But not everyone can master a Rubik's Cube, let alone the kind of leadership a vanguard company seems to require. The next question is, what skills are required to succeed at the new way of working?

WHO SUCCEEDS?

The rising stars of vanguard companies must have stamina, energy, long lists of contacts, an appetite for communication, comfort with ambiguity, and a belief that the company's values and principles mean they are part of something bigger than just a job.

Access across boundaries frees people from constraints, such as waiting to be told what to do, while adding to their responsibilities for taking initiative. A distributed organization has more ears to the ground, but people have to do something with what they hear. Success requires spotting opportunities, generating ideas, and getting them moving by identifying the people who should join the effort to develop or transmit them. The stakes are high, but so are the rewards. Those who can be connectors and integrators gain a feeling of autonomy and professional prerogatives once confined to those at or close to the top but now extended more broadly.

High performers are handed numerous opportunities to get even better—attend conferences, influence policy discussions, pursue more education, and represent the company at external events. They can invent aspects of their jobs, join groups reflecting their interests, use company resources to create meaningful innovations, and participate directly or by proxy in world-changing initiatives. That is why vanguard companies regularly show up on lists of the best employers in particular countries (IBM and P&G are ubiquitous on those lists and not only in the United States) and why their own surveys show high levels of overall engagement, the new buzzword for work motivation. But that's not the whole story, and some of those internal surveys also reveal pockets of dissatisfaction.

PAYING THE PRICE

The price for all this—a price many so-called top talents dismiss as hardly worth mentioning—is having to figure out how to navigate through a more complex and demanding work environment. This way of working puts the responsibility on individuals not only to work but also to work it out: to sell their ideas upward and sideways, and to entice other people to join and support their projects. In this mode, opportunity is wide open, but little is guaranteed except a chance.

For clever self-starters who are also good relationship builders and active learners updating their skills, a chance is all they need. They get that chance by working extremely hard and staying ever alert, wired 24/7. But they must be willing to be mobile and make trade-offs, as Christine Newman did at Cemex UK, deciding to commute for a great assignment, leaving her small child during the week.

However, formal structures have not yet caught up with the way that vanguard organizations operate in practice. Networks are zooming ahead, while hierarchies remain stuck in the past. Much of the horizontal dimension of connecting across the organization ends up being voluntary. It is easier to move activities and relocate people than to move mind-sets. Those empowered to execute might still see gravitational force exercised by headquarters or other hierarchies. It is harder to measure integrative work than technical or functional tasks. Some of the most important work people do in terms of external impact might not be listed among their formal responsibilities at all.

The new way of working contains a great deal of ambiguity, not to mention complexity. A matrix organization is hard to explain and hard to understand. People can get lost if they are new, inexperienced, or simply too remote to get the right connections. Even experienced managers can get lost. Gillette senior managers expressed initial confusion after the merger with Procter & Gamble about finding their way around P&G.

There is also a risk that opening up the world to people overloads them. The freedom to work anytime makes it tempting to work all the time. Thus, the liberation of mobility can produce the alienation of remoteness.

A middle manager in Chicago confessed something that immediately resonated with me: He sometimes envies his administrative assistant her nine-to-five job, boring as it is, because she can surf the Web during lulls, have lunch with friends just for fun, go home every day at the same time, and be totally off in her out-of-work hours. He has higher pay and more flexibility, but on a per hour basis, he said, he might not make more money because he works at home, on vacation, and while watching his children's soccer games. "The trick is to balance flexibility with the need for face-to-face interaction in ways that deliver the best result for the company and the clients," said Ron Glover, IBM vice president for diversity. He is right, but it is still a trick not everyone has mastered. Employees might not know how, and managers might not be willing or able to let go, preferring the people who are visible at all times and thus marginalizing those who choose flexibility. That is one reason for the common finding on surveys that women disproportionately take advantage of work-life balance programs such as caretaking leaves but also are disproportionately underrepresented in top jobs.

Not everyone sees opportunities in the new way of working. The people who work for Cemex in Mexico and the United States are often ambitious and see the company's growth and global opportunities as good for them. Not in Latvia, managers told us there. People who grew up under Communism, they said, have not yet caught up to the "Mexican work ethic" nor do they care about international connections. In Latin America, an executive recounted the difficulty of getting some IBM sales representatives to relate to the "innovation that matters" statement in the IBM values. He encourages them to spend more time with customers, to look for ideas to present in conversations with the company, and to get a higher level of contact in customer organizations. "But some people just want to be a hardware salesperson," he said.

A WORKPLACE IN PROGRESS

Dilemmas often accompany change. Vanguard companies have not resolved all of the dilemmas, nor have they answered all of the critics of globalization concerned about job losses or inequality (such as a high ratio of executive compensation to average worker pay), a matter I will take up later, in chapter 9. But the values and principles they espouse lead them to strive for a progressive agenda in other respects, for themselves and for the places in which they operate. Without having the answers, they confront the questions (sometimes because the public demands it).

Job insecurity is increasingly a fact of all companies and in nearly every country. Statistics for employment and unemployment hardly capture the variations in employment status; I want to add three new categories: underemployed, uneasily employed, and overemployed. Getting it just right—say, being happily employed using one's skills with lots of security and no overload—is harder and harder. The practice of "once in the family, always in the family" (unless there are significant performance problems) is harder even for the most familial of companies once they start acquiring and find someone better in the acquired company while having no place to put the person being displaced. A case in point is P&G's use of the principle of "field the best team" following its acquisition of Gillette; this was highly meritocratic in recognizing the talent that came from Gillette but was shocking to some longtime P&Gers who were not quite as good and were made redundant despite all the images of family.

Vanguard companies want to be employers of choice, so they are trying to reinvent portions of the social contract. Their leaders prefer not to talk about insecurity but instead call it flexibility. They say the challenges of global change require a shift of responsibility from employer to employee, while giving people opportunities and tools to succeed. Abundant training is good for both parties and is often one of the first big investments emerging vanguard companies make as they start to grow. Individual development plans are ubiquitous. These companies also attempt to help employees balance their family obligations with their work commitments, such as providing family leave for caretaking, day care centers, and lounges for breast-feeding new babies and reassigning husbands and wives so they can work from the same city.

Some vanguard companies are doing even more. Recently, IBM added other innovations to forge a new social contract for twenty-first-century workplaces. First in the United States but in process in Australia, Britain, and elsewhere, IBM offers Matching Learning Accounts to offer incentives for employees to invest in their own continuing education. IBM matches individual contributions into a portable individual savings fund that employees can use to further their education or get training to switch careers, inside or outside of IBM. When CEO Sam Palmisano announced this in a speech in July 2007, he received two thousand e-mails from IBMers within hours, much more, he joked, than he would get for a new dental or eyeglasses benefit. This is a company match, not an entitlement program, to make clear that individuals must take responsibility to be competitive—personal responsibility is part of the IBM values. IBM also helps people with transitions to new kinds of work outside the company. The company provides special support for people who want to move from IBM to public service, in programs called Transition to Teaching and Transition to Public Service, which help IBMers envision meaningful work in later stages of life after finishing their IBM career. IBM Europe has helped employees facing job reductions to get five-year assignments with business partners, after which they might also get the chance to come back to IBM.

Vanguard companies try to offer the best benefits if not the highest pay, especially in emerging markets where the war for talent is fierce (such as India and China) and newer hires from younger generations want to earn a lot fast and are willing to jump ship to get it (a common complaint by human resources managers in vanguard companies trying to keep turnover low by trying to get people hooked on values, reputation in the community, sports, and parties). They have a stake in raising standards toward world-class benefits in all the countries in which they operate for three reasons. One is their values; as leaders, they want to lead toward societal change. Second, in a connected world and extended family, word spreads quickly about what people are getting in one country versus another. Members of a women's network in a vanguard company might start comparing notes about their treatment, and discovering differences in policies across countries might pressure senior management to universalize standards. A third reason is even more pragmatic and not always stated explicitly. If the most progressive companies have to pay the cost of meeting world standards, their competitors should have to do so also. In that sense, certain kinds of regulation are their friends.

Raising standards can happen through infrastructure building, advocacy, or role modeling. P&G helped get Egypt's first health maintenance organization established so that the company could offer health insurance benefits. IBM has picked up practices from Europe to use in the United States, and it raised day care quality in Korea by insisting that centers used by IBMers meet higher U.S. standards. There are small actions too, such as the executives I met who volunteer to tutor at schools in the poor neighborhoods in which their menial service workers live, such as the cleaning or mailroom staff or the "office boys" in some countries who bring coffee, to show that they care about helping these workers improve their lives.

Vanguard companies often try to raise the labor standards of smaller companies that are at the fringes of the economy, as Cemex does through Construrama in Mexico. Banco Real assesses suppliers, including small companies, and tries to help them improve. The bank influenced the head of a motorcycle messenger company to take better care of its employees by adding safety gear and training. In the best of the vanguard, progressive policies give many employees the freedom to set their own schedules, sometimes their own vacation timing and length.

It is faster and easier to adjust policies than to change behavior.

Appearances can be deceptive, when people who have a right in theory can never exercise it in practice (do votes count in dictatorships that allow people to go to the polls?). Still, for professionals and managers in the vanguard, the new way of working puts a premium on distributed leadership and opportunities for voice. As more people in more jobs take advantage of this approach, it becomes more likely that policies will also emerge from what the people themselves want to do. Once a person is a self-organizing volunteer connector using a network to get his or her favorite initiative going, it is hard to settle for less. Jennifer Trelewicz can tell you that.

chapter seven

diversity and identity: dealing with differences

NOT ONCE during the first seventeen years of his successful management career could Jonathon Herbert have imagined that he would become the champion of a diversity effort on behalf of white male Americans.

On my several visits to his office in an older suburb of a major U.S. city, Herbert gradually told his story, after I promised to change his name and be vague about identifying details. Herbert had worked for an international investment firm after earning an MBA, then joined a growth company that was eventually sold to an Asian corporation (I'll call it AC), the target of his concerns.

The cabinet behind Herbert's desk featured photos of a smiling, tall Herbert shaking hands with various Chinese, Thai, Indonesian, and Indian CEOs to celebrate a deal—mementos of his investment days and proof of his international credentials. Herbert seemed to know people everywhere. He was ingratiating. He had excelled at college basketball and automatically joined social clubs in which he became a leader. He considered himself to be a tolerant, fair-minded person who befriended executive assistants and mentored two young women and an African American man, to whom he was passing on tips about how to follow in his footsteps. His career had taken him to California, where he brushed up on his high-school Spanish because of the burgeoning Hispanic population; London, where he gravitated to Asian restaurants and was especially fond of sushi and samosas; and Chicago, where he lived with his wife and two children. He flew coach as often as business class and carried his own luggage in hotels. He was not a prima donna.

But the world had always accommodated him. Everywhere he traveled, people spoke American. They knew American movies, they played American music, they were entertained by an occasional story about American sports, or they wanted to know about American politics. In terms that Simone de Beauvoir made famous, Herbert was the "dominant," and everyone else was the "other" who had to cater to Herbert-kind or lose out. Herbert was the model, the norm, the kind of person everyone wanted to emulate, his prosperous life the kind that the rest of the world envied.

Or so he thought. That is, until his company was sold to AC, which was just emerging as a player on the world stage. As a senior manager and leadership team member, Herbert was a prize AC wanted to keep. He became the head of North American operations, reporting to the CEO at headquarters across the Pacific, and the first American to sit on the corporate executive committee. Herbert was happy at first, and so were his new boss and colleagues. AC had a visionary founder much respected in the home country and a strong ethics code. AC had high market share domestically and in the region and was starting to grow in the United States, with the help of its new acquisition, so Herbert felt flush with the possibilities of additional investment in the United States. He was comfortable with international travel, and foreigners were not foreign to him.

By the three-year mark, however, he was feeling increasingly marginalized. He was tired of so much travel. He was constantly going to the head office; rarely did those executives come to see him. He was tired of phone conferences with Asian managers that extended past midnight, because he was one of the very few on the call so many time zones away. When he was at the head office, he was antagonized when other managers at lunch would lapse into their native language (he was learning it slowly) or have side conversations in regional dialects when out for a drink after work. The food was always drawn from the national cuisine, even at social events in the United States. The music was always the national music. Out on the streets around global headquarters, Herbert felt stared at as a tall blond-haired stranger. At home in the United States, he still felt surrounded by Asians, because AC placed North American offices in the areas where immigrants from the headquarters country were clustered. Those areas were often far from major customers, which was another irritant for customer-oriented Herbert.

Herbert felt that the Asian managers were arrogant, did not listen, and wandered off into irrelevant conversations. When he went directly into discussions of the task at hand, they bristled and told him he was trying to push his ideas too fast. When he questioned the longer-term viability of the current strategy when lower costs would no longer be the main customer consideration, he was told that the current direction was fine given the high margins, profits, and rapid growth rate and that he made trouble for himself by mentioning his concerns. Herbert thought the Asian executives were shortsighted and not very strategic, the growth rate in their home country could not continue indefinitely, and the rest of the world needed new business models with more local input and less dictation from Asia. The Asians seemed to feel that America was in decline, American business prowess overrated, and Asia would produce the next business superpowers.

What a turnabout for a man who for so long had been part of the dominant group. Could it be that his Americanness was no longer an asset, his white skin sometimes felt a bit uncomfortable, and even his sense of himself as a powerful man was not secure?

That is when Herbert became a diversity activist, pushing various proposals: The corporate executive committee should include more Americans and Europeans. The corporate training department should hire a U.S. diversity expert to run workshops on cross-cultural understanding. The CEO should engage a European expert on cultural differences to identify the issues . . . All were shot down. Others did not see that there was a problem. Herbert was one against many.

Herbert seemed unaware of two ironies. First, all around him at his office in the States were people who had felt marginalized all their lives by people like Herbert, such as the women and minorities who tried to please and emulate the dominant group of Herbert look-alikes. Second, in the past, it was often American companies that had been practically homogeneous at the top, marginalizing "foreign" managers in other parts of the world who were forced to take late-night phone calls to accommodate American time zones.

But Herbert was right too. AC was too new to global competition and too flush with early success for its executives to understand that blindness to differences could limit their international effectiveness. They might even lose rising stars like Jonathon Herbert.

They did. Herbert jumped ship. He accepted an offer from a vanguard U.S. firm, which I'll call Newco. Newco competed with AC but was older, internationally experienced, and known for progressive values; it could easily have been one of the companies in my vanguard project. I saw Herbert next when he visited me at Harvard Business School. He was a happy camper once again. It was not that he was back to being managed by Americans, because in fact, his new boss was Asian, and his peers were a mix of all nationalities. Newco long had a set of values and standards taught to all employees, and it made diversity a central focus, increasing the number of women and minorities both in the United States and abroad, offering training in cultural sensitivity. The company was moving the center of some activities to places outside of the United States, and Herbert was a candidate for leading one of those groups. Herbert was now secure again in his own identity and slightly more aware of how others might experience issues of exclusion and inclusion. But by now he was seeing that he could never assume that Americans automatically dominated. Newco was already moving headquarters functions to other parts of the world.

This chapter is dedicated to all the Jonathon Herberts whose identities are in flux. It shows why variety is the spice of the global information age and why vanguard companies are ahead in experiencing diversity and sometimes turning it into a business advantage. It will explore actions the best companies are taking to try to deal with diversity—how to respect differences without inadvertently encouraging fragmentation (e.g., by maintaining interest groups on the company intranet for every imaginable group) and how to build enough sense of community to enable cooperation across borders and identification with something bigger than one's own group. Stressing the "unity" in "community" is one way the vanguard contributes to social harmony.

everyone a stranger:
diversity and identity in a globalizing world

THE CURRENT WAVE of globalization brings the challenges of diversity inside companies in a significant way that is hard to deny or avoid. More people are likely to encounter strangers or to feel like strangers themselves as they venture across borders and beyond the familiarity of homogeneous groups.

In the past, international activities could be carried out with relatively few points of contact among operations in a variety of countries, because in the multinational model major countries tended to have a complete set of all functions. Within each country, companies could rely on relatively homogeneous local workforces. At the top of a country pyramid were expatriate home country representatives (e.g., Americans abroad running international units of American multinational companies, reporting to a group called "rest of world"), indicating that the big opportunities were still in North America or Europe. Those expats often lived in segregated enclaves echoing home country conditions and educated their children in American or international schools, thus remaining insulated from the local culture and conditions. Such enclaves still exist, but globalization has changed their character, along with so much else. Outside Beijing, for example, large detached houses in a suburban development near the English-speaking International School resemble mountain lodges in Oregon or Colorado, but the expat I visited there, whose four children attend the private school, is an executive from Singapore who moved to China to head the IBM PC business before it was sold to Lenovo. Now she runs the global desktop unit for Lenovo while her husband takes care of the children.

The traditional divide in industrial era companies between bosses from corporate and the locals beneath them with a ceiling on advancement mirrored stratification in the surrounding society. In many parts of the world, elites tended to form homogeneous closed circles and liked it that way. Although there often were (and still are) great differences within a country in ethnicity and race as well as gender divides, these were generally contained by segregation and subordination; if not contained, those divides became major sources of continuing conflict. Some of the divide stemmed from ethnic or tribal groups differentiated by history or religion and sometimes skin color. In Latin America, for example, differences in status ran along color lines, with those of European origin ("whites") garnering the most status, followed by two lower-status groups, those of indigenous origin ("browns") and those of African origin ("blacks"). People who wanted to succeed adopted the style of the dominant group and pretended that differences did not exist or did not matter. Eastern European immigrants to the United States Americanized their names, and so did immigrants to other countries; Chinese refugees in Indonesia took Indonesian names to avoid discrimination and violence (and some overseas Chinese survived to grow major companies under their new names).

Only relatively recently have even pluralistic countries recognized diversity as a matter of legal rights and overt discussion—meaning that people do not have to pretend that differences do not exist and can be overt about mentioning them. In the United States, the civil rights movement and the women's movement increased legal rights, and immigration increased attention to, and contention about, differences among ethnic and racial groups.

The global information era has increased both attention and contention. On the attention side, there has been continuing growth in the number of countries with equal opportunity legislation and growing attention to such diversity-related matters as keeping educated women in the workforce in countries that are hungry for talent owing to exponential growth in emerging markets or an aging population in mature markets. But at the same time, the major geopolitical conflicts of this era have involved ethnic or religious groups engaged in identity politics writ large, sometimes with a national dimension, sometimes with an ethno-religious one. Immigration has been a source of tension within countries, particularly when immigrants come from groups involved in those major conflicts or are simply visibly different and stereotyped as unskilled (e.g., North African Muslims in France, Turks in Germany, or Mexicans in the United States).

Groups and the differences among them reflect long-standing issues in the history of the world and can be easily seen as givens. Yet differences are a matter of social definition, a matter of prevailing tendencies in categorizing people. Groups chosen or assigned by social type can take on particular social meaning and produce distinctive traditions or cultural styles, sometimes reinforced by legal rules. There is a hoary saying in psychology about the twenty kinds of snow that Eskimos can recognize, while people from warmer climates see snow as just plain snow. In the global information age, how many kinds of differences among people should leaders and their companies recognize?

THE BUSINESS CASE FOR DIVERSITY

Let me start by suggesting that, as much as I champion diversity and inclusion, homogeneous groups can seem easier to manage than heterogeneous groups. People from the same group can talk in code, share secrets, immediately understand one another, and behave in a consistent, predictable manner. That is why for so many years major corporations were characterized by homosocial reproduction at the top, or what has familiarly been called cloning—managers reproducing themselves in kind. It is the World According to Jonathon Herbert: Everyone speaks American, and everyone wants to be like him.

Thus, there have to be some very good reasons for companies to want to introduce diversity. There is often a legal case, when discrimination is banned or companies are asked to take affirmative action to include people from formerly excluded groups. But is there a business case? I will run through some of the most common arguments, many of them well articulated by my Harvard colleagues David Thomas and Robin Ely.

The "fairness and justice" argument is the one enshrined in equal opportunity and other rights laws. People have the right to a chance to prove themselves, and discrimination is wrong because it violates that right on grounds other than performance. But for companies, once they do the minimum to comply with the law, the "war for talent" argument is more compelling. A preference for people of one kind over people of another kind reduces the talent pool by discriminating against otherwise-qualified candidates, and as competition for the best and the brightest heats up worldwide, companies need to widen their search beyond people who look like those already in the top ranks. The "signal of inclusion" argument involves making sure that the composition of the leadership ranks is sufficiently diverse that it raises aspirations. If people see that someone like them can achieve, they are motivated to work hard too. (This is the "Barack Obama effect" anticipated from the first African American U.S. president: that more African American boys will study hard and stay in school.)

"Match the marketplace" is another common argument, one that gets closer to the business. It is sometimes assumed that because customers prefer to deal with someone like them and, thus, to attract new customers from previously excluded groups, companies should have a diverse set of employees to cover all groups, matching the composition of society. In its simplistic form (e.g., that a woman prefers to buy from a woman or a Vietnamese from another Vietnamese), this hypothesis has received mixed support. For one thing, it seems to depend on whether the matched group is considered high status or low status—people often respond to high-status representatives even if different from themselves (an explanation for why so many whites preferred Obama and his Harvard Law degree over a folksy white candidate). But at least it makes sense to have people in the company who understand the context from which customers come and can intuit their thought processes.

The "innovation" argument for diversity is also invoked often: that diversity of social type means getting diversity of thought, which will produce more innovation by challenging conventional wisdom and generating creative alternatives. But that argument has weak support. Diversity of thought is important, and diverse experiences help innovators sense new needs and find new solutions, but does body type or ethnic background automatically produce a different way of thinking? There are numerous complications and contingencies on that one, including the fallacy of making assumptions about how people think from superficial conclusions about social category. (My Harvard MBAs of highly diverse origins come to think more like one another than like people in their home countries.)

A germ of truth in the innovation argument is connected to a more plausible and more often confirmed "learning argument." The learning argument holds that a deliberate attempt to understand differences of experience and opinions in a group can produce better solutions because the group has learned to learn and can thus make better use of one another's differences, whatever those differences might turn out to be.

Globalization has taken these considerations to a new level, especially as the vanguard marches toward emerging markets whose populations have often been among those discriminated against in the developed countries of North America and Europe. Thus, I hear all of the arguments I have just summarized used by vanguard company executives. Many feel that developing future leaders makes diversity a centerpiece, as John Chambers, the chairman and CEO of Cisco, says in every speech. Indeed, everything about vanguard companies makes acknowledging and dealing with differences a salient issue. They want to be tuned in to the surrounding environment, see the context, and find new opportunities through awareness of society—what triggers innovation for them is not the kinds of people they have inside the company but the ability of people to see new opportunities in meeting needs of which they might have been unaware and thereby seek contact with strangers from whom they can learn. They want to integrate people from acquired companies quickly and smoothly, and so they must work out cultural differences at company and country levels. They expect people at lower levels to assemble their own teams and initiate their own projects, which makes it even more important for people to communicate well and work out differences across big swaths of the world. They expect a large proportion of their workforce to communicate regularly with counterparts in culturally different locations. They seek new markets and move people across locations. And their values are central, including the ubiquitous "respect for people" value.

Taking diversity as a given and then finding ways to unite people even across categorical boundaries that might easily divide them underly the vanguard approach to doing business. Vanguard companies seek universal standards and a sense of community but recognize the varieties of identities that are brought to the workplace.

A THOUSAND AND ONE VARIETIES: DIMENSIONS OF DIFFERENCE

Globalization increases the variety of people who potentially interact as well as the dimensions of difference among them. That is a central fact with profound implications for many people and companies well beyond the cosmopolitan elite. Heterogeneity must be the new organizational assumption, and finding commonality in the midst of diversity the new leadership challenge.

Some kinds of differences are obvious and task relevant, such as language differences. Some reflect habits built up from societies with particular social systems and governments, which can affect how people approach tasks, such as differences in laws or infrastructure. Some, such as religious preferences, are matters of private life outside of work but reflect differences that are increasingly salient because of geopolitical conflicts and a surge in spirituality. Some are immutable, such as gender or skin color, with the meaning ascribed to them varying itself by differences based on location, nationality, or ethnicity. Some are variable over time, such as aging; generational differences are the latest hot area in diversity training. Some affect physical abilities, such as visual impairment or physical disabilities.

The structural point is merely that there are more dimensions of difference recognized, more types of bundles of those differences, and greater likelihood of encounters with strangers carrying those differences. Moreover, the rapid forming and disbanding of project groups and the increased mobility of people in a company mean that there will be more frequent encounters with people who are "different" in any number of respects, including in professional fields, some of those encounters for short periods of time, some of them as long-term coworkers.

The sorting of people into social categories carries assumptions about the attitudes, approaches, capabilities, and biases of people in those categories, and categories can become bases for self-identity and the formation of identity groups based on those categories. Differences can also become the basis for rankings of superiority and inferiority and thus for systems of dominance by people of some types over those of another type—such as a bias for home country natives or a preference for the approaches or interests of those who have typically held power.

For companies, external social identities are not the only set of differences requiring management attention. Organizational differences might also affect the ability to innovate or collaborate. There can be differences across functions (e.g., geek culture in the technology areas, buttoned-down culture in the financial areas), differences in approach or decision-making style among business partners, and differences introduced by mergers and acquisitions. Groupings of any kind can serve as the basis for loyalty and identification, with the temptation to close ranks and marginalize or exclude members of other groups. Differences among them can be rigidified into traditions, badges or uniforms, or inner circles with secret knowledge. These organizationally constructed identities can be remarkably enduring. It is common to find people still talking about themselves as working for a company that has disappeared into another one. As Digital Equipment Corporation (DEC) became Compaq, and Compaq became Hewlett-Packard, DEC people still refer to themselves as DEC and hold reunions. So facts of organizational life also present the challenge of how to manage differentiated identities and integrate people and their work effectively.

Identities, whether of individuals, groups, or an organization as a collective, become most vivid and salient when encountering others who are different. Identity is differentiation, so it takes the experience of an "other" for "me" to know what is "not me" and therefore "what I am." This holds at the organizational as well as the interpersonal level. Companies often don't bother with explicit articulation of what they are and stand for—their values—as long as they can recruit people for similarity and then slowly and carefully socialize them into their tacit culture, thereby assuring sufficient homogeneity for operating purposes. Procter & Gamble, for example, was long known for promotion from within and for a conformist culture; this was captured in the characterization of its employees as "proctoids." It was only when P&G made a very large acquisition (Richardson-Vicks) that the company formalized its institutional identity by crafting its purpose, values, and principles (PVP), as described in chapter 3.

Social and linguistic differences present a particular leadership challenge. They can produce miscommunication, misunderstanding, mistrust, divisiveness, distraction, inequalities, and resentment of inequalities—in short, centrifugal forces that threaten to tear an organization apart as people view how "people like me" are treated. Cultural differences can complicate the task of diplomacy across organizational boundaries, making it difficult to create favorable agreements with business partners, customers, or government. "Identity politics" of hostility and conflict occurs when people feel their differences go unacknowledged and their needs unmet, and they do not find points of commonality with a wider group.

What is a good company to do? There are three important issues: expression of self-identities, sensitivity to others' identities, and reinforcement of an overarching collective (company) identity.

individuality: allowing differences to surface

THE FIRST LEVEL of action is the one that Jonathon Herbert wanted at AC, when he said, in effect, *Pay attention to me! You're leaving me out! You're not listening to my ideas!* Not everyone wants to feel that he or she is different, but most people certainly do not want to feel that they are excluded. So the bottom-up, grassroots, self-organizing variant of diversity efforts begins when there are a few other people who feel the same way. If there is just one person who is different on some dimension, not much will happen. I call that one the "O" in a group composed of all "Xs." The O is more likely to want to hide his or her differences and try to look like the Xs than to speak up for change. But get a few more Os in the company, and they might find one another and start an e-mail trail. They might even be bold enough to form a group.

VOICE OR FRAGMENTATION? IDENTITY GROUPS IN THE WORKPLACE

If the traditional way to deal with diversity was to ignore it, the progressive way is to emphasize differences by letting people wear their social identities on their sleeves or their name badges, if they want to. Diversity offices target and track even more possible groups than governments require in equal opportunity programs. In the United States, these departments facilitate networks to help people of a particular category find one another, support one another, give voice to concerns, and recruit others like them, so that everyone has a "home" identity group in which not to feel alone, regardless of what job the person does or what the composition of particular work groups might be.

In Newco, the American company Jonathon Herbert joined after feeling discriminated against by Asians, there are networks for just about everyone: women, mothers, parents, African Americans, Hispanics in general, Mexicans, Asian Americans in general, Indians, recent immigrants, gays and lesbians, and the physically challenged. The diversity department is considering networks for reading difficulties, eating disorders, and single dads. The diversity staff tolerates but does not encourage Bible study, Torah study, and Koran study groups.

Newco counts more than forty networks in the United States alone, not including the ones it is in the process of establishing in other places as global vehicles for the expression of identity. These are aboveground and far from subversive, although they often pass on criticisms, recommend changes, and take bold stands. Their presence in the workplace—meeting on company time, using company communications—is part of a bargain: the groups name names, and people can be tapped to recruit others like them or serve as a resource for training programs about their group.

Newco has increased the numbers of people from previously excluded categories and given them a vehicle for meeting others like them, trained managers about what various groups might want or need from the workplace, and spread some U.S.-originated policies (e.g., around work-family issues) to other countries. Critics who want even greater people power in companies might say that this is a form of co-optation that resembles divide-and-conquer strategies to prevent change—people are too busy in their own identity groups to think about their collective interests. But to the people in Newco, the policy changes are all for the good. The networks are ready to air more grievances and get more changes.

But wait a minute. Jonathon Herbert is not so sure that this proliferation of networks makes sense. He has gone from championing cultural diversity at AC because the Asian bosses did not acknowledge it at all to being a diversity skeptic at Newco, thinking it has gone too far. He wants the people working for him to find common ground, not to be preoccupied with which interest group to join. He is concerned that people who do not want to join will feel railroaded. He is concerned about implicit stereotyping. He observes that people often have multiple identities, and which one should they emphasize? He wonders how Newco will develop global leaders capable of working across countries in a globally integrated fashion, because Newco's approach to diversity has resulted in fragmentation.

Banco Real has chosen another, more promising way to acknowledge diversity at the company level: to let people first choose what they want to emphasize about themselves and then to get their support for paying attention to one another.

THE OPT-IN STRATEGY:
CHOOSE YOUR IDENTITY

For Banco Real, diversity is a potential competitive advantage, helping the bank attract a broad segment of the population that was poorly served in other companies, stimulate employee creativity, and live up to its values of serving society by opening opportunities to people from all parts of the community. Perhaps new products and business opportunities would emerge, leaders reasoned, from looking more broadly at demographic groups and cultural diversity.

The bank's starting point was similar to that of companies in any country with relatively homogeneous elites: Banco Real employees were not representative of the Brazilian population, and Brazilian laws pushed nondiscrimination. In the late 1990s, only 10 percent of the bank's employees were African Brazilian, only 9 percent of managerial positions were held by women (all of them white), and a mere 10 percent were over forty-five years of age. The disabled population was close to zero, though a 1991 nondiscrimination law required larger employers to have the physically challenged constitute 5 percent of their staff; with nearly 15 percent of the Brazilian population suffering from some kind of disability, Banco Real was leaving a potentially large pool of talent untapped.

Banco Real's official diversity program started in 2001, with the appointment of a committee. Diversity goals were communicated through written material, lunch seminars, and videotapes, but nothing much happened, as is typical in many companies. For one thing, the human resources department did not want to go too far in making accusations about biases and probing individual attitudes. Instead, they took a gentler approach that made expression of identity a matter of personal choice and added a bit of fun that built community spirit. A Friday in June 2002 was designated Diversity Day. The entire staff was encouraged to wear a shirt that showed a side to their identity, any side. It could be frivolous or serious—Carnaval in the office. Thousands of employees exposed their political, sport-related, religious, and social preferences. I think that permitting sports themes probably put it over the top in soccer-mad Brazil. Certainly, sports reinforced the idea that we might play on different teams, but we're in the same game. This wasn't the revolution of the oppressed; it was just making the office more colorful.

The idea that everyone did not have to look the same or, occasionally, dress the same made it easier for people to feel comfortable being different. Soon, staff with different sexual orientations began to go public, and religious minorities felt freer to appear in religious garb (e.g., Muslim women in chadors or Jewish men in a *kippah*). Now diversity was less emotional and confrontational, becoming more like an international food festival. The diversity committee was expanded and divided into five subgroups on specific action areas such as recruiting or training. The groups presented forty-four consensus proposals to top executives, and implementation took off in 2003. Community organizations were invited to the bank and asked for help recruiting African Brazilians. Wheelchair access ramps were installed. Specific banking products were developed, such as financing adaptation of cars for disabled people.

Some bank employees said that the greatest impact came from the hiring of a visually impaired employee, a woman with a bachelor's degree in law who had been blind since the age of four. She worked in a department that analyzed customer information. Maria Luiza Pinto, a senior leader, described the reaction: "No one in the company knew how to deal with a visually impaired person and a guide dog. Some people were extremely attentive while others tried to be politically correct, avoiding expressions that involved sight. Everyone had to adapt. But exposing problems and deficiencies was seen by many as a growth process and not a weakness anymore."

Now that diversity is established not as group-against-group identity politics but as individual expression, the bank can assess the impact of diversity on customer relationships. For example, one survey focuses on minorities, in order to learn more about the embarrassments these groups encounter and their expectations regarding treatment by the company. In short, employees are learning to see things from the perspective of others. They are moving to the second level of action.

identifying with others: living with variety

AWARENESS OF OTHERS is the next issue. Skillful interaction across differentiated groups and cultures is even more important than a chance for people to express their individuality. Vanguard companies tend to emphasize this skill because it facilitates the interaction, attraction, collaboration, and integration that the new way of working requires. To their leaders, "respecting differences" means finding ways for people coming from different groups to have relatively equal weight in deliberations and decisions based on their expertise—that cultural differences or other socially induced differences should not get in the way and that people can look beyond them or utilize them, as the situation warrants. That's the ideal, anyway. The goal is pluralism, not singularity. It is accompanied by an attempt at both organizational democratization and ties that cut across groups, giving more people more group memberships in common.

In attempting to flatten the hierarchy and lower the center of gravity, vanguard companies also attempt to moderate any one group's dominance over decision making. Certainly, there remain vertical chains of command and pecking orders, but the goal is to make them less important than the circles of influence that include more people bringing knowledge to the table.

It is still a struggle for many global companies to get away from home country dominance, even when other countries account for most of the revenues or profits, as was the case for AC, as Jonathon Herbert experienced it. P&G people talk about Cincinnati, IBMers about Armonk, and Cemex people about Monterrey as though these places were persons. I often heard personification associated with headquarters in interviews in remote field locations, sometimes confused with home base nationality. Some Europeans in Cemex operations in France and Germany discuss Cemex as though divided between "Mexicans" and everyone else, although they use the word *Mexican* loosely, to encompass all native Spanish speakers whether from Latin America or Spain. Omron has a dramatically shrinking proportion of its business in Japan and about a third of its workforce in China, but in other respects it is a headquarters-dominated Japanese company; although it strives to be more global in its leadership, it is still far from achieving that goal, as evidenced by people in other countries who acknowledge a certain pressure to learn Japanese preferences.

Favoritism can be manifested in numerous ways, including such simple things as time zone politics: who gets to be on a conference call in the office and who is awakened in the middle of the night. It is impossible to create policies for handling all of the many things that can become signs of which group is on top or which people always get it their way. Thus, as in other aspects of their operations, vanguard companies must count on their values, on structures that give more people more contact across boundaries, and on developmental experiences that make people want to reach beyond differences to treat one another with respect.

FINDING COMMONALITY:
SEEING BEYOND STEREOTYPES

People in vanguard companies who have worked across geographies have stories about cultural tendencies, some told with admiration (e.g., an American expressing appreciation for Japanese culture because of team members who are punctual, courteous, and willing to talk in the middle of their night).

But here's an interesting finding: For the most part, the people I asked about the differences they encounter in working with people from other countries and ethnic groups began by downplaying differences. They wanted to find more similarities than differences. They looked for commonalities with coworkers and customers on a human level. They stressed the multiple aspects of identity, that rarely is there a "pure type." And when they did mention differences, they itemized first the ones that stem from impersonal factors such as political systems or past history. The belief seemed to be that they can reach beyond obvious differences to come to a common understanding. That does not always work in practice, but it is a stated goal for many vanguard company managers and professionals: to feel at home with anyone, anywhere, because at some level we are all the same.

Jennifer Trelewicz, the American IBM veteran we met in chapter 6 leading a technical function in Moscow, joked in response to my question, "What's different about doing business in Russia?" "They speak Russian here," she deadpanned. Only then, after establishing that people are people, did she mention Russia's unique historical legacy of Communism and shaky business practices that needed to change to an international model. A Brazilian at IBM in São Paulo who led implementation of a global model in Italy, Ireland, and Vietnam could point to the differences in how governments were organized or differences in accents but was most inspired by the similarities everywhere in people's passion for their children and families.

Other IBMers similarly downplayed country differences and were quick to point to cultural differences within countries that require equal or more sensitivity—regions in the United States, ethnic suburbs outside major suburbs, or north versus south in the United Kingdom or Brazil. They mentioned that sometimes differences across functions are more difficult than national differences. A British engineer working in Russia described adjusting his style to differences between research teams and customer-facing teams; that was more salient than any differences between British and Russian colleagues, he said.

SHOES AND EGOS: ADJUSTING TO FIT

Like the British engineer, effective leaders in the vanguard companies are good at reading cues that tell them how to adjust their styles to make interactions smooth and produce the outcomes they desire. They are able to put themselves in the shoes of others, as the saying goes, and, after walking around in those shoes, to see their own actions from the points of view of others and adjust them accordingly. Empathy of this sort involves reasoning rather than mere compassion. The reasoning helps people develop a strategy for action in particular situations that is likely to be well received by others. It involves interpretive skills.

Part of the art is acknowledging that differences exist without making a value judgment, adjusting expectations and responses to fit. A Mexican IBMer based in Brazil, who headed a Latin American function spanning ten countries, commented that staff meetings required constant calibration. "People from certain countries are very direct and very passionate to say something. And from another country, very soft and tentative, but it is not because that person is not involved or interested in his or her point," she said. "I tell my team to listen hard for the ideas and to ignore how the person speaks."

Listening also involves catching the meaning in a range of accents.

When Patricia Menezes was given a global assignment to manage from Brazil, she asked an English teacher in her neighborhood to give her lessons over the phone rather than in person so that she could learn to recognize words in different accents on telephone calls. An executive in Egypt is also sensitive to accents, even within his country. He told me he deliberately uses a thicker accent with English words when talking with government customers, to make them feel at ease.

Thus, to flourish under pluralism, leaders do not need a set of stereotypes about countries or types of people; they need the ability to see people as individuals while weighing how they might experience the world because they are part of particular categories. In vanguard companies such as P&G, people say that the ultimate benefit of a focus on diversity in the workplace is that they have permission to talk to one another more openly, to learn what it is like for other people with a different life experience. Productive conversations about life experiences facilitate comfort that differences can be bridged, and they also increase leadership skills for working with customers and even for their own lives. A senior manager in the United States said, "They take the learning home, to their neighborhood, to families. Some people say it helps make them much better people."

In its highest form, putting oneself in the shoes of the others and including them as partners rather than subordinates requires a suppression of ego and a leveling of status, in order to truly "read" others and put them at ease by managing their perception of the situation. Recall Maurice Lévy, the CEO of Publicis Groupe, whom we met in chapter 5. In leading the courtship of advertising agencies considered unattainable, he went by himself, unaccompanied and unadorned, to meet with their CEOs. He made himself vulnerable by revealing details of his own family history (his father's wartime difficulties) to show his values, and he also observed carefully to see what mattered to each of the CEOs.

The courtship metaphor is often used, but Lévy went deeper, and he saw how they—from each of their vantage points—viewed a Frenchman and the feelings they would have about being part of a French company. (The Saatchi & Saatchi acquisition was reported in the British press as group against group—the French conquering the British.) When Saatchi's CEO, Kevin Roberts, a brave New Zealander born in England, said that he didn't want to have a boss, Lévy took note and, seeing the value of many Saatchi practices, proceeded to treat the merger as a reverse takeover. Lévy's empathy built so much rapport that Roberts wanted to please Lévy, and Lévy did not have to pull rank as Groupe CEO to steer Roberts; all he had to do was hint, which made Lévy the boss without anyone losing face.

Gestures of respect involve adjusting one's own habits or traditions to honor something important to others. This works best when there is reciprocity involved; each person or group makes a gesture and receives one in return, the way that national leaders exchange gifts as a matter of protocol in international diplomacy. Because of the respect that Lévy showed to Roberts and Publicis to Saatchi, Saatchi executives reciprocated. At the first postdeal meeting of Publicis and Saatchi executives, Saatchi chairman Robert Seelert, who is British, made his opening speech entirely in French. Even though he did not consider himself fluent, and the Publicis executives were all good English speakers, his doing so was a gesture of respect that required humility.

Inclusion means respecting others' traditions and making room for them. For relationships that are important, the signs that the company is more diverse get bigger and clearer. After Mittal Steel, originally from India, acquired Arcelor, a French company, the new entity, Arcelor Mittal suspended Mittal's rule of no alcohol at work to serve French wine during the workday at its facilities, including those in India. After moving into Europe through the RMC acquisition, Cemex changed the whistle-blowing clause in its companywide code of ethics, which asked employees to report actions or behaviors that violated the code. The feature was both legal and well accepted in Mexico and the United States, but a number of European countries discouraged mandatory whistle-blowing clauses owing to painful histories with government informants. Cemex executives considered this change a gesture of respect for European colleagues. "Cemex is demonstrating that we listen to newly acquired employees. If there are improvements to be made, we do it, and we export it to other operations," said Guillermo Martinez Sans, vice president of human resources in Europe and the United Kingdom.

a common identity: finding the unity in community

IT TAKES A GREAT DEAL of effort to overcome centrifugal forces that diversity can introduce into organizations. Some observers hold that tribalism is a state of nature, part of the human condition, and that given a choice, people will revert to preferring their own kind. The optimistic view that contact across tribes will produce understanding, tolerance, and better relationships is undermined by the fact that some of the bloodiest conflicts of recent decades have been between groups in close proximity, whether in the Balkans or Africa. In some U.S. communities, diversity has been found to reduce rather than increase social capital; people who perceive other groups as being on their territory became more closed, exclusionary, and protective of their own. Democratic pluralism works to hold such tribal battles at bay largely because of cross-cutting ties that break up the singularity of groups and create subgroups for tasks or interests that combine people in a variety of ways. That is what the matrix organization and the fluid set of project teams from overlapping departments does for vanguard companies. But while cross-cutting ties break up monolithic identities and provide a basis for person-to-person and group-to-group interactions, they do not by themselves meet the goal of vanguard companies.

The vanguard wants to unite people and help them identify with a larger whole: one world, one enterprise, one human community. This is important for operations, so that people can communicate, form project teams, and disseminate and apply innovations and best practices quickly and effectively. It is also important for institution building, whereby people feel that they are members of a community beyond the job, which helps attract, motivate, and retain the best talent. Thus, while vanguard companies might encourage people to express individual identities and become sensitive to others' identities, they seek, above all, to build an overarching company identity with a sense of common purpose at its heart. They want people to see themselves as global citizens and global leaders.

Helping people to work as members of a broader community rather than isolated in fragmented groups has both technical and emotional components.

THE COMFORT OF CONSISTENCY:
COMMON PLATFORMS

The impersonal technocratic side of community building is simply providing an infrastructure for communication. That is not enough, but without it, it is difficult to unite diverse people behind a common effort. When I start talking about IT systems or meeting protocols as part of a diversity and inclusion effort, some human resources managers might roll their eyes, but in fact the infrastructure makes a difference, and vanguard companies emphasize it. They seek consistency of environment and process. This puts everyone on the same page, as the saying goes—or rather, the same e-mail system, the same models and templates, the same metrics and data, the same problem-solving tools, the same language, the same common vocabulary, and the same values and standards. This is efficient, like a single currency for Europe, and it facilitates faster transactions as well as objective analyses of the whole.

"One Cemex. I always wanted only one Cemex," CEO Lorenzo Zambrano declared to me in his New York office, in explaining why he organized the creation of the Cemex Way soon after Cemex made its first acquisition outside of its region. While the cultural differences between Mexico and Spain, or Mexicans and Spaniards, were not as great as between other companies without a common language, there were enough differences that Zambrano determined to create a single global platform or set of operations. This was not intended to reduce innovation—always a danger of standardization—but it would be the consistent background music as innovators sang variations on a theme. Cemex created the Cemex Way to make explicit and easy to learn all of those routines that would help people in acquired companies feel part of one Cemex and work out differences without contention. The technical infrastructure is important, because it increases objectivity and makes certain routine processes givens, not arenas for conflict.

Periods of adjustment are required to bring everything up to one universal standard. Upon taking over European operations, Cemex leaders found that Europeans highly valued personal time whereas they felt that Mexicans emphasized personal improvement, making the Mexicans more willing to sacrifice personal time and accept Cemex's demanding work ethic. It was very common at Cemex to have meetings on Saturday and for people to get up at 3:00 a.m. There were clashes over Cemex's practice of closing the books on every month before the fourth day (not business day) of the following month, which could require working on weekends—a sore point in France, where thirty-five-hour workweeks had legal support and managers guarded their autonomy. Legacy Cemex personnel initially handled closing the books by the fourth of the month until people from RMC caught on that they might miss out unless they showed up. Cemex rolled out its Web-based potential and performance assessment platforms in the region so that people could define objectives, set targets for projects, and measure financial performance in the same consistent way that was done everywhere else.

Cemex seeks consistency down to the factory level, including the color coding of pipes, so that any Cemex employee from any part of the world can walk in and find his or her way around. No distractions before getting down to work. I heard this theme of comfort and familiarity throughout my interviews with the most global of the vanguard. Hans-Ulrich Maerki, former chairman of Europe, the Middle East, and Africa for IBM, a region that encompasses the maximum national and cultural diversity in the world, says he can walk into any IBM office anywhere in the world and feel at home. Maerki, who is Swiss and speaks five languages, is an example of the cosmopolitans who increasingly populate vanguard companies. His colleague Bruno di Leo, raised in Peru by Italian parents, head of Latin America and then southern Europe, and now running an emerging markets group from Shanghai, China, echoes the comfort of consistency within IBM.

In a sense, the common platforms in vanguard companies replace the homogeneity of social type—managers reproducing themselves in terms of country of origin, color, or gender—with homogeneity of profession or company identity. Engineers speak engineering everywhere in the world, and when English skills are halting or accents hard to understand, a few mathematical notes or physics expressions help people recognize one another as doing the same thing. My Harvard Business School MBA students referenced earlier are an educated global elite speaking the language of spreadsheets and PowerPoint. Companies such as Procter & Gamble have so many buzzwords and acronyms that it would take a small dictionary to explain them outside of this community of people who cover almost every imaginable type and yet are united in their ability to speak the P&G language and who attribute everything to the PVP. If, in addition, there is a template for every process, as tends to be the case at IBM, and an improved template immediately becomes available to anyone anywhere with access to the IBM intranet, then acting in unity is facilitated.

All this can seem like washing away differences in one bureaucratic tide, and sometimes the number of processes and procedures and standard decision-making hoops can feel that way, as some people complained in my interviews. But having one platform for doing things is better for most people than having multiple platforms, which is what the vanguard are trying to get away from. IBM is still working on making key processes globally integrated. And not having to think about every background detail before getting to work frees the mind for more creative endeavors. Consistency of process can enhance rather than stifle innovation. It simplifies life.

So far this is "community" at a very superficial level. But modern business is inherently superficial, and it should be. Luckily, people do not have to know one another deeply in every single respect to know one another as colleagues. In fact, having common business processes and languages can permit joining together of people whose personal lives outside of work, if exposed, could lead to conflict. Managers at P&G Near East, covering Egypt and Lebanon, can talk in P&G-speak about product features or packaging modifications with colleagues in Israel even though there are political and religious tensions among the countries.

Discouraging, if not banning, workplace discussions of religion or politics (the most divisive issues in a world of diversity) can focus attention on the tasks and goals that unite people, and that is what they are supposed to do at work anyway. If this seems to contradict the formation of identity groups or networks that I discussed earlier, it simply puts an outer limit on the kinds of differences that can be expressed productively. But those boundaries are shifting too in a globalizing world. The Somalian Muslims working at the Rochester, Minnesota,

IBM factory have presented a challenge. After it was noted that they used the sinks in the men's rooms to wash their feet before midday prayers, IBM added footbaths, but that led others to ask why they couldn't display Christmas decorations at their workstations. The challenge is to keep seeking common points of reference and universal values. The technical stuff of platforms and templates is not enough: While the common language of engineering or of managerial processes can provide a basis for connection, they cannot fully produce a sense of community. Something more transcendent is required.

I have already discussed at length the benefits that vanguard companies get from their values and principles. Let me just reprise the role they play in creating a common identity that can transcend group interests and make people want to feel connected because together they are accomplishing something important for the world. People not only share Web-based tools to run processes in a consistent way, they also come to share a consciousness, a way of seeing the world. Values statements become almost like religious texts, and they satisfy at least some of the same human desire for meaning that religions do. Omron employees, as I have said, recite the Omron motto to begin every workday, reminding them that they are part of a community of higher purpose than today's tasks. So even if spirituality is something more than what can happen in a company or workplace, at least a portion of that connection can be made. And that phenomenon both creates a shared identity and reduces conflict.

P&G and IBM managers use almost the same words when asked to explain why overt conflict is so rare and why people insist they do not take it personally if a request is turned down. One said: "It's the notion of an IBMer. We understand one another really very well, and we speak the same language, and we share the same beliefs and values. When issues arise, we are making some business decisions, and it's just done. Everyone understands."

RELATIONSHIPS FOR THEIR OWN SAKE: COMMUNITIES FOR COMPANY SPIRIT

Forging a common identity is not a matter of rhetoric, though anthems can help. When Novartis was formed out of the merger of Sandoz and Ciba-Geigy, I lightheartedly suggested that they sing a company song. To my surprise, a Swiss executive wrote one, and four hundred slightly inebriated managers from around the world sang it over dinner at their first conference in Bermuda. But beyond that onetime evening of emotion, Novartis reminds people of their membership in a community through global days of community service on the anniversary of the merger. When I suggested both ideas to European executives, I thought that they would write them off as too American. But they understood that building a company identity involves going beyond tasks and transactions to help people make relationships that have no immediate instrumental business purpose.

For Shinhan Financial Group, the emotional integration activities described in chapter 5 were considered extravagant at first but later viewed as a wise investment. When fifteen hundred managers of two former rival banks climbed a mountain together in historic shrine-filled Serabol, South Korea, the powerful imagery provided a common reference point, and the shared experience outside of formal roles forged emotional bonds. Recall the shaved heads and hair pile Chohung left for Shinhan as the opening sign of antagonism by employees who did not want to feel inferior. The Serabol Summit was the first time managers from the two groups were together without any assumption of superiority or inferiority and no pressure to do anything but talk (and climb).

A feeling of common membership is reinforced by activities that lie outside of formal responsibilities, so they are not viewed as purely utilitarian. That is why community service projects are a powerful way to transcend the many things that can divide people. The "community" leaders build overlaps with the organization but is not identical with the formal structure and boundaries. The community can encompass the entire extended family of alumni, retirees, and business partners. The business advantage is flexibility and speed—being able to mobilize people quickly for projects, including inviting alumni back to the company.

Communities can be so important that vanguard companies are willing to invest in building them even without a task-oriented or business-related justification. That has been the case at IBM in North America.

In 2006, in response to declining numbers on its employee pulse survey, Bob Zapfel, head of Global Technology Services (GTS) for the Americas, hit upon a new idea. He would create communities of enjoyment to lift the spirits of IBMers residing in the same neighborhood who might be working at home and feeling isolated and who probably did not even know that there were other IBMers around. Who knows what else they were feeling, as IBM increased its investment in emerging market countries. Some managers worried, as one told me, that the sense of identity as IBMers could be weakening. Zapfel, a technical executive who also understood the value of emotional leadership, called his vision spirit communities. Helping people feel connected to one another as members of the IBM community was sufficiently important, he felt, that he allocated $1 million for anything people locally wanted to do—pizza parties, gatherings at a museum, or something that would be fun and help IBMers know their neighbors who lived in the same postal zone, regardless of their job. Every location under GTS formed an executive steering committee, but the real work was done by volunteers, led by one appointed "mayor" per postal zip code.

The concept of spirit communities spread quickly. The country general manager for Canada did the same thing nationwide across Canada. Ann Cramer, director of corporate citizenship and corporate affairs for North America, got wind of it and took the idea to Americas president Mark Lauterbach. Lauterbach enthusiastically endorsed it for the whole United States and went door knocking for contributions to a budget from several of the business units. By March 2007, the program was up and running throughout the United States. It soon became clear that there were many side benefits. Some of the mayors were people who had "sit at desks" jobs; this pulled them out of the daily routine and gave them chances to show and develop their leadership skills. Mentoring and networking were also expected to take place, with senior executives participating in activities alongside other employees. In a spirit community, everyone could be equals. The shared identity as IBMers was the important thing.

Mayors consulted their colleagues and created many different kinds of opportunities, from fun and games to inspiration and community service. In Atlanta, spirit community mayors led over forty-four events. The most successful were informal local events in various zip code communities. Thirty or fifty people would go bowling, to a ball game, or meet for pizza and drinks. In Raleigh, North Carolina, a back-to-school drive to collect materials to donate to disadvantaged public schools was tied to registering to volunteer for the schools using IBM's On Demand Community online tools. In California, seven hundred people gathered from six IBM sites around San Jose for a town hall meeting on diversity. Discussion was followed by performances by IBMers: a dance concert using wheelchairs as a prop and a musical performance by Thein An Nguyen, an IBMer of Vietnamese origin, on a Chinese instrument called the *guzheng*.

A year later, the spirit communities had raised morale and productivity, promoted commitment and cohesiveness, and helped foster a common culture among a remote, mobile, and diverse workforce. On a survey, 97 percent of the executive members of the spirit teams concluded that the spirit program improved the sense of community at their location. In March 2008, funding was increased.

The interesting thing about spirit communities is that they are intensely local yet speak to something bigger. They unite people by stressing their commonalities and connect them to a larger sense of purpose that the company espouses. In this most global of companies, a sense of broader membership is built one neighborhood at a time. Inclusion is not an abstraction; it is experienced on the ground.

toward universalism

THIS CHAPTER BEGAN with a story about feeling different, in which a person who had been among the dominant group, even while working internationally, experienced what it was like to have the tables turned. (He is not the only American to feel that way today.) It concludes with examples of ways that vanguard companies try to build a sense of community compatible with their values of respecting individuals yet seeking broader common purpose. Dominance-subordination models are fading from the best global companies. The culture and work practices of vanguard companies are aimed at a tricky balance: recognizing differences but not taking them as signs of superiority or inferiority. Differences become so matter-of-fact that people expect them and, over time, learn to adjust to them.

Horizons are enlarged by the mere fact of contact and communication across dividing lines, whether of functions, departments, groups, and projects, or race, ethnicity, regions, and nations. A Cemex manager in London, who had worked for Cemex's big European acquisition, speaks to this. "If you asked anybody in Europe where Mexico was, most people certainly knew roughly where it was on the map, but we would have had a hard job putting a cross on the country, and even a harder time when it came to places like Costa Rica and the Dominican Republic," he said. "But all of a sudden you have people from these countries working with people in Poland, Latvia, and the rest of Europe, and it opens up the world. We now feel part of a truly global company."

Vanguard companies are on a trajectory toward universalism—that is, finding those standards, values, and practices that can unite people even in a world of differences. That is certainly good for business when they can meet this ideal. It can help companies attract and motivate talent, help people with diverse identities find commonalities, create empathy with customers, and ensure consistency while encouraging expression of different ideas. At least, that is the goal.

In its largest manifestation, the vanguard approach has the potential for smoothing the pathway for businesses to become more global and also for allowing global sensibilities to be taken home, when employees act as citizens.

chapter eight

grounding: bringing the best to communities, countries, and the public

OTHER AMERICANS BEFORE me had lifted a shovel for a tree-planting ceremony outside a foundation headquarters, a small oasis in steamy Hyderabad, India, including *New York Times* columnist Thomas Friedman and University of Michigan professor C. K. Prahalad. The saplings bearing our names reside in a corner of the garden. This is not yet a forest, but it is a good metaphor. Business and local leaders, in partnership with government, are trying to ensure that some of the world's best ideas and technologies take root in local soil to help children grow and poor villages thrive.

I was there with a colleague because IBM was deploying KidSmart workstations for preschool-aged and young children in innovative classrooms for the tiniest and poorest of schools. These are the same workstations that IBM gives to disadvantaged public schools in the United States. For IBM, whose corporate home is New York State and its India headquarters a plane ride away in Bangalore, this intensely local project is the essence of global citizenship, as IBM focuses global values and resources on one small part of India. The partnership is also an asset in corporate diplomacy.

One paradox of globalizing is that it is accompanied by the need for deep national and local connections. Those connections have to occur in many more places, in plural public spheres with multiple and sometimes conflicting agendas. To thrive in diverse geographies and political jurisdictions, companies must build a base of relationships with government officials, public intermediaries, community organizations, and business partners that can ensure alignment of interests even as circumstances (and public officials) change. These stakeholders do not want to be used and abandoned. They are interested in the quality and sustainability of the company as a local contributor—especially if the company has ties elsewhere.

For their part, companies want both an extended family of relationships with high-quality business partners and a seat at the policy table for matters affecting their ability to do business in the future. For example, Arcelor Mittal built a church in Romania as a goodwill gesture to show that a foreign company is committed for the long haul to things the Romanian public cares about.

Vanguard companies have an advantage in the public sphere. Their values and principles tend to make their leaders more attentive to societal needs and more willing to support innovations and investments to address those needs. Their track record of operating to high standards makes public officials and the public less suspicious of their motives and intentions. That is not all. At the same time that vanguard companies "internalize society," bringing consciousness of the societal context and the business ecosystem inside the organization, they also "externalize" their business capabilities, using the same tools and frameworks that make them successful innovators to benefit the business to create community innovations to benefit the public—innovations that can later be adopted by governments. And they can gain a seat at the policy table where the public agenda is discussed.

Vanguard companies are certainly charitable, but this model is not corporate philanthropy in the traditional sense of giveaways, nor is it corporate social responsibility as a passive matter of meeting standards. It is corporate social innovation and entrepreneurship combined with corporate diplomacy, a powerful combination that Klaus Schwab, the influential founder and chairman of the World Economic Forum, has urged companies to adopt, because they have capabilities that can address some of the world's most challenging social and environmental problems. Thus, in this model, companies show that they are acting in the public interest by actively creating tangible improvements in communities. I call this the shift from "spare change" to "real change." Instead of giving spare change, left over from business proceeds, they aspire to make real change that raises standards and improves communities.

In this chapter, I describe this model, show it in operation, and derive lessons about how companies pursue their business interests while serving society. They choose issues with strong signaling power, think systemically with awareness of the local context, leverage unique capabilities and work with multiple partners to ensure effective outcomes, and use diplomatic skills with government and the public.

That brings me back to IBM and helping the poor. The villages I visited are a good starting point for considering the creation of public benefits by private companies, through actions across sectors that build on business capabilities. Civic engagement involves many circles and networks.

engagement rings: partnerships for world-class local change

To GET to some of the KidSmart-endowed villages, the van leaves the highway for a series of dusty roads alongside fields still bearing an early summer green, even though the temperature is over 100 degrees Fahrenheit. The first stop is always the schools, because the children are the greeters and the proof of change. The buildings are very small, featureless concrete structures in courtyards or up narrow stone steps. The teachers and principals, who are government employees, are young, slender, and proud to be learning and teaching in a school with world-class technology. But the children bring it all to life, with their big smiles, gifts of flower necklaces, offerings of drawings, and shy words in English. The most impressive sight is the small bodies at colorful plastic-sheathed workstations keying commands and using the same multimedia interactive educational software that is found in U.S. public schools.

The problem of poverty in India is huge, and, at the time of my visit, the new model and tools had reached two hundred poor villages, a number that can sound high but is just a drop in the bucket and covering only six districts in one state. Improvement goals for education are ambitious in a country with school dropout rates of 50 percent to 60 percent in villages and 10 percent to 15 percent of village children who never go to school at all. This is not just an education problem. Children cannot learn if they are not healthy, and they cannot be healthy if drinking water brings disease. Education is not valued without jobs, and no change will occur without good leadership in the community.

In one village, we entered the two-room health center to talk to the visiting physician. An older woman in a sari, she had finished her weekly office hours and was making notes at a small desk in the examination room, while the health aide, who was on a daily shift, showed off the medicine and equipment closet. Internet connections permit remote diagnoses, such as electrocardiograms (EKGs), which cost less than $1 per person compared with $25 in a hospital and can be sent to physicians around the world to read; Boston's top medical centers are on the system. The health center is not as busy this year, the doctor said, because the water purification plant halted childhood illnesses from bad water.

A water sanitation process is another social innovation for these villages. The plant requires little space. A small reservoir lies underneath. Two small rooms are crammed with purification and storage tanks and a large number of two-gallon jugs that community members use to carry their water home each day. Home delivery is the eventual goal. Meanwhile, the children are educated in school (which they now attend religiously) to understand why fresh water needs to be acquired daily. Community members working at the small treatment plant are also communicators. The village council, which has received extensive leadership training, proudly supports all initiatives—as members showed in their enthusiastic swarming around the American visitors, eager to talk through interpreters and proud that the children are learning English.

FORMING INNOVATION PARTNERSHIPS

The new social entrepreneurs, in India and around the world, want the best solutions, connected to other solutions—open innovation, a vanguard principle that means taking the best from anywhere. They do not settle for yesterday's solutions. Thus, it is not surprising that a local group aggressively pursued the IBM partnership.

Beginning in the 1990s, IBM has donated KidSmart early learning centers in collaboration with key nongovernmental organizations (NGOs) in the United States, Europe, Latin America, Asia, and Africa. These workstations for preschoolers and up have proven impact on

early literacy and numeracy, and they have become an effective starting point for IBM's contributions to education and the community. In
India, KidSmart partnerships began ahead of the growth of the IBM
business and were one element in IBM India's discussions with government. By 2004, IBM had deployed KidSmart in city schools in
Bangalore, Chennai, and Mumbai, expecting the schools to take over
responsibility for running the program after a year, so that IBM could
add more schools.

Partners' capabilities leverage IBM's contributions, but only if
the partner can meet IBM standards. In places with significant social
needs, traditional nonprofit organizations are not always up to the
challenges in terms of their own skills; in addition, government bureaucracies can be difficult to deal with, and administrator or teacher
skills may not be at a level to make a KidSmart installation effective.
The utmost diplomacy is required to leave doors open but walk away
from an unsuitable project or partner. When the right partner is available, however, the impact of IBM's role can be multiplied to produce
noticeable social value.

IBM had not yet run the program in a rural area, so Julie Coyne,
an IBM Asia-Pacific manager based in Australia and responsible for
education initiatives, and others wanted to know how confident potential local partners were about making it succeed. They expressed
confidence and committed to running the program for a minimum of
five years in every school, with the support of the state government
education department. And unlike the city model, which primarily
comprised a donation of computers to schools and teacher training,
the new village approach would involve a strong community partnership model with high involvement of both village leaders and government schools, with program management from a foundation. It was a
broad coalition.

KidSmart goes beyond technology, observed Jalaji Pillai, an IBM
India manager; it also enables multigrade teaching and classroom management and provides a widely used community learning center. The
KidSmart facility is open to children from neighboring schools and,
in evenings, to any other child, including older ones, and it is kept
open year-round and used for summer camps. After the first eighteen
months, the seventy-five centers had become the prime tourist

attraction in many of the villages. School enrollment increased dramatically and teacher attrition dropped. "For a rural area, this is almost like leapfrogging into the future overnight, and to get a facility like this in a place like that, even much ahead of the city schools, is a very, very motivating factor," a local observer said. Pillai saw potential for huge impacts in India, such as decreasing school dropouts and reducing child labor. "Everyone likes to be associated with corporates who have a heart and who want to share their prosperity with the lesser-privileged in the society," another participant said.

The building where I planted a tree houses the Center for Rural Transformation, complete with a Solutions Design Center to create technology innovations, a Mission Control Center to collect and analyze data, and a Learning Center to train field agents and community leaders. It is similar in look and advanced technology feel to Silicon Valley companies or IBM offices. And technology is advancing through social innovation. Just after my visit, in June 2008 at a dinner in Washington, D.C., the remote EKG system for heart monitoring received a Twenty-first Century Achievement Award from *Computerworld* magazine (its highest honor) for innovations in technology to meet social needs. The project had also received an IBM award for the best rural education program.

real change, not spare change: the ibm model of strategic corporate citizenship

THE RURAL TRANSFORMATION project is only one of many IBM KidSmart applications in the United States and around the world, and KidSmart is just one of dozens of programs in IBM's Global Citizenship Portfolio. Although IBM is extraordinary, even among the vanguard, the evolution of its model and the principles it employs are worth examining in detail because they can be emulated.

IBM's approach to corporate citizenship is closely connected to its business purpose: to harness the power of innovation in service to the social and educational goals of the broader society. "I see a change in the way we think about social responsibility," Sergio Xavier de Brito, a Latin American executive, said. "Twenty years ago, I think the focus was, do the right thing internally. Before, it's like I see a problem in the society, in the community, and I don't care, because this is not inside IBM, so I have nothing to do with it. The change right now is to leverage the size of IBM and do the right thing outside our organization, into the whole supply change with providers and customers, and in the community. Right now, if I think that I can help, I can do something. That is the kind of company that we want to be."

In 1993, IBM's new CEO Louis V. Gerstner Jr., undertook to transform the company from an inward-looking to a more open environment. He focused IBM's philanthropy on American public education reform and recruited a former deputy chancellor of the New York City schools, Stanley Litow, who had also worked in banking, as vice president of corporate community relations (renamed corporate citizenship and corporate affairs in 2007) and president of the IBM International Foundation. As it played out, this function came to be considered so strategic and innovative that for several years, from 2005 to 2008, the group became an integral part of the technology and innovation community, under executive vice president of technology and innovation Nicholas Donofrio. Donofrio later told me, with a broad smile, that "Stan hasn't done anything but make me look like a genius ever since."

IBM's Reinventing Education initiative was launched in the United States in 1994, operating by principles that run through subsequent projects joining company and society. The approach is not to give away "spare change," using leftovers after revenues and profits are secured as an afterthought, but to promote "real change"—innovation that makes a discernible difference on a problem. The following tenets underlie this approach.

- *It is not about the cash.* Unlike traditional philanthropy, the major contribution is expertise, not money.

- *It is about the change.* The goal is solutions to significant problems that can be spread and sustained. The issues should matter. The public should care about the problems and be willing to support the solutions.

• *Innovation is the pathway.* Technology—IBM's core competence—is used in creative ways to develop the solution. The best and latest technologies are used and improved, and new learning and new technology emerge, oriented to sustainable smart solutions, not one-off contributions.

• *Recipients are ready for change.* Targeted recipients are those most likely to succeed, not necessarily the neediest. Recipients must be active investors and participants, adding their own time and even resources to the mix.

• *The most talented people get asked first.* The work is not for burned-out or mediocre employees; it requires the highest skills and thus the best people.

• *The work can be managed just like other work.* Projects involving grants and donations use the same processes of assignment, measurement, and compensation as any project. They are simply internally funded—so-called blue projects, after IBM's signature color—instead of revenue-producing green projects, named for the color of U.S. currency.

• *Solutions emerge as the work proceeds.* Agreements stress a process of joint discovery rather than following detailed preordained specifications.

• *The best partners round out the change coalition.* By working with a variety of nonprofits or NGOs that are linked to the community, IBM can specialize on what it does best and multiply its impact.

• *Results are the prize.* As wonderful as the handshake photo opportunity can be, the work is not finished when the public relations spotlight ends. The goal is to produce measurable results and sustainable solutions.

Reinventing Education began with two rounds of projects in twenty-one large American urban school districts (or, in some cases, whole states), including Boston, Charlotte, Chicago, Memphis, San Francisco, Florida's Broward County, Vermont, and West Virginia. IBM also convened three U.S. national education summits with federal officials and nearly every state governor; Reinventing Education lent credibility by giving IBM skin in the game. By the year 2000, Reinventing Education solutions such as Wired-for-Learning (a platform later licensed to an external company for commercialization as Learning Village) and Reading Companion (the ultimate version of Watch-me!-Read described in chapter 4) had spread to over a dozen other countries and resulted in numerous technological innovations, thus contributing to IBM's globalization and innovation agendas.

Educational solutions such as KidSmart workstations became vehicles for assisting with market entry in countries where public support for IBM's presence is a critical ingredient. For example, in Russia, although deploying KidSmart required delicate work with cumbersome socialist-legacy systems and adapting methods to local conditions (preschools in Russia were really nurseries, with staff that had not been trained to teach, let alone work with computers), IBM gained valuable relationships and insights into navigating government bureaucracy. In China, work on KidSmart began in 2000 and was formally announced in 2001 in Beijing; by 2007, there were two thousand KidSmart workstations in four hundred kindergarten and early education schools in remote regions of all thirty-one provinces of China, including Tibet and Inner Mongolia, and training programs for role model teachers who train other teachers. KidSmart is among twelve education-related programs that bring IBM into partnerships with the powerful central Chinese Ministry of Education. Globally, IBM estimates that its noncommercial public education programs serve over eighty thousand teachers and over eight million children.

Litow's business-strategic, high-leverage strategy mirrors IBM's go-to-market trends: emphasizing services rather than products; pushing open source and open access; offering business transformation, not just processing power; integrating resources throughout IBM; relying on external business partners to extend reach; and reinforcing goodwill with high-ranking government officials. "Litow sees his group as a stalking horse for the business," an executive said. "He always looks for a customer—someone in the business with a stake, who wants to invest in a project because it is a strategic business opportunity." Litow explained the rationale: "Progressive companies see their social investments and policies as being intrinsically linked to their core values, and sustaining them requires them to be linked closely to the business strategy and purpose of the company."

For societal impact, it is equally important that the issues on which the company works be visible and important, so that they send strong signals of the company's intentions, principles, and prowess. Education is generally first on the list of what the public cares about in every corner of the world and high on the list of areas to which companies of all kinds contribute, including IBM's peers and competitors such as Microsoft, Oracle, Intel, Hewlett-Packard, and Cisco. In addition to education, IBM supports health and science projects through World Community Grid (described in chapter 4) and has leaped onto the green bandwagon with Smarter Planet activities aimed at energy efficiencies and a Great Rivers project oriented toward environmental preservation.

Perhaps most illustrative of how IBM works strategically with neighborhoods and nations is a series of cultural heritage projects. These put IBM's brand on an issue central to concerns about the global information age, dear to the emotions of the public, and strategic for governments trying to attract international investment. The cultural heritage projects use the Web and the latest interactive technologies to keep unique cultures alive and well.

NATIONAL PRIDE AND GLOBAL TECHNOLOGY: CREATING THE FUTURE BY PRESERVING THE PAST

A project in Rome got Litow's group and regional leaders thinking about cultural heritage preservation projects, with the same approach that lay behind Reinventing Education, that is, significant projects involving technology innovation. Digital reconstruction of Michelangelo's *Pietà*, an application that later proved useful in telemedicine of the kind used by the villages in India, deepened relations with the Vatican. Continuing conversations led to an initiative to scan the Vatican Library, which helped pontifical colleges in other countries access the holdings in Rome remotely. IBM was approached by many museums for charitable contributions, but IBM wanted to invest in something that was business strategic. So the next effort involved a partnership in Russia to scan the Hermitage Museum collection in three dimensions and make it accessible through a website, www.hermitage museum.org, which earned the gratitude of government officials just when IBM was increasing its investment in Russia.

Word spread quickly throughout IBM about the Hermitage achievement, and in 2001, IBM Egypt broached the idea of doing a similar thing with even more advanced technology. IBM Egypt, established in 1954, had high-level connections with government ministries, especially around IT. Egypt wanted to increase foreign investment and tourism as strategic priorities. The initiative, dubbed Eternal Egypt, would digitize the cultural treasures of Egypt and use unique technology solutions to connect museums with cultural and historic sites and re-create, virtually, large-scale structures or places that no longer existed. Robotic cameras were placed around Egypt so that visitors could connect current-day sites with the reconstructions. There was cell phone access to the website throughout Egypt, which turned out to be one of the most valuable points of access, as Egypt's treasures were found in many locations; people could continue their tour while on the move between historic sites and get references to things they had seen previously. On my trip to Egypt, I could walk around the outside of the pyramids of Giza, near the highway linking downtown Cairo to IBM's offices in a new suburban office park, but avoid claustrophobia by going inside the pyramids virtually in a futuristic technology showroom with large screens providing the 360-degree experience.

Eternal Egypt is a very high-profile public-facing project that started as a social contribution, involved joint development teams with government ministries, linked IBM to the highest officials, and ended with commercial payoff. The Egyptian prime minister spoke at the launch of Eternal Egypt from the foot of the Sphinx. It was much acclaimed in Egypt and became internationally known. Eternal Egypt became part of the "chat item" for sales reps—"Much better than talking about the weather," IBM Egypt's general manager said, "and it demonstrates that the company cares about more than maximizing sales, especially important for an off-shore company." It was viewed as a critical ingredient in IBM's winning a very large commercial contract from the Egyptian government to digitize the Library of Alexandria.

Word traveled to the global marketplace. A customer in Chile, the finance chief of a four-country retailer, mentioned Eternal Egypt to an IBM executive in Brazil; his daughter had heard about it while studying in Paris, so the customer went to the Eternal Egypt website. This opened new discussions with IBM about future business. "When you receive this kind of phone call, it's the prize—this is the momentum that outsiders see, a company that is here helping society," another executive commented.

Each successive opportunity for a significant project is also an opportunity to develop and showcase the best and latest technologies—an example of "blue" corporate citizenship projects contributing to the public ahead of profit-making "green" commercial projects. This is definitely not a case of spare change being donated to a cause; if it were, government officials would never become partners.

IBM's next project is in an even more strategic country with even more advanced technology, so new that its commercial applications are still emerging. Beyond Space and Time, the project in China that digitizes and creates experiences around the Forbidden City in Beijing, adds virtual worlds and interactive applications to the mix (demonstrated by CEO Sam Palmisano when he sent his avatar into the Forbidden City at the project's announcement), and it solidifies important relationships with the Chinese government at high levels in Beijing.

High-profile national projects such as Eternal Egypt and Forbidden City are joined by other cultural initiatives that strengthen IBM's relationship with a key constituency. In the United States, the Smithsonian Institution's new Museum of African American History and Culture is an oral history website as much as a place. In Brazil, IBM is a participant in the new Museum for the Portuguese Language, a Brazilian government initiative above the central train station, with futuristic exhibits based on IBM's WebSphere; on the day of my visit, it was swarming with schoolchildren who came by bus and train from all parts of Brazil. Each is a source of considerable pride for the country. Each highlights the company's desire to build long-lasting relationships with particular groups and honor their cultures while demonstrating an important new technology.

Such projects reinforce the company's internal commitment to diversity and a community that respects differences, as I showed in the previous chapter. They also respond to fears about globalization by showing that a global company can support the deepest emotions of national and local pride. Note that the public that benefits is not just citizens of a nation or members of a group who feel that their traditions are honored and preserved but also the global public: People anywhere there is an Internet connection can travel virtually to experience and learn about history and culture.

Litow and his team have also moved in parallel with business needs to rethink employee volunteerism to increase its impact. In 2003, when IBM's business emphasis had shifted to On Demand Computing, the company launched On Demand Community, an intranet site for technology tools designed to improve schools and community organizations. A mere three years later, seventy-five thousand employees (over 20 percent of the population) had performed nearly 3.5 million hours of service using IBM tools. IBMers could clock their volunteer time and at fifty hours get a certificate of recognition from their country head and be eligible to apply for a grant for that organization based on IBM worldwide standards; many people love the service for its own sake and forget to clock their hours.

In 2007, IBM announced a new IBM corporate service corps (mentioned in chapter 1), which goes beyond volunteerism or brief sabbaticals to deploy IBMers in teams on full-time four-week service projects, organized through NGO partners wherever the world has needs, regardless of whether IBM had much business in that region. When launched, over five thousand applications were received in three weeks; a year later, fifty-five thousand applications had been received for fifteen hundred opportunities. In July 2008, the first team of eight headed for Romania to lend expertise to a furniture manufacturer, a nonprofit foundation working with the disabled, a university, and a textile company. These are strong examples of service beyond the business.

Far from finding corporate citizenship programs a distraction from the business, IBMers in a variety of business roles and geographies want the company to do even more. Inderpreet Thukral, India's strategy director, called community initiatives essential to ensuring the future, saying: "If we are participating in the community, people see that we are willing to make commitments for the long haul, that we're a company oriented toward building long-lasting relationships." An executive who oversees the Latin America retail industry sector finds societal initiatives so important that he wants IBM to expand its scope, court more companies as partners, make projects even more significant, and multiply their impact.

Overall, the success of community programs has encouraged many people in the company to get involved themselves, to spot opportunities where the company can make a difference, and to submit proposals for "blue projects," some with a green tinge not of raw commercialism but of environmental sensibilities, such as the Great Rivers project, a consortium dedicated to mapping worldwide rivers so as to be able to identify and control environmental damage. Projects like these are considered a gift to governments and the world. They are fundamental to giving IBM a voice in the public agenda.

CORPORATE DIPLOMACY: SERVICE, NOT LIP SERVICE

Around the world, IBM professionals and managers in various roles report that they see the connections among community programs, innovation, and positive relationships with government. This nexus is the essence of corporate social entrepreneurship to raise standards and improve society. Dravinda Seetharam, government programs executive for India based in Bangalore, commented on the close linkage between his work and community programs. "There is an expectation that an organization like IBM contributes to the community. More and more, the social programs give us leverage. The best part of it is, most of the bureaucrats now, they listen to us. Government wants ideas from us. They want to know how to improve things."

In every part of the world, demonstrations of corporate citizenship help secure a seat at the government policy table for issues such as education and IT strategy, but also to discuss IBM's agenda of trade liberalization, open-source standards, data privacy, and mobility of people (e.g., visa policies). There are synergies when a project in one area opens the door for IBM leaders to discuss other areas. Government connections for IBM education initiatives help IBM get a hearing in other government departments for human resource executives to discuss workplace issues, for example in Europe, where IBM seeks more flexibility on labor policies.

This is just as important in the United States. In its home nation, IBM makes numerous high-profile national as well as community contributions that are directly tied to government policies and actions. CEO Sam Palmisano leads the National Innovation Initiative of the U.S. Council on Competitiveness—a clear sign of commitment to America's continuing success. IBM's corporate citizenship executive for New England, Maura Banta, chairs the Massachusetts Board of Education at the request of Governor Deval Patrick, in a volunteer position that is very important to the governor's agenda for the future.

"What we want to be known for is first to be an employer of choice and next to be treated as a national asset," said an IBM India executive, describing the long-term vision for building IBM's presence in India. Country staff find the connections between the company's global agenda and national interests. In India, for example, three people based in Bangalore, Mumbai, and Delhi, respectively, focus on national and seventy state governments "to understand what's happening and to see our priorities, and then to work with the key thought leaders, getting the global practices to these individuals and help them to shape public policy," Seetharam said. That includes advising the minister of commerce on India's competitiveness.

In Egypt, where IBM's population is almost without exception Egyptian, the challenge of proving commitment to the country's interest is entangled with geopolitics. IBM has a long history in Egypt and has supplied many of the key IT executives in other companies as well as the retired IBMer crafting Egypt's national IT competitiveness strategy. When Egypt decided to actively seek foreign direct investment, IBM already had close working relationships with many ministries. But all that still did not prevent questions about a "foreign" company. An insider reported, "We were working closely with the Ministry of IT, helping them, trying to convince them of the international view of Egypt as an investment destination. After the meeting of our chairman with the minister of IT and the minister of Industry and Trade, a task force was formed in order to see how we can take Egypt further to more liberalization. We gathered the stakeholders, and we tried to convince them of the pros and cons. And we discussed it openly and we told them our view. But sometimes you will find them asking, well, what is in it for IBM? What is the hidden agenda? Tell us, why are you doing this? Is it a kind of invasion? Is it a kind of flood?"

IBMers have to understand the underlying concerns and make the case diplomatically that projects or policies are in Egypt's interest—an imperative also for P&G and Cemex in their own expanding operations in Egypt. "Their [government officials'] worry is about having a lot of expats working and taking the places of Egyptians, so the unemployment rate will increase. And our counterargument is that if a lot of expats will come, they will come in a profession that is not there in Egypt, so that is why we are asking them to do this, to transfer the new know-how," the insider concluded.

It is a balancing act similar to what multinationals face in other countries: how to bring perspective and expertise from outside Egypt while being Egyptian in other respects. In 2003, there were numerous anti-American protests about the invasion of Iraq (although there were also long lines at the U.S. embassy for visas, an IBM leader pointed out) and then a boycott of American products and protests because of the Palestinian situation, targeting mostly consumer products. But IBM managed to remain above the fray. An American, John Tolva, project leader for Eternal Egypt, traveled to Egypt from his base in Chicago before, during, and after the terrorist attacks in New York on September 11, 2001. "A year after September 11, support was great for America's actions, and then it began to deteriorate. But it never influenced IBM. Even though IBM's headquarters is in the U.S., we are perceived as a global company. That has served us well," Tolva reported.

"IBM is not seen as a company that is tied to a specific government or works for a specific cause," commented Ahmed Tantawy, an Egyptian who had returned from years of work for IBM in the United States. Government relations head Dina Galal has a telling example: "We asked a journalist, who said, 'No, you are perceived as a local company. However, you are an American company.' So we chitchatted with him that if we can as Egyptians get a better alternative than IBM products, then we should do it. We always give them the impression that we are Egyptians before we are multinational."

Egypt is a relatively small market. In China, however, the vast population, strong central government power, and strategic importance of the nation make IBM's local embeddedness even more vital. IBM can contribute global expertise to discussions with government officials and often does. Leaders of IBM China are rarely asked questions that imply that IBM is a U.S. company and thus might have a different agenda for China when there are disagreements between the countries. But some indicated that they know such questions exist below the surface and that ideas are scrutinized through that lens. "We talk about open standards and IP policy," an IBM China insider said. "Different companies in the industry have different views depending on the business model. Given that IBM has a very complicated business portfolio, IBM is in the middle. While the government will take into account the perspective of your company, that happens less for us. Given that IBM has been in China for two decades, our position is well received, and in many cases we are the sole company in policy discussions."

Others felt that nationalism among the general public and government officials could mean that foreign enterprises would be excluded once their expertise is applied. "China's eleventh five-year plan on innovation is talking about indigenous innovation, developing technology with China's own intellectual property," a manager said. "So whether companies like IBM will be included in China's national innovation system, we don't know. This is why we did lots of things in the past years to show them that we are very committed, that we want to be China's innovation partner."

It is not as simple or easy as these comments suggest. There are conflicts between company goals and public priorities, trade-offs among countries, risks stemming from problems among governments, and internal disagreements about how to handle situations inside a country. Still, what puts IBM in the vanguard is the awareness that community engagement is linked to voice in a national agenda and that credibility comes from service, not lip service. More people at more levels understand that the company is not just a business but rather a social institution that is part of society, not apart from it. They exercise diplomacy on behalf of the company to the public in particular places, and they also can think about diplomacy in multiple public spheres.

That is what Henry Chow, chairman of IBM Greater China, did in

May 2007, when he took it upon himself to contribute to improving U.S.-China relations. Chow is a Chinese national raised in Hong Kong who has worked for IBM in Asia for his entire career, mostly in China. He has been honored as one of the most respected CEOs in China. He also acts as a global citizen and informal international diplomat trying to broker collaboration among powerful nations, using the same sensitive attention exhibited in his hundred mentoring relationships I mentioned in chapter 6. We could rename a classic movie in his honor: *Mr. Chow Goes to Washington*.

Chow had previously visited Washington on executive trips organized by the American Chamber of Commerce in China. Once China became part of the World Trade Organization, Chow wanted to use his experience as a Chinese executive for IBM to facilitate positive development of the U.S.-China relationship and find areas of collaboration, such as environmental issues. With the help of IBM's government relations office, Chow spent four days calling on senators and congressmen, some who supported China and others who had grave concerns. He met a deputy secretary at the White House and gave a number of speeches. Discussion focused on principles, not details. "There were no specific agenda and topics; otherwise it would get too sensitive and political. Nonetheless it was still very meaningful to understand more how the U.S. government works and the sentiment of officials," he said. Chow felt that the trip was so productive that he wanted to repeat it in 2009, after the 2008 U.S. elections.

Business as a force for world peace and harmony? That seems a stretch. But it is not far-fetched to see a step toward this in the range of corporate citizenship efforts, from community projects to diplomatic outreach: that values-infused vanguard companies can be a force for raising standards.

can anyone do this? win-win values and societal benefits in the course of doing business

Vanguard companies' actions in the public sphere acknowledge two important realities of the global information age: the importance of governments and the emotional pull of place. Strategies and tactics to address them require thinking beyond a market logic of profit maximizing. Leaders must also see the social logic involved, that relationships matter and that long-term societal investments build a sustainable institution.

Corporate citizenship has become a common function in an increasing number of companies not simply because it is the latest fad, public relations opportunity, or necessity as a source of legitimacy with the public. Community and societal initiatives are investments that can trigger innovation and showcase it to the public, in a manner consistent with both values and business priorities. They can demonstrate capabilities and commitments. They attract media attention, seats at the government table, top talent, and prime partners. They signal intentions and alleviate concerns. The generic term *goodwill* hardly covers all of this.

The bigger and more visible the company, the more the public expects and the more that governments call upon them to do. In Egypt, for example, the first lady, Suzanne Mubarak, has called on foreign multinational companies to help with the education of women. The national government also wants large companies to contribute to the development of the country by building schools. There is no stated quid pro quo, but executives understand that they want help from the government, too, for a variety of licenses and permits.

Many companies have responded to government calls for contributions. In line with its values, Procter & Gamble has built several schools in Egypt by funding construction and turning the schools' buildings over to the government. In addition, P&G Egypt has taken the unusual step of providing employees with two hours of release time per week to volunteer in the schools. In China, P&G partnered with the China Youth Development Foundation, one of China's first nonprofit organizations; by 2008, the partners had built 140 schools in rural areas, with the help of more than a thousand P&G volunteers. From the company's standpoint, national initiatives such as these in a developing country fit P&G's global Live, Learn, and Thrive focus for its corporate contributions. Some of those contributions are global in scope and significance, a far cry from the days when civic engagement meant lending executives to the Cincinnati Chamber of Commerce and volunteering in Ohio schools. The Children's Safe Drinking Water partnership highlighted in chapter 3 is a prime example of putting society first: P&G converted an unprofitable product, PuR water purification powder, into a nonprofit initiative.

But it is not just giants that can get involved, nor do the projects have to be gigantic in scope. Companies of any size can tackle something in the neighborhood. Recall the iconic alley next door that symbolized Banco Real's commitment to serving society, as described in chapter 3. It was just an alley, but it gave the public a safe, enjoyable, environmentally friendly space. One alley does not change the system. But the mind-set of responsibility infuses many other aspects of the business.

Every principles-led company can create public benefits in the course of doing business. I will start with Cemex, because Cemex's social contributions began before it was a global giant.

PAVING THE WAY AND CEMENTING RELATIONSHIPS: CONTRIBUTIONS TO DEVELOPMENT

Cemex started its Patrimonio Hoy program in 1998, while it was still a relatively small regional cement company. Patrimonio Hoy organizes poor families into peer groups and offers them access as a group to special financing with payment terms they can afford, low-cost building materials, technical expertise, and customer service. Community residents were hired to run the programs locally, thus creating jobs that also primed the market for Cemex's core products. By removing obstacles that hinder low-income individuals from building their own homes and helping them work collaboratively, Cemex claims to have improved the quality of life of over one hundred thousand Mexican families. Cemex's reputation for caring about Mexico has been enhanced, even as it has increased its investment outside of Mexico.

Operating across the supply chain, Cemex offers training that raises the standards of the even smaller companies with which it does business, and that not only helps those businesses succeed, lifting local economies, but it also reverberates throughout society. In 1999, Cemex bought an Egyptian government-owned cement company in the southern city of Assuit, in what has been called the first model of a successful privatization of an Egyptian state enterprise as the Egyptian economy liberalized. Cemex wanted to use its Cemex Way tools to make the factory more efficient, and that would mean eliminating jobs in a unionized environment in a recently socialist country. Corporate diplomacy kicked in. Cemex raised wages, to reward the greater productivity of the best workers, the ones the company wanted to retain, thus beginning to raise the standard of living. For the community, and the laid-off workers, Cemex aided in the formation of new businesses that would offer services the community lacked, such as dry-cleaning establishments. Cemex built a school and set out to improve it. These were all major investments in Assuit.

Elsewhere, Cemex helps distributors improve their businesses and operate to higher standards, which include small-scale corporate citizenship. Recall the discussion in chapter 3 of Cemex's Construrama distribution program for small hardware stores. One important feature is involving them in community contributions such as school construction using tools and materials from the stores.

Another Cemex program gets a bit more political, in light of the touchy subject of Mexican immigration to the United States, legal as well as illegal. In 2000, Cemex bought Southdown, a U.S. cement company headquartered in Houston, Texas, not far from the border, and then launched a program called Construmex. Construmex serves Mexicans working in the United States who want to buy a new home or remodel an existing one in Mexico but lack access to credit. Construmex grants them loans of up to $50,000 for purchasing a home and $8,000 for buying construction materials. Through its distribution network in Mexico, Construmex delivers the loans to the workers' relatives supervising the construction project. By improving quality of life in Mexico and formalizing what might otherwise be an informal cash economy, could Cemex's actions help ease tension with the American public?

CEO Lorenzo Zambrano educates Cemex managers in corporate citizenship and diplomacy, as he explained over coffee in his New York office. A Cemex manager in his first country post expressed surprise to Zambrano about how much time he had to spend fostering relationships with government officials and wondered if he should be doing it. "Welcome to top management!" Zambrano said he replied.

The first thing the public wants from any company is that it do no harm, that it operate its business to comply with prevailing rules and standards. For a cement company, the primary imperative is to reduce emissions and refrain from polluting the neighborhood. Cemex has won awards for environmental responsibility, going beyond compliance to innovate in the use of alternative fuels. That is a big effort, organized internationally and guided by its environmental research laboratory in Switzerland.

If a basic commodity like cement can create public side benefits, why not any product? Under the right circumstances, the public benefits can be unexpected and enormous, all in the course of building a market, with government relationships and the whole distribution chain in mind. Consider another dramatic example.

THE BEER THAT SOLVED SOCIAL PROBLEMS

It was not Diageo's original intention to solve a public health problem for Africa through marketing a new beer. Whatever social contribution Diageo leaders thought they were making to health in Africa was through its charitable foundation's donations to clean water initiatives. And as an alcoholic beverage, beer itself is considered part of a "sin industry," one that is outright banned in some places. But in Kenya, beer is a national beverage. People like their beer and like it cheap—to the extent that unregulated home brews using impure water and sometimes laced with ethanol or battery acid became a serious public health problem. Diageo's team at its East Africa Brewing Limited (EABL) subsidiary was merely looking for market share. But as part of an aspiring vanguard company, values also led them toward wondering if they could do something about this.

Diageo was formed through the 1997 merger of Grand Metropolitan and Guinness. While the new company's brands stretched back over 250 years with the invention of local spirits and beers such as J&B scotch whiskey and Guinness porter stout, the new entity had to forge a new corporate culture to guide its global expansion. The first step came when the company rebranded itself as Diageo—stemming from the Latin word for "day" and the Greek root for "world"—to represent the everyday, everywhere ambitions the company had for its products. The new name also gave leaders a clean slate for identifying a core set of values, principles, and processes in 2001. The values stress pride and the freedom to succeed, with customers at the center. Diageo followed with new marketing, corporate citizenship, and re-cruiting policies. It created a Diageo Way of Brand Building (DWBB, pronounced "dweeb"), developed a global code for responsible mar-keting, and nurtured talent in places like Africa by recruiting from the internationally educated African diaspora and sending such cosmo-politan Africans back at expatriate pay rates that were higher than prevailing local market rates. All three organizational developments became crucial to the success of Diageo's Kenya subsidiary.

Diageo entered the Kenyan market in 1998 with a large invest-ment in EABL, but it could not match the low price of the competi-tion. That was because the home brew competition was subject to no standards or inspections and was sold out of *busaa* clubs or *chang'aa* dens, unlicensed and unregulated drinking establishments. Illicit beer is downright dangerous in a country where water supplies are often contaminated—it is known to cause blindness as well as the intense hangovers and related illnesses that routinely lower productivity in Kenya's labor-intensive industries. But cheap home brew accounted for over half of national alcohol consumption. With no government taxes added to its price, it offered the most sips for the shilling. De-spite EABL's modest success with Citizen Lager, a low-cost unmalted barley beer that used local and, therefore, untaxed ingredients, the company still could not lower the price far enough to compete. EABL distributed the beer in bottles, which subjected it to a surtax, and dis-tribution and retail costs remained too high.

Diageo had the benefit of local talent who recognized an opportu-nity and seized it. EABL understood that the answer lay in producing a safe, low-cost beer and making it widely available, giving the buyers of illicit beer a reasonable alternative. Success, however, depended on convincing the government to cooperate on lowering taxes. In line with Diageo's values statement, the company focused on the best out-come for society and was therefore able to open lines of communica-tion with the national government to negotiate a reduced surtax. But the government wasn't interested in corporate charity. As the third-largest company listed on Kenya's stock exchange and the country's largest tax payer, EABL had to convince the government that lower taxes would be a win-win situation. Lower taxes would make EABL's low-cost beer competitive with illicit home brews. If more people bought legal beer, more tax revenue would be collected on a greater proportion of the alcohol being consumed and the society would be healthier for it. With this combination of fiscally responsible and values-driven argument, the government agreed to reduce its tax burden on bottled and keg beers.

EABL used the Citizen Lager formula as the basis for the new beer and rebranded it as an aspirational product, one that was not illicit but of premium quality, which lower-income consumers could afford. Local and global marketers used Diageo's DWBB process to identify a new name. They preserved the "Citizen" frame but upgraded the rank to "Senator." Local marketers wanted to give a second name of Challenger, but corporate team members invoked the company's responsible marketing commitment, cautioning that the term implied potency, as if it were stronger than illicit brews, a comparison the company did not want to make. The team settled on Senator Special instead for the bottles and Senator Keg for the draft distribution.

Diageo values influenced decisions throughout the process. "We have adopted the Diageo beliefs around how we market and the passion for understanding consumers," Peter Ndegwa, an EABL sales director, said. "Obviously complying with international codes in a local market can feel constraining at times. But this company is open to dialogue, and that's why it works. So Diageo controls EABL from the international marketing perspective but gives EABL a lot of leeway, particularly on business decisions around brands that are regional or local." Senator Keg pilot tests began in 2004.

To extend market reach and protect against cannibalization of existing sales, EABL redesigned its low-income go-to-market strategy for keg distribution, focusing on lower-income urban areas. "This required a whole new sort of thinking, a whole new level of product innovation, a whole new organizational structure, a whole new set of logistics to transport the product to market. It was a huge thing for us," Billy Indeche, EABL marketing director, said. Until then, EABL recruited distributors through newspaper ads, while the business depended on a small number of high-volume sales to outlets. EABL could be found in hotels and restaurants but not in lower-income urban areas. Its absence was particularly apparent in *busaa* clubs and *chang'aa* dens, where the negative impact on public health was especially pronounced.

EABL used Diageo's "search-and-spin" knowledge-sharing process to tap the company's global network of people and practices to devise a new go-to-market strategy. EABL sent a team of twelve into the cities, to identify potential distributors who were locally known and trusted citizens. The company worked even more intensively with existing shopkeepers and *busaa* owners, many of whom either had never sold keg beer or operated illegally. Support included helping the owners legalize their establishments, an arduous process that was eased with government support, as well as training in quality management, hygiene standards, and stock control. *Busaa* owners were given classes, equipment, including keg-cleaning kits, and upgraded bathrooms.

Senator Beer is a success for the company and for Kenya. In two years, sponsored establishments ballooned from three hundred to three thousand outlets, and the beer gained a 10 percent share of EABL's volume in Kenya. The figure rose to 18 percent by 2006 and continued to grow, eating into the illicit beer market. In 2004, the product received an unexpected marketing boost when Barack Obama, the son of a Kenyan man, was elected as a United States Senator, and Senator Beer became informally known as "Obama Beer." When Obama was elected president of the United States in November 2008, EABL had already planned to offer a special edition President Lager to celebrate the occasion. The pub network was also highly successful and slated to expand into Uganda and Tanzania. The societal benefits were immeasurable. Diageo was recognized for contributing to reduced rates of blindness and increases in workplace productivity. Meanwhile, thousands of new small businesses flourished, standards for sanitation were raised, and government policies were nudged in a new direction. Kenya remains a troubled country with outbreaks of violence. But even so, a business bringing global standards and values has made a small contribution to economic and social development.

terms of engagement: seven rules for success in the public sphere

VANGUARD COMPANIES ASPIRE to have impact beyond the donation of spare change, but they also recognize the limits of the real change they can make, even with the best set of partners in the ring. To succeed as businesses, companies must stick close to their own capabilities and serve their customers. Moreover, even the largest of the giants is dwarfed in size by the budgets and employment of most national governments. Governments set the rules, legitimizing them as the will of the people, even where governments are inefficient or corrupt.

Still, through their corporate citizenship efforts, companies in a range of industries, including a "sin industry" like alcoholic beverages, are in a position to exercise diplomacy on some issues, change lives by improving communities, and perhaps even raise standards. Corporate citizenship and diplomacy also have some potential to ease tensions where country interests differ or in the face of troubling historical memories or recent conflict, as evidenced, for example, by the high respect the Japanese company Omron is accorded in China and by the way U.S. companies such as P&G or IBM can export their values to foster social progress that benefits people and communities in the Middle East. When company leaders conduct themselves in a society-serving manner and remain unmarried to the political regimes in the countries in which they're based, they might subtly shift perceptions that influence relationships not only within countries but across borders—that is Henry Chow's goal in flying from Beijing to Washington.

Perhaps the best contribution companies can make is to lend their expertise. Companies can contribute innovations to public services, as IBM and its local partners do for education in Indian villages, or innovate in the public interest.

The most effective projects carried out by vanguard companies in the public sphere serve multiple purposes: helping people achieve better health, education, and standards of living; making a contribution the public cares about; demonstrating significant capabilities and building new ones; signaling positive intentions and alleviating concerns; becoming insiders; reinforcing and demonstrating values; building relationships with community leaders, government, and NGOs; gathering intelligence about needs and opportunities; weighing in on the policy agenda; bringing world-class tools and best practices from other places; and raising standards.

To get these benefits for both company and country requires a strategic approach, a citizenship mind-set, a broad perspective, and a great deal of diplomacy. Let me translate that into seven guidelines that summarize vanguard practices.

1. If the first lady calls, answer the phone. If given the chance to advise or contribute, show concern for the public agenda and public good, looking beyond your own interests.

2. If you say you are serving society, mean it. Claims of good citizenship are credible and tangible when leaders allocate time, talent, and resources to national or community projects without seeking immediate returns. Any instrumental goal would not be achievable without first contributing to efforts clearly benefiting the country.

3. Be deeply local. Go native. Draw people from the community, and be part of the community. Participate beyond the immediate tasks. This is the best way to overcome suspicion of outsiders and concerns about hidden corporate agendas.

4. See the whole system. Social and environmental problems are complex, and it is hard to have impact by poking at one corner. Understand the interconnections among aspects of the problems, to ensure that your contributions add an important ingredient that will make other parts add up to a better whole.

5. Bring the whole family. Reach out to partners, to your networks, to your own supply and distribution channels. Think end-to-end. Involving the whole extended family can magnify your contribution and ensure more comprehensive solutions. Find the best nonprofits and NGOs to serve as intermediaries and/or implementers.

6. Look inside. Make sure that your values are clear. Use the mirror test—do we look like what we espouse? Ensure that your culture and practices are models for the kinds of changes you want to produce for society.

7. *Provide your best.* Use your core capabilities and your best and latest ideas and technologies. Deploy your best people for community projects. Train many diplomats and involve many volunteers.

To behave as a local company fully committed to the success of the country, corporate leaders need to encourage a citizenship mind-set in managers, professionals, and associates at many levels. While top executives of the largest of the vanguard circumnavigate the globe to meet with business partners, government officials, and community leaders, employee diplomats on the ground help make the company an enduring institution contributing to particular communities and countries. By keeping society in mind as part of their daily job, they can turn more passive social responsibility into active, innovative corporate social entrepreneurship. "Corporate social responsibility" thus melts into a broader notion of "corporate responsibility," which is itself a step on the path toward progressive corporations that meet high standards in every aspect of their business and embed social good in everyday work.

This is work that spans departments and develops the broad perspective future leaders will need. Vanguard companies certainly have staffs dedicated to government, community, and public relations, but they keep those staffs relatively small, augmenting them with employees who care about an issue. Indeed, the work of corporate citizenship and diplomacy is sometimes less effective in terms of impact on external stakeholders when it appears to be "just a job." Instead, many others perform institutional work as volunteers, giving public meetings or community service projects a ring of authentic motivation. Getting involved is not a hard sell for people either native to the area or long-term residents, because there is an emotional pull of place that makes institutional work desirable. People in those positions are willing to volunteer personal time to serve communities and nations, sometimes initiating efforts and taking others in the company with them. For others whose careers take them across geographies, institutional work is a way to connect their internal roles with the place they now live in, making them feel less rootless and more at home.

The motives of a company setting up in foreign countries are always going to be questioned, at least initially, by the local community.

Let us acknowledge that and move on. Of course companies are try-ing to secure advantages for themselves! That's what it means to be strategic in corporate citizenship.

But competing to be the first with a solution for schools, the first to reduce greenhouse gases, or the first to apply technology to lift people out of poverty is qualitatively different than crass advantage seeking. That is the kind of competition the public can embrace. The village children I met in India whose lives are being transformed by IBM partnerships would be the first to applaud.

part four

agenda *for the future*

chapter nine

unfinished business: confronting the dark side of globalization

To skeptics, the vanguard company model could seem like an American comic-book caricature of a superhero. People in distress look up at the sky and shout as they view their rescuer drawing near, "It's a bird. It's a plane. No, it's SuperCorp!" Is there a tsunami in Asia? A hurricane in Louisiana? A need for clean water? Public health problems in Kenya? SuperCorp to the rescue! SuperCorp can leap tall country boundaries at a single bound. SuperCorp has X-ray vision to see future trends. SuperCorp is vulnerable only to political kryptonite. SuperCorp has the strength to save Metropolis from the evil Enronman or rescue mortgage holders from the perils of the Derivates Gang. SuperCorp always wins the merger partner . . .

To caricature the vanguard companies is misleading. Vanguard companies are neither larger than life nor invulnerable. As individual companies as well as a collective model for business, they are exposed to attack. The most visible are the most vulnerable. Before we headed out on research trips, my team prepared detailed briefing books about the lawsuits and negative press on the vanguard companies, akin to the "opposition research" conducted by political campaigns. I wanted to know what got them in trouble. I found weaknesses that were quickly corrected (e.g., environmental problems of hazardous chemical use), ripples on the surface (e.g., lawsuits by disgruntled employees about discriminatory managers), and historical problems stemming from decades earlier. I found nothing that undermined their values and very few, if any, problems that arose in the twenty-first century, when they followed the vanguard model.

Their endurance and generally stellar financial performance, despite occasional setbacks and industry downturns, is largely because they nurture their cultures—the values and principles that inform their practices and organizational models. Even during fall 2008, when the worst financial crisis since the Great Depression hit the world, most, though not all, of the vanguard companies in this book suffered less than their counterparts and generally had better performance between December 2007 and early December 2008. The companies I have examined set goals that indicate that they aspire to excellence: P&G wants to be "the best consumer products company in the world," not just the largest, and Banco Real wants to be the number-one bank in Brazil in profits and reputation, not in asset size; but they do not say they have reached those heights. They are careful in their claims about their impact on society, relying on third-party assessments and working with partners, such as nongovernmental organizations (NGOs), which often get the more visible credit.

Many of them have chosen new CEOs in recent years with humble, collaborative styles who present themselves as down to earth, flaws and all. I was in the front row of the old Opera House in St. Petersburg, Russia, in 2007 when IBM chairman Sam Palmisano, arguably one of the top CEOs in the world, stumbled on the steps leading up from the audience to center stage, then joked about his clumsiness. Maurice Lévy of Publicis Groupe said those three magic words that usually do not trip lightly off the tongue of CEOs, "I was wrong," when he told a thousand of the world's elite at the World Economic Forum in Davos, Switzerland, about his mistakes in the failed alliance with Foote, Cone & Belding. Low profiles can be protective coloring, but they also signal awareness of limitations.

Furthermore, vanguard companies do not have powers unavailable to the average company. Sometimes they have the clout of size, but their growth itself stems from factors rooted in their cultures. There is no mystery about foresightedness. When they appear to be faster or more visionary, it is the result of simply getting more eyes out looking for needs and opportunities; and when they stop doing that, innovation decreases. Their prowess at mergers comes from human sensibilities about treating others with respect, not from a magic formula. It is also clear that the vanguard model of attention to values and culture, combined with empowerment of diverse people, helps a company perform well at any life stage from different nations, including recently emerged leaders (Shinhan, Cemex, Banco Real) or established American and European giants (IBM, Procter & Gamble, Publicis).

The vanguard model has proven good for the companies I have studied, but how far can we take it? Globalization, which the vanguard companies enthuiastically embrace and master, is accompanied by many rumblings of discontent. During my research, I also paused to examine antiglobalization arguments, scholarly analyses, and the perspectives of distinguished critics (not ideologues), which I summarize in this chapter, weighing and responding to each criticism.

Concerns about globalization are also expressed within vanguard companies themselves. In mid-2007, IBM solicited comments from a set of managers worldwide about the implications of becoming a globally integrated enterprise (GIE). The managers had predictable business questions about go-to-market strategies and organizational structures in geopolitically/culturally different regions and about risk management when local crises that take down a function could have much broader impact on global activities because functions were no longer duplicated in several geographies. But the Americans and Europeans also had numerous questions about the downside of globalization. Would there be local job losses and outsourcing to emerging nations? As investment grows in emerging markets, would there be job creation strategies for mature markets? From France, a place with considerable country pride, managers asked how a GIE could communicate effectively with French stakeholders who are very nationalistic. They asked whether the GIE implied standardization (e.g., of language and culture and in terms of contracts with smaller local partners and relations with local governments) and how a GIE could commit to being a long-term business player in a country and contribute to the country's development. A Swiss respondent asked about whether cultural heritage would be lost. From Australia came questions of whether a GIE has a separate responsibility in each nation in which it does business or whether nations are irrelevant. And these questions were also raised by Americans: Is IBM no longer a U.S. company? Do we all have to learn to speak Chinese?

For an IBM or other vanguard companies, such questions trigger a search for solutions. Those who are fortunate enough to work for those companies or their best partners will find help making the adjustments (e.g., IBM's various transition programs outlined in chapter 6), and if they adapt to the new ways of working, their opportunities could increase.

But for people who do not work for enlightened employers, or those who do not have regular employment at all, anxieties about global change are not easily allayed. The people eliminated first from games of musical chairs cannot stand back to think that it is a wonderful game. And even if new jobs replace the ones that leave for foreign shores, the people who get the new ones are not always the same people who lost the old ones, and the jobs themselves may vary in quality.

Furthermore, some problems have been getting worse, if not in absolute terms then in terms of public pressure. Environmental issues remain to be addressed. Public health issues threaten to bring pandemics across borders. Income inequality is widening in many parts of the world, especially in the United States, with the United Kingdom a close second, and secure middle-class jobs are disappearing. People measure themselves in relative, not absolute, terms. Even if the bottom is better off in standard of living, the widening gap between the bottom and the top makes people feel miserable. And the global financial meltdown affects everyone.

A wage premium for education and skills occurs everywhere. As we can see from the profile of success in vanguard companies, the Fortunate Few tend to be cosmopolitans with an international outlook, educated and English speaking, and mobile in terms of location or able to join broad networks, who can work well with people of diverse types. The Miserable Masses tend to be local and left out. That's why basic education is the most crowded arena for social contribution made by vanguard companies.

Business leaders are aware that disparities in income and growth within and across regions, along with international conflicts and environmental degradation, pose threats to the future of global trade, which has aided prosperity in general, although it has also widened the gap between richer and poorer. According to focus groups with chief executives on three continents conducted by my Harvard Business School colleagues, Joseph Bower, Herman Leonard, and Lynn

Sharp Paine, leaders say that something more than corporate social responsibility is needed, that there should be a more radical reformulation of business.

Against this backdrop, exactly what claims can be made for the vanguard company model? I have offered the positive arguments throughout this book: that they operate in a new way informed by values and principles; that this approach helps them succeed as businesses and deal with uncertainty, complexity, and diversity; and that they generate societal benefits as well as strong financial performance in the process. But now I want to stand back to put them in perspective, by addressing the critics concerned about the role of business in society.

doubts and detractors: answering the skeptics

DETRACTORS COVER a contradictory range, from those who think big companies do not do enough for society to those who believe that they should not spend shareholders' money trying. The latter have missed the point about how many benefits the best companies get from putting society at the heart of the enterprise and thus why goodwill is more than just a balance-sheet item.

It is easy to condemn companies that break the law, violate moral standards, use underhanded or corrupt tactics, exploit, or pollute. For progressive companies trying to do positive things, the criticisms are more subtle, falling into three escalating categories:

- They are not all that good; they still have problems and flaws.
- Even if they are very good, they are rare exceptions. Most companies will never change.
- Even if companies do change and adopt vanguard practices, that is the wrong path toward improving the state of the world, because the system itself is flawed.

I will explore the grain of truth in each set of objections and then respond with the arguments for a positive, central role of vanguard companies in society—why business leaders in the vanguard should make sure they are leading the parade and why public policies should encourage them to do so.

IMPERFECT?

Although they have large numbers of engaged and satisfied stakeholders, vanguard companies have not built a business Utopia. They are ahead of the pack, but their models are still works in progress. In numerous places throughout this book, even while telling success stories or showcasing particular practices, I have indicated that these companies are heading toward a destination they have not yet reached. They are surrounded by ethical dilemmas about which observers and their own employees disagree (e.g., should a global company engage in "gift-giving" practices traditional in some countries but questionable in others? The answer in most is no.). Top leaders have set processes in motion to build or reinforce the desired culture, but the long march to align all people and practices is just under way.

Scratch every successful outcome and you will find controversy and difficulties below the surface. At Procter & Gamble, the Básico products for lower-income families did not win support easily; it took repeated tries and undeniable frustration. The formation of a non-profit organization for the commercially unsuccessful PuR water purification powder was not a sure thing; internal skeptics fought it. The integration of Gillette, which P&G considers highly successful as corporate mergers go, involved various stumbles along the way: the need to revise certain communications from the top that were misunderstood, the discovery of surprising differences in business approach that had been hidden by the emphasis on similar values, and departures of executives whom P&G might have liked to keep. Attempts to bend over backward to welcome Gillette's talent made some P&G people feel left out, something that also happened when Shinhan absorbed Chohung Bank in Korea. You cannot please all of the people all of the time.

The workplace is not a workers' paradise either. Daily work life can be a stressful grind even when working toward lofty goals. Cemex includes work-life balance in its values, but those who succeed at Cemex work extreme hours, and executive women are scarce. Even if Christine Newman, the British accountant from chapter 5, chose to leave her young family to commute a hundred miles to Rugby, England, during the week, her work situation can still be considered stressful and family unfriendly. Sometimes the goals are not even that lofty. Cemex, for example, while praised for Patrimonio Hoy and other economic development contributions, has also been accused of using its market power to charge higher prices in its home market, which can raise costs for customers.

Empowering, network-oriented companies that permit self-organizing and volunteering for projects can also be confusing. Tasks that are agreed to but not urgent can fall through the cracks without a strong champion or high-level sponsor constantly pushing them. People who are less skillful at making themselves known to others or developing reputations that precede them can get lost. A matrix organization can push decision making lower for daily actions but also seem like a complicated bureaucracy in terms of approval points and resource allocations. An IBM internal survey, for example, shows that a high proportion of employees have favorable views of their immediate managers but a less favorable view of the company as a whole. I was privy to internal disputes that I was asked not to repeat. They did not take the form of overt power struggles, but people sometimes disagreed vociferously or dug in their heels, withholding something from colleagues even if they had agreed on the general goal.

Vanguard companies do not offer every form of voice to employees—some are unionized, some are not, for example, depending on countries' labor laws. But they offer more voice than is the norm for traditional companies. IBM's ValuesJam and Innovation Jam are prime examples. For people from places with strong democratic traditions or interest in trade unions, this can seem trivial—a limited form of voice that does not change worker subordination. For people from countries where freedom of expression is discouraged, however, being able to voice ideas within a corporate context can be a really big deal.

Diversity is an area in which company policies are often well ahead of the capacity for individuals to change their behavior. MTN's international buffet reflecting national cuisines and religiously oriented food preferences across Africa and the Middle East is an easy step; changing the racist attitudes of the few white Afrikaners with whom I spoke at the buffet table is much harder and more complicated. And effectiveness in some countries does not guarantee effectiveness in all. MTN is tight with the government in South Africa and successful in

West Africa, but it became embroiled in a major controversy with the Nigerian government in East Africa.

Practices that solve one problem sometimes lead to others. IBM's dynamic workplace of mobility and remote work options is a boon for anyone who wants to control her (or his) own work hours and work at home. But it can also make people feel lonely or isolated, thus undermining work relationships. In addition, some changes happen faster than others. For example, shifting work to horizontal networks before determining exactly how performance appraisals, which are still vertically oriented, are handled—and by whom—can cause confusion and anxiety.

Vanguard companies are not so far ahead that they have avoided every problem. IBM seized on "green computing" relatively recently, and that is now part of the company's Smarter Planet sustainability strategy. Yet many decades ago, every company in the IT industry used what later turned out to be toxic chemicals in chip production. IBM was among those sued by victims—but the company also acted quickly to make changes once the problems were known.

"Best" is said to be the enemy of "good." Perhaps we should get rid of the phrase *best practice* because it implies a standard of perfection impossible to attain. It might be more accurate to say that vanguard companies have "better practices," subject to further improvement.

It does not undermine the case for the vanguard company model to raise concerns about imperfections, because they reflect continuing dilemmas that plague all organizations. It takes time for changes in human behavior to catch up to corporate policy changes. Add to that the trade-offs between empowerment (many voices deliberating about decisions) and efficiency (a small group forging ahead). Or consider other dilemmas: Making values and principles into sacred texts does not prevent religious wars over interpretation. Work that is intrinsically satisfying and fulfilling can also be more demanding, making the perfect balance between work life and family life difficult to attain on a daily basis.

Progressive companies might not be perfect, but they head in the right direction. They seek high standards and evolve with new issues. And they enjoy positive Rubik's Cube moments when their resources align to improve the world.

EXCEPTIONS?

Even if exemplary, critics say, vanguard companies are mere exceptions to the rules that guide common business practice. So what, they say, if there are a few good companies. Every era and every country has a few exceptions. They are not leading a parade; they are walking alone. Vanguard companies are at the head of a parade with no one behind them. For every IBM, this cynical argument runs, there could be thousands of Enrons waiting in the wings. Thus, the vanguard does nothing to change the image or the reality of business.

But the trend line does not support the argument that these companies will always be exceptions, even if some of their practices are still exceptional. In every major country, there is growth in the number of companies choosing to join associations espousing progressive practices; joining does not mean anything, except that this kind of club is more likely to exert positive influence by making companies conscious of high standards and encouraging peer comparisons. When Business for Social Responsibility started in the United States in 1992, its membership consisted of relatively small companies slightly out of the mainstream and considered quirky; today we might see Ben & Jerry's or Tom's of Maine as ahead of their time, but they were certainly not giants—although Ben & Jerry's is now a subsidiary of giant Unilever. There has been dramatic change since the early 1990s. The companies highlighted in this book are decidedly mainstream heavyweights.

Some critics go further in making the "exception" argument. They imply that vanguard companies not only fail to influence their peers, but they also leave their suppliers and partners to do their dirty work. Some companies might maintain their own image of high standards, the argument runs, by, in effect, outsourcing problematic practices such as worker exploitation or pollution to other companies, especially anonymous ones farthest away in the supply chain. This is conspiracy theory to the max: Far from raising standards, this criticism says, large companies actually exploit lower standards in poor countries or among captive low-cost suppliers while appearing to be virtuous themselves.

But that is simply not the general practice in vanguard companies. To the contrary, the values and principles of vanguard companies encourage end-to-end responsibility, as I showed in chapter 3. Vanguard companies such as Banco Real take it upon themselves to screen suppliers and customers to make sure they meet high standards. IBM and Cemex offer training for suppliers or distributors that raise their practices to high international standards.

Too many eyes are watching vanguard companies for them to get away with a failure to take responsibility across the business value chain, from their suppliers' suppliers to their customers' customers. Transparency will reign. As successful companies among the most significant in their industries and countries, they are in the spotlight, and because they espouse high standards, they can seem like soft targets that will give in easily. Nokia's head of global corporate responsibility in Finland was told by the head of an NGO with which Nokia partnered on projects in Africa that if his advocacy group went after the telecommunications industry, Nokia would be the first target, regardless of the Nokia-NGO close working relationship, because Nokia is the industry leader. Despite national pride in Publicis as a successful French company and respect for Maurice Lévy as an activist against anti-Semitism in France, Publicis expects to be picketed during anti-capitalism demonstrations.

Vanguard companies keep score themselves. They measure their own compliance with standards. Banco Real asks NGOs such as Ethos Institute to conduct internal audits against benchmarks for social and environmental responsibility. IBM, starting in 2002, and growing numbers of other companies, issue comprehensive corporate responsibility reports. European vanguard companies regularly report on a triple bottom line. And as activists request more information, companies learn to provide it. As governments see what some companies are willing to do, they can require it of all companies. Vanguard practices are likely to become the standard to which all companies are held.

Of course, critics and activists pushed companies to undertake these forms of reporting; they did not arise spontaneously out of the goodness of the hearts of the accounting departments. John Elkington, founder of the U.K.-based consultancy SustainAbility, coined the term *triple bottom line* (TBL), a reference to financial, environmental, and social concerns, in the early 1990s, and gradually TBL reporting took hold, propelled by crises, mostly of an environmental nature.

Two years after the row over the disposal of Shell's Brent Spar platform, Elkington and his organization worked with Shell to include a "people, planet, profits" framework in its first corporate social responsibility reports in 1997 and 1998.

The concern is also raised that values and principles and the practices expressing them are luxuries of good times, for those companies large enough to have the extra resources to afford them. The minute times get tough, skeptics say, principles will be abandoned. Or perhaps some vanguard contributions are loss leaders to entice the public to support a company, especially when entering new markets, but without true commitment to act on those values when exiting a community or a line of business. That line of argument is based on the assumption that cutthroat greed is the default position for business. It therefore misses the mark for most vanguard companies. Values are part of the offer they make to employees, and employee motivation depends on living up to values that make people feel good about themselves and their standing in their communities.

How one views the role of vanguard companies depends on one's theory of change. Exceptions can prove the rule and thus not change anything, or they can be instances of "positive deviance" that are a harbinger of trends to follow. I find that the latter is more likely. A departure from tradition points the way to how things can be done differently. Communication of better practices enhances the reputation of those who work that way, which encourages others to adopt these practices too.

Vanguard companies take it upon themselves to lead and educate their peers. They are at the front of the pack and onstage for industry associations, speaking about their practices and opening their doors to other companies that wish to visit. Fabio Barbosa, Banco Real's CEO, became president of the Brazilian banking federation in 2007, after having already enlisted other banks in Brazil behind environmental initiatives. Leaders of progressive companies say that they gain benefits from giving away knowledge of their practices. As practices are copied, they are legitimated, which makes it easier for vanguard companies to take progressive or long-term actions with a clearer justification, unlike the situation when IBM's Palmisano had to explain the Values-Jam to a board member who thought it was "socialism" because he had no frame of reference for it. Any extra costs borne by vanguard companies for meeting higher standards merely become the cost of doing business if others adopt the same practices. And if a vanguard company wants to remain distinctive, then imitation becomes an impetus for innovation, which keeps a vanguard company marching ahead.

A WRONG TURN?

A third set of concerns focuses on the system. International trade and information technology, the twin forces of the global information age, have raised prosperity in general but left wide disparities in income and standard of living as well as significant environmental problems and a financial system run amok, without adequate controls. A little local good, this argument runs, does not do much to change the state of global problems, and in fact, turning to private sector companies might undermine efforts to improve conditions, these critics say.

Two of the criticisms can seem contradictory. One is that even the best companies are too powerful, distorting the public agenda. The other is that they are not powerful enough—that all their efforts do not make much difference on significant problems. To some detractors, these are not contradictory at all. By influencing public policy in their favor, they say, big companies deflect resources and thus undermine action to address significant social and environmental issues. This problem is magnified, the argument runs, for foreign companies with no loyalty to the country or community, and so they take the money and run.

The trend in practically every part of the world, until the global downturn, which required government bailouts on nearly every continent, was toward smaller government. That generally meant privatization of public services or state-owned enterprises. But does the increased action of companies in the social sector represent privatization of the public agenda as well? When large companies or other private sector actors, such as foundations, contribute to communities and steer local action toward the projects they wish to fund, this constitutes a de facto setting of the public agenda, as nonprofits drop other things to chase the money. When corporate diplomats get seats at the policy table because of their industry expertise or global experience, they gain a bigger voice than representatives of the public.

There are legitimate concerns about ceding the public agenda to companies, however enlightened or progressive the company is, be-cause companies have, by law, a duty to their shareholders as primary stakeholders, not to the public at large as the first premise, as long as they obey the law. There are even bigger concerns about ceding public priorities to companies of other kinds whose cozy relationship with top officials can lead to actions that hurt the long-term public interest (e.g., many view that the U.S. Bush administration ties to Big Oil re-sulted in the unpopular war in Iraq—a modern version of the military-industrial complex said to dominate America after World War II). And even if schooled to incorporate the country's or community's interests, corporate diplomats want to get their standard adopted as *the* standard and advocate for superiority of their own ideas, or they would be dis-loyal to their company.

According to this line of criticism, companies also might distort the democratic process or undermine the public sector if they employ lobbyists to push their agendas and drown out those without compa-rable resources. Worse to some is lobbying for lower taxes or failing to pay taxes, which support public services that they consume. Former U.S. Treasury secretary Lawrence Summers, who is President Obama's chief economist, declared to an audience of Harvard Business School faculty that the best thing companies can do for education, for example, is to fire their lobbyists, pay high taxes, and let governments run the schools, since government is more likely to seek just outcomes with the greatest social benefit (reflecting his faith in government despite years of decline in U.S. inner-city schools). And to ensure that their tax money fills the public coffers, this reasoning goes, companies should keep their eyes focused on the business to maximize financial returns and employment, both of which generate tax revenues.

But this critique misses several big points on both sides of the equation. First are the business benefits vanguard companies derive from their engagement with societal problems. Second are the public benefits added from private sector contributions, often mediated and guided by NGOs and community-based nonprofits. In short, both parties—businesses and the public—can get a great deal from the en-gagement. Consider IBM's Reinventing Education projects described in chapter 4, which brought innovations to schools that they could never develop themselves.

The private sector definitely adds an important element to social or environmental progress when government providers are inefficient or ineffective, not to mention corrupt, or may otherwise be constrained in their capacity to innovate. To avoid unbridled corporate bullying, civil society, the realm of nonprofit organizations and voluntary citizen action, is often the sector that channels corporate contributions, not direct action by the companies themselves. P&G and IBM work through nonprofit or NGO intermediaries, or they create separate nonprofits with arm's-length boards (e.g., Children's Drinking Water or World Community Grid), to engage the public without commercial interests getting in the way.

The vanguard model emphasizes societal purpose embedded in the business enterprise, but that by itself does not represent a business takeover of the public agenda. Instead, employees (who are also members of the public) are encouraged to seek opportunities to create new benefits for the public through innovation, as I described in chapter 4.

Moreover, in the vanguard model, priorities are increasingly set democratically. Self-organizing networks from the bottom and middle of organizations can get items put on the agenda that are concerns of a broad public rather than a few elite. Digital technology enables many people to weigh in on company priorities, including their societal activities. The IBM ValuesJam and Innovation Jam are examples, as is the American Express Members Project on which Digitas worked, in which customers (cardholders) voted on where American Express money should go and awarded $2 million to P&G's Children's Safe Drinking Water initiative. Vanguard companies are also likely to have internal checks on how much power they exercise in the public arena and of what sort, because their business models center on listening to customers and employees. Vanguard companies take their cues from the marketplace and the public they serve. They do not want to get too far ahead nor tangled in issues that would cause their products and services or their jobs to be viewed in an unfavorable light. If their voice on the public agenda appears too self-interested, they jeopardize other stakeholder relationships.

A related set of doubts about vanguard companies concerns their stated aspirations. To some critics, values and principles, with the occasional charitable gift or community program, are a cosmetic add-on masking other motives. Cynics contend that CEOs use shareholders' money to make contributions to their favorite causes, then get honored at charity benefits as though they have done something wonderful on their own. There is also suspicion that community projects and philanthropy are an acceptable way to "buy" public and government support as an alternative to bribing corrupt officials. The fact that businesses can get strategic benefits from their corporate citizenship activities is considered to be negative evidence of self-interest rather than a positive feature that makes such activities sustainable. Indeed, some economists define "corporate social responsibility" as actions companies undertake with no profit. But that would rule out a large number of possibilities for contributions to well-being that come from the core of the business, such as Omron's innovations for industrial safety or women's heart health. If the impact is positive and the benefits to people clear, then the fact that businesses get something out of it is not only acceptable but desirable, because then the company is likely to do more of it.

The other side of the excessive-power-concern coin is one about insufficient impact. Even with the best will in the world, this argument runs, companies are not powerful enough to make a dent in major societal problems. The hope that they will, skeptics say, is false hope.

Certainly if we look at the relative size and resources of governments in most countries compared with the size and resources of private companies, it is clear that governments in major countries dwarf what the top companies might spend. In 2006, total U.S. corporate philanthropic contributions, including foundation grants, amounted to $13.8 billion, which is about the size of the gross national product of Bolivia. IBM's biggest education initiatives reach only a small fraction of the world's children, despite the impressive eight million children its programs serve. Even the Bill and Melinda Gates Foundation, now the world's largest private philanthropy, which made $17.3 billion in grants between its founding in 2000 and 2008, is a dwarf compared with governments, although its $2 billion of contributions in 2007 was about the gross domestic product of Suriname and was larger than the GDP of thirty poor countries. Adding individual contributions, total philanthropic giving in the United States managed to reach $295 billion in 2006, still just a fraction of the of the U.S. government bailout package during the 2008 global financial crisis, which was $700 billion.

But this misses the point in terms of what progressive companies can actually contribute. They are catalysts of innovation and change. Their progressive workplace practices can become the basis for new government programs to take those practices to more companies and more places. Corporate innovations in technology or product standards can stimulate new action by government, including significant investment to spread the innovations widely. The expertise that companies bring from deep knowledge of their fields and comparative experiences across countries can be a way to transmit high standards. Vanguard companies can often be faster and more responsive than government bureaucracies when the need arises, and their positions are often apolitical, reflecting a pragmatic sense of what will get the job done.

The ultimate concern of detractors is that while progressive companies might make worthwhile social contributions far from their home base, they are not doing enough about the problems in their own backyards. If a U.S. company, for example, brings great societal benefits to an emerging market country while cutting jobs in the United States, are they helping others at the expense of workers at home? And where is the progressive CEO voice on excessive CEO compensation, or the company pushing for an end to unpopular, costly wars? Of course, it is difficult for a business with multiple stakeholders and customers covering a range of political views to push a controversial agenda. This means that vanguard companies are unlikely to champion unpopular causes, and therefore, even when they act on certain values inside their own organizations, they are unlikely to use their megaphones to try to get laws changed—for example, about gay rights in Muslim countries even while championing those rights in North America and Europe, or about same-sex marriages in the United States even while offering partner benefits to same-sex couples. Companies whose own practices are decidedly green did not try to convince the Bush administration to sign the Kyoto Accord on reduction of greenhouse gases, although approximately one hundred medium-size U.S. businesses took out an advertisement in the *New York Times* to voice support for the protocol. However, U.S. Fortune 100 companies, even those not in carbon-heavy industries, did not express vociferous opposition, prompting Greenpeace to write to the companies.

Yes, but within the constraints of their obligations to multiple stakeholders, vanguard companies still make courageous efforts to change norms in society. There are examples throughout this book. IBM filed a brief supporting the University of Michigan's affirmative action program when it was under legal attack, because of the company's diversity values, joining a handful of other progressive companies. ABN AMRO stimulated the World Bank to convene ten large global banks to create the Equator Principles, an environmentally sensitive code for project finance. Omron's representative to the Keidendran, Japan's major industry association, is working on the issue of wage disparities between top and bottom in Japanese companies. Banco Real has walked away from customers that could not meet its environmental standards, and it has pushed suppliers as well as customers to make their practices more socially and environmentally responsible. Although studies show that voluntary codes of conduct rarely change behavior as much as official regulations, the very fact that some companies work to create codes raises the ante, and such voluntary codes have the potential to shape eventual laws.

Some problems are systemic in nature, and innovations or courageous actions by companies will not necessarily have much impact unless many other players are engaged and act together. Partnerships and coalitions are a central part of the vanguard model. Employees are encouraged to put actions in wider societal context and to work collaboratively across boundaries. Vanguard companies partner with governments, global institutions, NGOs, and community-based organizations, and they are thus able to magnify their impact.

Just as the public sector is said to fill gaps owing to market failures—that is, to serve those who would not be served by market mechanisms—the private sector can help fill gaps in public services, especially when government is inefficient, weak, or corrupt. Vanguard companies can plug a hole in the system and work with others to produce positive societal outcomes on many fronts, as the examples in this book illustrate, whether through workstations to educate disadvantaged young children, beverages that reduce disease, biosensors that improve food safety, or even the occasional ride to the rescue after a disaster like the tsunami.

shedding light

DESPITE DOUBTS AND DETRACTORS, imperfections and limitations, I conclude that vanguard companies and the humanistic values-based model they exhibit offer hope for solving problems in a troubled world, especially if aligned behind an agenda that reflects the areas that people in general care about. The success that they exhibit as businesses as well as social institutions makes it more likely that others will follow their lead in adopting more progressive practices. Vanguard companies survive and flourish under difficult conditions by building profitable, sustainable enterprises that also keep their eye on their role in society. That's the big prize for steering a course through all the potential pitfalls I have just cataloged. Along the way, vanguard companies also win the smaller prizes, such as the national and international awards given to Cemex, IBM, P&G, Omron, Diageo, and others in this book.

Because vanguard companies stand for universal high standards while striving to preserve the heritage of local cultures, and because they espouse openness, inclusion, and empowerment, there is even an intriguing, if grand, possibility. If the vanguard model spreads, and a critical mass of progressive companies grows, perhaps they could serve as a buffer against oppressive or corrupt governments and oppressive or restrictive religions and a force for peace by linking activities across borders.

"It is better to light one candle than to curse the darkness," an old Chinese proverb asserts. Perhaps wisdom from the Chinese will not make North American and European readers feel better about the changes in their economies (and because Chinese state-linked industries are not at all vanguardlike in their actions, it might not make sense to quote a Chinese proverb!). But the saying makes sense nonetheless. Although it could be foolish to pin hopes for the future of the world on a few projects by multinational companies, why not appreciate them for their candle lighting? That is the strategy used by the

United Nations in enlisting companies to commit to contributing to the Millennium Development Goals of ending world misery and by the World Economic Forum in calling for even more active corporate social entrepreneurship, as its founder Klaus Schwab advocates.

The vanguard model has been slowly taking shape over the course of the past two decades. Until the twenty-first century, it represented an ideal type rather than a living organizational approach adopted by major companies in major countries. Now it reflects a movement that could gain momentum. The message of this chapter is that the leaders of vanguard companies need to step up to the challenge of making sure they not only operate to high standards themselves but that they also finish the job by bringing many others along with them.

chapter ten

the triumph of the transformational enterprise: leadership for the future

Consider how much can be wrapped into a single memorable moment. When Sam Palmisano's avatar entered a virtual version of the Forbidden City while he stood in Beijing celebrating IBM's partnership with the Chinese Ministry of Culture, the real Palmisano also announced IBM's global innovation priorities, which were informed by the input of 150,000 people on a Web chat.

Leaders deal in symbols as well as strategies, and the symbols reinforce commitment to the strategies. That day's events reflected IBM's transformation and goals for the future, highlighting its core value of "innovation that makes a difference, for our company and the world." Palmisano's trip started with MBFA—management by flying around—which put the top leader physically on the scene in a highly strategic location, halfway around the world from corporate headquarters. The priorities he announced would guide the next wave of business offerings, from green computing to social networking tools. One major priority, virtual worlds, was demonstrated for the world to see via a corporate citizenship project in partnership with government, an example of societal contributions coming ahead of commercialization. Those strategic priorities had been set by an open process of dialogue throughout the company, heavily influenced by the bottom-up work of self-organizing networks. Behind the scenes, shaping the avatar idea, were other leaders who argued and door-knocked, in the new way of working, until a consensus emerged.

The impact on IBMers who witnessed this event, mostly via information on the Web, was profound. They felt ownership of the priorities and values; their voices had been heard. They were reminded of the short leap from today's job to changing the world. They saw that they were part of something grand, that the vision and clout of their company could tackle big problems and big challenges, some of them acute like the tsunami, some of them new opportunities. Perhaps they too could volunteer to apply company resources from anywhere in the world to make a difference in their home community or beyond. It is worth putting up with trivial annoyances of daily life in a big company and the constant change and uncertainty about the future, some told me they thought, because the collective impact could be so powerful and meaningful.

A noble purpose can energize mundane work. That's one of many secrets of vanguard success.

leadership for the vanguard

THE ART OF LEADERSHIP is to inspire action and guide people in productive directions. Sometimes it is to personify and symbolize the will of those people. The global information age increases the challenge of both sides of leadership. Finding symbols that create meaning becomes more difficult and more important when dealing with multiple stakeholders in multiple countries. Leaders' ability to send messages, that is, communicate their themes or visions, must be augmented by their ability to receive and interpret messages from a diverse set of others. Leaders can no longer take for granted that people will think the same way or share a perspective; they must be deeply attuned to multiple contexts. Under these circumstances, the vanguard model of values-based humanistic leadership, as practiced by IBM and other companies, becomes a necessity, not just a choice.

THE VANGUARD ORGANIZATIONAL MODEL

The dictionary definition of *vanguard* is "the forefront of an action, an example of change to come." Leaders of vanguard companies must be transformational leaders, turning their companies into forces for changing business and the world. Sometimes there are trade-offs—you can't satisfy all of the people all of the time, the saying goes. But for the most part, the vanguard model is on the rise because it is good for business, it is good for communities, employees want it, and the public approves of it.

As we have seen in numerous cases throughout this book, values-and-principles-based leadership makes strategic business sense. The company gets business opportunities, market position, innovation, employee motivation, company solidarity, and the pick of the best business partners and acquisition targets. The company also gets social legitimacy—reputation, influence, connections to information networks, and a seat at the policy table.

The vanguard model is transformational; it represents an approach to doing business geared to change in a world of uncertainty, complexity, diversity, and transparency. Purpose, values, and principles provide a guidance mechanism that can be internalized by individuals, thus permitting autonomous decisions and a basis for fast mobilization. The anchoring effect of values helps balance the alienating effect of mobility. Providing clear principles on common platforms means that people can move across projects and go to work immediately with the same understanding of how to operate. The vanguard's emphasis on connections across an extended family of partners helps them strategically. A stress on end-to-end responsibilities triggers awareness of opportunities for new solutions. Open innovation widens the search for new ideas. Internal integration and a lower "center of gravity" shorten the loop between need and solution, between innovation and application. Vanguard companies are able to change internally with fewer stumbles and less resistance because they empower people to make change themselves. They favor integrators who can forge relationships, catalyze networks, and work well with people who come from different backgrounds or from newly acquired companies.

The organizational paradigm can be summarized in terms of five *F*s for the future. Their organizations are *focused*, with clear statements of values and principles to guide strategic choices and common platforms and tools to guide operations. They are *flexible*, organizing work into a series of projects, mentoring and training people to work collaboratively in projects that cut across structural boundaries, encouraging employees to self-organize, and giving people control over work hours and places. They are *fast*, shortening the loop between society and solutions, developers and users, to speed innovation into implementation and mobilizing quickly in response to crisis or change. They stress being organizationally *friendly*—open, affable, responsive, welcoming. Finally, they include an element of *fun*, not in the frivolous sense, but to enhance motivation, build relationships that increase team spirit, and offer the deeper satisfaction of connecting tasks to the excitement of acting toward a meaningful societal purpose.

Viewed this way, as condensed in the five *F*s, the vanguard model is generalizable well beyond the giants and emerging giants I examined in America and throughout the world. Leaders at vanguard companies encourage managers at every level to apply principles like these to their divisions and departments. They want to transmit similar leadership standards to suppliers and distributors, both at home and abroad. In Brazil, Banco Real invited me to speak to a set of its business customers from major industries such as regional jet manufacturer Embraer to smaller local businesses. Back home in Boston from one of my international swings, I found vanguard values and principles resonating with a wide swath of entrepreneurs and leaders of small and midsized businesses. In fact, one of my candidates for Vanguard Leader of the Future is a Boston real estate developer of residential properties with just sixty employees now but with big growth ambitions and a firm commitment to end-to-end responsibility, community service, innovation in green building technology, and a happy workplace.

With aspiring vanguard members in mind, I prepared a starter kit, a list of "Ten Things Anyone Can Do to Be in the Vanguard."

1. Make values and vision a part of the daily conversation, until it is automatic to include mentions in every message.
2. See your work in the context of the large system surrounding it. Consider the whole chain from suppliers' suppliers to your customers' customers, and ensure that all meet high standards.
3. Stress innovation; keep your eye on societal problems, imagine unique new solutions, and grab ideas from anywhere to implement.
4. Think in terms of networks; be a connector who opens new possibilities by forging partnerships.
5. Create routines, consistent processes that can be adopted easily by anyone and free their time for more creative tasks.

6. Stress projects over fixed positions, and include people on teams or councils that cut across the organization.
7. Treat employees as though they are volunteers; encourage them to self-organize, and give them some control over when and where they work, as long as they get the job done for their team.
8. Cultivate empathy and understand the power of emotional bonds when other people feel respected as individuals.
9. Invest in the human community; help people have fun together.
10. Allocate time for external service, to causes that your employees and customers care about, and connect that back to your values.

Like all deceptively simple principles, these are easy to articulate, harder to do. They require leaders willing to work through circles of influence rather than chains of command. They require enlightened leaders strong intellectually, physically, and emotionally.

LEADERSHIP COMPETENCIES

Vanguard companies are hungry for leaders. Not only do they want to attract and retain the best people, they also want more people to exercise leadership at more levels and to do it earlier in their careers.

For every CEO mentioned in this book, hundreds of other leaders appear by name or by implication. At Procter & Gamble, for example, I listened to the chairman and CEO A. G. Lafley and the vice chairman and COO Robert McDonald in Cincinnati, Ohio, and watched them in meetings in Boston and New Hampshire. But the proof of the leadership principles they espouse lies elsewhere, in the people we spoke to who are doing the work in the United States, Brazil, India, Britain, and the Near East. Some of them appear in action in the stories of this book. We saw Juliana Azevedo in concert with her colleagues in São Paolo, innovating in outreach to low-income families (and handing out candy), and we lunched with Tarek Farahat, who rose from a category head in the Latin American region to become Brazil's country general manager. We saw how Mohammed Samir in Cairo, the manager in charge of distribution in a small region, turned global principles into fast action to help families after the 2006 war in Lebanon. We viewed the passion of American leaders such as Charlotte

Otto, a senior executive, and Greg Allgood, a midlevel professional, for products that would help children, as they championed Children's Safe Drinking Water. Lafley and McDonald, who practice MBFA, were their guides and coaches.

Tasks are specific, but leadership competencies are generic. Whatever their technical expertise, the best characteristics of leaders at all levels in vanguard companies can be distilled into the ultimate job description for the future. It could run something like this:

• *Intellect: Systems thinking.* Can see things in context, can understand complex interactions among many variables. Has tolerance for ambiguity. Is skilled in pattern recognition, seeing similarities and differences, framing and conceptualizing. Has intellectual curiosity; the desire to learn and understand. Has a cosmopolitan outlook and is able to put local actions or places in a broader perspective.

• *Action: Initiative taker.* Has a bias for action and a desire for solutions. Seeks problems to solve. Sets big goals, then breaks them down into practical tactics. Abhors passivity; wants to get moving, to find steps to take in any circumstance. Can envision a sequence of actions and their consequences. Understands what drives or impedes change, can strategize around barriers. Is energetic and has physical stamina. Is results oriented.

• *Relationships: Persuasion and diplomacy.* Can communicate, listen, and inspire. Likes to connect, to collaborate, and to find solutions that are good for many people. Can enlist people in projects and motivate volunteers. Is partnership oriented, seeing opportunities to leverage resources by tapping networks. Work as an effective, enthusiastic mentor.

• *Emotion: self-awareness and empathy.* Has strong self-knowledge, awareness of limitations as well as strengths. Can put self in others' shoes and analyze their perspective, respect their individuality. Can hold own ego in check while making gestures that address others' emotional reactions. Is willing to invest in activities that build emotional bonds.

• *Spirituality: Values driven.* Is a good steward of resources for all stakeholders, including investors, while remaining attuned to long-term sustainability. Is attuned to a higher purpose beyond only making money. Cares about values and ethics, about the impact of the business on society. Believes in the transformative power of service.

Effective leaders have always possessed some measure of these qualities. But now they must exercise leadership with so many more variables in mind, with resources they cannot fully control, with attention to the hearts and minds of other people who might come with different assumptions or interests, and with the utmost of diplomacy. Leaders must invest time and effort in building enduring institutions infused with values and meaning beyond particular tasks and transactions. The vanguard model not only demands more leaders; it demands more *of* them. They function as integrators, identity managers, and institution builders who can master complexity, diversity, and uncertainty.

populating the vanguard

WHAT WILL IT TAKE to produce transformational leaders to start, change, or guide values-led flexible enterprises? Moving more companies into vanguard mode, whether they are small suppliers in developing countries or large enterprises in North America, requires new kinds of education, incentives, and career paths.

The education system, at every level, is the biggest factor in determining whether the vanguard model will take hold. It is not simply a matter of teaching basic skills such as literacy and numeracy, although those are critical; speaking English, the increasingly universal language of science and commerce, tends to divide those with opportunities in the global economy from those at the bottom of the wage scale. Reducing school dropout rates is critical, and that covers American inner cities and rural areas as well as the masses in India or Africa. Ensuring sufficient human talent to lead the vanguard is also a matter of adding an understanding of civic virtues to the elite with advanced technical skills. Colleges and universities throughout the world, as part of every degree program, including the most technical, could prepare future leaders to care about their own society and yet gain a global perspective via exchange programs. If such programs become a valued credential signifying the best talent, then they will take hold. Business schools could increase their focus on leadership across functions such as marketing or finance, emphasize collaborative projects benefiting communities, and encourage open discussion about values. Executives could go back to school to learn about advanced leadership for highly complex global problems that require delicate public-private partnerships and nongovernmental organization (NGO) intermediaries, such as poverty alleviation, public health, or the environment.

In short, leadership sensibilities need to be added to technical training, from preschool to postgraduate programs. Vanguard companies are already demanding both, but education systems lag in their ability to meet these standards.

To encourage companies to change, new incentives are in order. Competitions and prizes already publicize some of the virtuous, but there is more work to be done here. The companies featured in this book have already won awards, and, of course, virtue is its own reward, when it shows up in strong financial performance, as is also the case for the companies I studied. But the media tend to focus on lapses more than on successes, unless they are big visible projects. Moreover, even with the rise of "triple bottom line" reporting on financial, social, and environmental impact, public reporting and auditing systems barely scratch the surface of the activities of vanguard companies, and the majority of businesses do none of this. Lists of the best companies on various values-connected dimensions could be expanded, and indices such as the *Financial Times*'s ranking of good companies could be expanded to reach parts of the world where standards remain to be raised. Just as vanguard companies take the lead in public education reform, their presence as innovators could stimulate public investments to take promising innovations to more of the places and populations that need them.

Career paths and leadership development programs are another arena that could support the development of leaders to populate the vanguard. Programs that enable people in businesses to experience life in the public or nonprofit sector and transition across sectors enlarge horizons while building skills. Temporary placements in the organizations of business partners would serve some of the same purpose. Some companies offer sabbaticals that permit their employees to work for a period of time for the cause of their choice. Performing public or community service on company teams is another opportunity.

Building community service into every major corporate activity—orientation for new hires, training programs, executive conferences—could not only signal values but change perspectives. To do this requires a receptive public environment.

Favorable external conditions also help vanguard companies to flourish, and they often choose locations for their activities based on them. Three items should be high on the public agenda in all nations, not just because of the preferences of global companies but also because it is hard for societal improvement and world betterment to proceed without them.

• *Twenty-first-century infrastructure*. A starting point for a "smarter planet" is a ubiquitous digital infrastructure. Broadband should be the rural electrification counterpart for the twenty-first century, permitting communication to reach everyone, everywhere. So much of the work of vanguard companies depends on mobility and fast communication connections, including tapping common platforms; disseminating information rapidly across borders; and the ability of working parents, primarily women, to remain working by being able to do so from home. As a corollary, it is time to reinvent the workplace for the twenty-first century. Industrial-age assumptions about work taking place in fixed locations at fixed times are increasingly obsolete, and government policies and infrastructure investments should recognize and support change.

• *A robust civil society*. A large number of nonprofit organizations, voluntary associations, foundations, and NGOs in developed countries, especially the United States and nations with Anglo-Saxon heritages, fill market gaps and government gaps while also broadening the meaning of democracy beyond voting to active citizen participation. In theory, these organizations are focused only on social good, and they are connected with community interests and knowledgeable about social needs in ways that companies are not. Vanguard companies depend on such organizations to serve as partners and intermediaries; this includes not only community service projects but also innovation-critical scientific or technical research with universities (as is the case with Omron and IBM). Furthermore, organized service opportunities, whether community events or individual actions (e.g., to recycle and reduce carbon footprints, tutor children in public schools, visit AIDS orphans in hospitals, plant trees in drought-ridden areas), make it easy for companies to get employees involved.

• *Open government and global governance forums.* The best businesses depend on an underlying framework set by government that helps establish the rules of the market, providing a basis for trust. If the rules are clear and fair, it is easier for companies to abide by them or at least for progressive companies to feel that they are not bearing disproportionate costs. If standards are clear and performance is rewarded, then companies can invest with greater certainty, thereby making deeper commitments to those places, which ultimately benefit the wider public. To this agenda should be added well-functioning global governance systems to address cross-border issues. Vanguard companies already want to operate by common standards in diverse countries. And global interdependence is obvious in so many issues. Diseases are carried by travelers from one place to another, making it possible for pandemics to start within hours. Winds blow and rivers flow across borders. And as the global financial crisis that started in the fall of 2008 made clear, the financial system is interconnected in significant ways. Global institutions do not have to undermine national sovereignty, but they are essential forums for coordination and establishing common standards. This is not to say that there should be one overarching global organization. Sometimes it is better to have multiple groups for multiple purposes. Small groups of nations, such as the G8, should become larger groups, such as the G20 nations that met in November 2008 to discuss actions to solve the financial crisis.

marching toward the future

THE VANGUARD MODEL turns organizations upside down and inside out. They become less hierarchical and more driven by flexible networks. They become more open and transparent to the outside world while bringing society and its needs inside. As an ideal and an aspiration, the vanguard model attempts to reconcile contradictions: to be big but human, efficient but innovative, respecting individual differences while seeking common ground, global in thinking but concerned about local communities.

The march led by the vanguard is still in an early stage, taking shape in the companies I studied primarily in the first years of the twenty-first century. Thus, many questions remain about what the next years will bring and how vanguard companies and others that aspire to be like them will handle new challenges. For example, can a social contract be forged with the public across diverse countries with conflicting societal needs and requirements? As the ecosystem for business reaches its theoretical limits, encompassing potentially the entire world, how can leaders maintain the national/local bonds that provide legitimation? Will the bases for legitimacy shift, as global bodies legitimate if not authorize companies, and will something resembling a global culture be created even while national sovereignty remains strong? Will universal values truly guide the behavior of the best companies? And will that create convergence among countries or merely provoke particularistic backlash?

One possibility is that countries will snap shut, favor their own, and seek power, as Russia appears to be doing as I write this, or that the mercantilist enterprises of China, for example, could swamp all attempts by Western nations and their companies to address environmental issues or improve lives for the poor in Africa.

Anything is possible in a world where surprises are the new normal. But there is another scenario already in motion because of the actions of vanguard companies that involves more positive change. National contexts will continue to range from open and tolerant to closed and restrictive, but as companies adapt to varieties of governments and cultures, they will also exert an influence by virtue of the growth of de facto international standards. As leaders are developed and mobilized by companies that operate under more universalistic values, those leaders themselves have enormous potential to improve the state of the world.

Ideas will inevitably come from many countries, and that will require adjustment by those who consider dominance an entitlement. Americans, for example, once a primary source of most management wisdom, will learn banking practices from India (e.g., ICICI's mobile banking) or Brazil (Banco Real's environment-friendly lending), factory management from Mexico (Cemex's cement plant productivity), or merger management from Korea (Shinhan's emotional integration process). American and European companies will increasingly cede top positions within countries and for global functions not to expatriates on international assignments but to local managers with regional education and experience, and they will then include those culturally different managers in global decision-making circles. Mobility will become the norm. Within organizations, teams at all levels will increasingly become more diverse, including the exclusive clubs of once-homogeneous top management. The development of leaders with a global mind-set will inevitably become a priority. Strategic choices, process preferences, and public engagement will continue to be shaped by the national or industry context, but transformational leaders will increasingly carry practices from one place to another. And vanguard companies will continue to fly to the rescue when disaster strikes anywhere in the world.

The inexorable march of global change confers advantages on the vanguard. Their innovation capabilities put them in the forefront of new ideas. Their partnership orientation and commitment to high standards bring relationship advantages essential for a networked world. The opportunities they provide for people to thrive in empowered workplaces help them attract and retain the best talent. Their values that put societal purpose at the center help them build deep local connections even as they globalize. And their powerful models of success give them the influence to steer that global march in positive directions.

APPENDIX
THE SCOPE OF THE RESEARCH

As a colleague once wisecracked, collect a hundred anecdotes, and suddenly you have real data. For this book I found hundreds of stories about leading-edge companies and used that as a set of naturalistic observations from which patterns could be discerned.

This book is based on a multiyear study of about fifteen companies with international scope, headquartered in the United States, Latin America, Europe, Asia, and Africa. Eight of them were studied in sufficient depth to be featured prominently in this book: Banco Real, Cemex, Diageo, IBM, Omron, Procter & Gamble, Publicis Groupe, and Shinhan Financial Group, and twelve others were also studied, including ABN AMRO (before its sale), Cisco Systems, Digitas (before its sale), Garanti Bank, Gillette (before its sale), ICICI Bank, Nokia, MTN, an anonymous Asian company (kept anonymous for reasons that are clear in chapter 7), and several European and U.S. pharmaceutical companies. A few other sets of interviews were conducted with Avon, Eli Lilly, Lenovo, and Timberland to get informants' views of their own company practices compared with the outlines of the vanguard model.

The list of the main eight companies is not intended to be an exclusive set of vanguard companies but rather a broad, diverse representation. I consider companies not studied, such as Cisco Systems, Novartis, and Toyota, equally excellent reflections of the vanguard model, and I have been fortunate to have worked with Cisco and Novartis and to have shared the platform with their highly regarded CEOs, John Chambers and Daniel Vasella, respectively.

appendix

One aspect common to the eight focal companies is that they solidified their top standing in their industry in the twenty-first century. The companies were chosen opportunistically because of their expressed interest in globalizing further and their willingness to allow access (in several cases, I was invited as a consultant), but all were externally identified by at least one group as high reputation and high performance, sometimes subsequent to their inclusion in this project, which helped confirm my selection. All of them made significant changes to their strategies and structures starting around 2000, in response to global challenges and aspirations. The companies anchored in developed countries increased their investment in emerging market countries, and several of the companies from emerging economies increased investment in the developed world. Even the oldest companies in this group, with international operations for a hundred years or more, changed their international strategies and organizational structures and processes after the year 2000. Many of the companies have CEOs who are widely admired, some of whom led turnarounds following predecessors who stumbled.

The companies can be arrayed along a continuum in terms of degree of globality. At the least global end, though the company earned 90 percent of its revenues outside its home country, about 80 percent of its employees were natives of the headquarters country, even those working in international facilities. The company anchoring the most global end of the continuum in my research operated in 170 countries and was reshaping its organizational model to be "globally integrated" rather than "multinational."

Over 350 structured and semistructured interviews were conducted by my researchers and myself over three years in more than twenty countries. In addition to the United States, the countries included (alphabetically) Australia, Brazil, China (Mainland China and Hong Kong), Egypt, Finland, France, Germany, India, Israel, Japan, Kenya, Latvia, Mexico, Netherlands, New Zealand, Russia, Singapore, South Africa, South Korea, and the United Kingdom (Great Britain). I also met with executives in Switzerland, Denmark, and Dubai, and one of my researchers interviewed managers from Ukraine while he was in Moscow. Country variety served as context in which to view (1) the consistency with which companies behaved (was a universal model developing that could be applied in places that were culturally and politically different?) and (2) how companies managed the connections across geographies.

Interviews were accompanied by collection of company documents, CEO speeches, and statistics. Statistics included aggregate financial performance metrics and other data such as employment figures, geographic locations, and related issues that were publicly disclosed at the corporate level. We also sought specific indicators for countries in which we were following events, such as Procter & Gamble's financial results for Brazil and its performance compared with both local and multinational competitors. In some cases, we were shown numbers but asked not to disclose them (e.g., IBM in Egypt); sometimes we found competitor information via public sources.

The largest number of formal interviews took place with employees of the largest company, IBM (eighty); the smallest number of interviews among multinationals took place with employees of Nokia (eleven, in three countries). The vast majority of interviews took place in person at a company facility, which permitted observations of settings and artifacts and provided an opportunity to obtain documents. There were also informal discussions at meals, sometimes with larger groups, and invitations to participate in conferences (such as Publicis Groupe's "digital day" in Paris in June 2008 or IBM's CEO-led Business Leadership Forums in St. Petersburg in June 2007 and Istanbul in November 2008), which facilitated additional information gathering.

Visits were sought in three kinds of locations: (1) corporate headquarters and the home base region, (2) a major market (for non-U.S. companies, this was generally the United States), and (3) a "culturally remote" country as defined by the company liaison—one that was viewed by managers as maximally different from the home base. (That is how my research team ended up interviewing global company subsidiaries in Egypt, Latvia, and Kenya.)

Interviews were conducted with the CEO and top corporate staff, country general managers, and senior managers representing major functions at both corporate and country levels (product or brand management, production, technology and innovation, marketing and sales, procurement or supply chain relationships, human resources, public or government affairs, and community relations). In many places, senior financial and strategy executives were also interviewed. Some interviews spanned several meetings.

In addition, where feasible, focus groups were held with a cross section of professionals and/or technical workers; we requested two kinds of groups, one of customer-facing employees, one of technical or production workers. In some cases, customers and business partners were also interviewed on their premises, including officials of government ministries and small company distributors. Showrooms, retail stores, and others places where company products or services were operating or on display were also visited wherever possible.

Information gathering focused on two kinds of situations: events requiring change management skills (acquisition integration, crisis response, product or service innovation) and routine ways of working that illustrated the connection between overarching global frameworks and local actions. For events, we talked to key players and constructed chronologies of actions, confirming the event history through the eyes of more than one source.

To understand routine ways of working, interview guides were constructed to gather information from people representing appropriate functions about areas with which they had experience (i.e., topics were divided by interviewee). Topics included the following.

- Business fundamentals—the business mix, key competitors, market share, financial performance and trends, employment profile, customer profile, recent innovations and their sources and process of creation, and current business challenges
- Employment—company policies regarding recruitment, employment, training, career paths (within focal countries and globally), communications, benefits (e.g., health care, family leave) and how these affect the workforce and the public; that is, what national differences are taken into account or how the company works (alone or with other companies) to ensure that its employees in various countries get comparable treatment to employees in other parts of the world, which might mean influencing traditional practices in some countries and trying to influence changes
- Supply and distribution chains—how the company chooses suppliers and distributors, both globally and nationally, and how the

company works with them as business partners and attempts to influence the standards by which they operate their businesses

- Community initiatives in which the company contributes its resources and expertise to make a positive difference in particular countries; examples of activities the company engages in alone, with other companies, or with partners from other sectors and how this determination is made; the challenges of being a leader in these initiatives if they are not common practice, and any evidence about the company's reputation in focal countries
- How employees (both on the technical/production side and customer facing) view their company's role in their lives and their communities and how they compare their careers to those of friends outside the company
- Any role the company plays in shaping the thinking and policies of the government, first with respect to the industry but then more generally; the behavior of the industry, through key relationships and membership and role in business associations and policy forums; and any particular policy initiatives or public debates to which the company has contributed

In all interviews, informants were first asked about their own careers and history with the company. This not only provided a basis for weighing the credibility of the source, but it also proved a valuable source of information about the organizational system and workplace culture. They were next asked about major accomplishments in the past two years in their own work, followed by major challenges. That line of questioning provided grounded narratives with specific examples about both events and routine ways of working.

To augment interviews with external stakeholders (which were few in number compared to internal interviews), we looked at public sources to examine reputations and to identify problems the companies had encountered, such as legal problems, public controversies, or negative incidents. Briefing books were compiled on the eight major focal companies including news clips, analyst reports, summaries of lawsuits, and their place on award lists from various countries and locally. Many publications prepare annual lists for their countries of the best companies overall and for particular purposes (e.g., the best places to work).

Analysis was qualitative and inductive. The first task was to capture the essence of each company with respect to how events are handled and how the business model operates; this took the form of case studies reviewed by representatives of that company. The next task was to find patterns as well as differences across companies through comparisons among subsets—for example, extracting key themes from one situation and seeing whether they were found elsewhere. This is a creative mental process that cannot be expressed in a formula. Though the process was sometimes like comparing the proverbial apples and oranges, there were enough similarities to permit generalizations. Because the case examples are so varied, the generalizations take on greater significance.

After most of the book was written, the global financial crisis of the fall of 2008 led to precipitous declines in markets everywhere. We checked the fate of the focal companies in this research through financial reports and public sources. The extent of the damage depended on the industry, but most did better than their peers. Using public reporting services, such as Hoover's and OneSource, and basing comparisons on company statements about their competitor set, we found that Shinhan, Publicis Groupe, P&G, IBM, Omron, and Diageo were among those that had outperformed their peers in terms of stock price for the shaky months leading up to the crisis and holding their own or outperforming them during the crisis, which meant, given the magnitude of the market crash, that they did better by losing less. (Cemex suffered more, due to general industry conditions and its debt burden from financing big acquisitions.) Although stock price is only one indicator of the value created by the vanguard companies, this is a helpful sign that the companies in this research project are sustainable and, thus, that the vanguard model is useful for business and society.

NOTES

chapter one

11. *science fiction fantasy* Frederik Pohl and C. M. Kornbluth, *The Space Merchants* (New York: Ballantine Books, 1974 [first published in 1952]).

13. *December 2004 tsunami* The facts in this story, and the facts in other company accounts throughout this book, come from my own research interviews (more than 350 of them), direct observation of events, and review of company documents. Facts have been verified by company review.

22. *worldwide community donated* One month after the Indian Ocean earthquake and tsunami, the BBC News reported, on January 27, 2005, that at least $7 billion in aid had been pledged from governments and organizations. See BBC News, "Tsunami Aid: Who's Giving What?" http://news.bbc.co.uk/1/hi/world/asia-pacific/4145259.stm (accessed November 26, 2008).

22. *Pfizer, Deutsche Bank* See UNICEF, "U.S. Fund for UNICEF Annual Report 2005," 8–13, http://www.unicefusa.org/news/publications/annual-report/2005_Annual_Report.pdf (accessed November 26, 2008).

chapter two

30. *series of geopolitical events* Fareed Zakaria uses 1979 as the year when massive change began. See Fareed Zakaria, *The Post-American World* (New York: Norton, 2008). Influential authors in the exuberance camp at the end of the 1980s included a Japanese politician, Kenichi Ohmae, and a former chairman of Citicorp, Walter Wriston. See Kenichi Ohmae, *The Borderless World: Power and Strategy in the Interlinked Economy* (New York: HarperBusiness, 1990); Walter Wriston, *The Twilight of Sovereignty: How the Information Revolution Is Transforming Our World* (New York: Scribner, 1992).

30. *facilitated by information technology* Lists of the largest global companies at that time were dominated by U.S.-headquartered firms. Some of the American giants underwent restructuring in the 1980s to meet the challenge of Japanese competition. See Rosabeth Moss Kanter, *World Class: Thriving Locally in the Global Economy* (New York: Simon & Schuster, 1995), but American firms remained the largest and most powerful global players overall. The recent demise has been gradual but notable since 2005, as the number of U.S. companies on the Fortune Global 500 list has fallen every year from 176 (2005) to 170 (2006), 162 (2007), and 153 (2008).

30. *deregulation of industry* Margaret Thatcher was elected prime minister of the United Kingdom in 1979; Ronald Reagan was elected president of the United States in 1980. Deregulation of the airlines had begun in the late 1970s under President Jimmy Carter.

31. *European community deliberations* Post–World War II European integration had its roots in the European Coal and Steel Community, an agreement signed by six western European countries. It served as the basis for future cooperative initiatives, including the European Economic Community. The European Union was formed through the 1992 Maastricht Treaty to house three pillar institutions: the European Community, Justice and Home Affairs, and Common Foreign and Security Policy. The European Union's creation, which formally took effect in 1993, led to the launching of the euro currency in 1999.

31. *"new economy" of* Historical trends based on the Money Tree Report, a quarterly study of the venture capital industry authored by PricewaterhouseCoopers and the National Venture Capital Association and based on data provided by Thomson Financial, show that VC funding rose from $1.7 billion in Q1 1995 to a peak of $28.3 billion in Q1 2000 before falling to $4.5 billion in Q4 2002. Since then, it gradually rose to $8.1 billion in Q4 2007 before falling to $7.1 billion in Q3 2008. See https://www.pwcmoneytree.com/MTPublic/ns/nav.jsp?page=historical (accessed November 26, 2008).

31. *North American Free Trade Agreement* NAFTA signatories included Canada, Mexico, and the United States. The agreement was signed in December 1992 and took effect in January 1994.

31. *Developing countries grew quickly* IBM, for example, had operated in India from 1951 to 1977, when it pulled out due to disputes with the government over equity participation and intellectual property. The company did not return until 1992. See Rosabeth Moss Kanter, "IBM (A): The Coming of the Globally-Integrated Enterprise," Harvard Business School case N9-308-105.

31. *prosperity in the United States* See Lawrence Mishel, Jared Bernstein, and Sylvia Allegretto, *The State of Working America, 2006/2007* (Ithaca, NY: ILR Press, 2007). Mishel and his colleagues at the Eco-

nomic Policy Institute have tracked the growing inequality of both consumption and income. While the lowest and middle fifth of household incomes grew just 6.1 percent and 12.3 percent, respectively, between 1979 and 2000, the highest fifth grew 70 percent, with the richest 1 percent expanding its income by an astonishing 184 percent. These trends continued during the first decade of the twenty-first century, when wages stagnated. Between 2000 and 2004, the average family income, measured in inflation-adjusted terms, fell by 3 percent.

31. *1997–98 Asian financial crisis* In P&G, for example, net earnings in Asia fell from $275 million in 1997 to $174 million in 1998, before recovering to a record $279 million in 1999. See Procter & Gamble Company, *P&G Annual Report 1999: Embracing the Future*, 18. Gillette likewise reported lower sales in the region. Its overall international sales had fallen 12 percent compared with 1997 owing to weakness in Russia and Asia. See Gillette Company, *Gillette Annual Report 1999*, 17.

32. *World Trade Organization* Rosabeth Moss Kanter, *Evolve! Succeeding the Digital Culture of Tomorrow* (Boston: Harvard Business School Press, 2001).

32. *Protests at the 2001 G8* Nick Davies, "The Bloody Battle of Genoa," *Guardian*, July 27, 2008.

32. *Protests were benign* The U.S. 9/11 attack killed 2,974 people plus the nineteen terrorists. The 11-M Madrid train bombings took place on the morning of March 11, 2004, just days before Spain's national elections. It killed 191 people. The London 7/7 attack occurred on July 7, 2005, taking the lives of 56 people, including the four bombers. Related attacks have occurred in North Africa, the Middle East, Indonesia, and India.

32. *socialist regimes returned* Hugo Chavez was elected president of Venezuela in 1998 and has since consolidated power and actively promoted the spread of what he considers a Bolivarian Revolution in Latin America. His closest regional allies include Evo Morales, elected president of Bolivia in 2006, Rafael Correa, elected president of Ecuador in 2006, and Daniel Ortega, who returned as president of Nicaragua in 2007. Ollanta Humala, the Chavez-backed presidential candidate for Peru, narrowly lost a run-off in 2006.

32. *analysts posited a dire* Samuel Huntington, *The Clash of Civilizations and the Remaking of the World Order* (New York: Simon & Schuster, 1996). This polemical book was based on an equally controversial 1993 article with a similar name. Samuel Huntington, "The Clash of Civilizations?" *Foreign Affairs* 72, no. 3 (1993): 22–49.

32. *Enron's fast rise* Enron's problems first became public in late 2001. See Malcolm Salter, *Innovation Corrupted: The Origins and Legacy of Enron's Collapse* (Cambridge: Harvard University Press, 2008).

32. *Revelations of excesses* The Tyco scandal broke in 2002, as did the MCI WorldCom accounting fraud. The Parmalat scandal became public in late 2003. Samsung, South Korea's largest *chaebol* or family-run conglomerate, had weathered scandals in the past, but bribery allegations in 2007, followed by a tax evasion indictment, brought down the CEO.

32. *October 2008 global financial meltdown* See Julio Rotenberg, "Subprime Meltdown: American Housing and Global Financial Turmoil," Harvard Business School case 708-042.

32. *Countries such as Brazil* Tarun Khanna, *Billions of Entrepreneurs: How China and India Are Reshaping Their Futures and Yours* (Boston: Harvard Business School Press, 2008); Tarun Khanna and Yishay Yafeh, "Business Groups in Emerging Markets: Paragons or Parasites?" *Journal of Economic Literature* 45, no. 2 (2007): 331–372; Tarun Khanna and Krishna Palepu, "Emerging Giants: Building World-Class Companies in Developing Countries," *Harvard Business Review* 84, no. 10 (2006): 60–69; and Tarun Khanna and Krishna Palepu, "Strategies That Fit Emerging Markets," *Harvard Business Review* 83, no. 6 (2005): 63–76.

33. *By the mid-2000s* This figure was reported in National Science Board, *Science and Engineering Indicators 2006* (vol. 1, NSB 06-01; chap. 2, p. 6). (Arlington, VA: National Science Foundation). See http://www.nsf .gov/statistics/seind06/pdf/c02.pdf (accessed November 26, 2008).

33. *Emerging champions from developing countries* See Arindam K. Bhattacharya and David C. Michael, "How Local Companies Keep Multinationals at Bay," *Harvard Business Review* 86, no. 3 (2008): 84–95; and Tarun Khanna and Krishna Palepu, "Emerging Giants: Building World-Class Companies in Developing Countries," *Harvard Business Review* 84, no. 10 (2006): 60–69.

33. *Companies emanating from emerging markets* According to an A. T. Kearny study cited by a World Economic Forum report prepared for its Annual Meeting of New Champions in China in September 2008, companies from developing countries—including China, India, Malaysia, Russia, United Arab Emirates, and South Africa—executed 19 percent of the merger-and-acquisitions transactions between developed and developing nations in 2007; and overall, the number of deals they executed in developed countries grew by nearly 20 percent between 2002 and 2007, roughly four times the rate for within-country deals. By 2008, the World Economic Forum expected that the deals would get bigger, with nearly 10 percent exceeding $100 million. World Economic Forum, "Annual Meeting of the New Champions 2008: The Next Wave of Growth," http://www.weforum.org/pdf/ tianjin/Tianjin_report.pdf (accessed November 25, 2008).

35. *youthful employees coaxed veterans* Rosabeth Moss Kanter, *Evolve! Succeeding the Digital Culture of Tomorrow* (Boston: Harvard Business School Press, 2001), which discusses the need for organizational changes and

refs to the challenges Digitas faced in its client work, including those with Bausch & Lomb.

37. *into the 2000s, American companies* A comparison of the Deloitte Technology Fast 500, an annual survey of the fastest-growing technology companies in North America, Asia-Pacific, and Europe–Middle East–Africa regions, finds that a larger number of the top 50 and top 500 in the United States register faster growth rates. Reports are downloadable at http://www.deloitte.com.

38. *China and India were home* The International Telecommunications Union provides national, regional, and global telecommunication penetration and usage statistics. See http://www.itu.int/ITU-D/ict/statistics/ (accessed November 26, 2008).

39. *David Kenny wrote* David Kenny and John Marshall, "Contextual Marketing: The Real Business of the Internet," *Harvard Business Review* 78, no. 6 (2001): 119–125.

chapter three

58. *range of advantages* Numerous studies have outlined the benefits of values-driven corporate social performance (CSP) initiatives. See Lynn Paine, *Value Shift: Why Companies Must Merge Financial and Social Imperatives to Achieve Superior Performance* (New York: McGraw-Hill, 2002); Ira Jackson and Jane Nelson, *Profits with Principles: Seven Strategies for Delivering Value with Values* (New York: Currency/Doubleday, 2004); and Bradley Googins, Philip Mervis, and Steven Rochlin, *Beyond Good Company: Next Generation Corporate Citizenship* (New York: Palgrave Macmillan, 2007). For reviews of the vast research on the relationship between CSP and financial performance, see Marc Orlitzky, "Corporate Social Performance and Financial Performance: A Research Synthesis," in Andrew Crane, Abagail McWilliams, Dirk Matten, Jeremy Moon, and Donald Siegel, eds., *The Oxford Handbook of Corporate Social Responsibility* (Oxford: Oxford University Press, 2008), 113–134; Joshua Margolis and James Walsh, "Misery Loves Companies: Rethinking Social Initiatives by Business," *Administrative Science Quarterly* 48 (2003): 268–305; and Joshua Margolis, Hillary Anger Elfenbein, and James Walsh, "Do Well by Doing Good? Don't Count on It," *Harvard Business Review* 86, no. 1 (January 2008): 19–20. In their meta-analyses, Orlitzky, as well as Margolis and Walsh, found a "small" or "mild" positive relationship between CSP and financial performance, but it was also highly variable.

58. *report about everything* The push to make companies take responsibility for its subcontracted supply chain began in the 1990s. See Debora Spar, "The Spotlight and the Bottom Line: How Multinationals Export Human Rights," *Foreign Affairs* 77, no. 2 (1998): 7–12. This responsibility expanded to include environmental, labor, and human

rights concerns. For a review, see Andrew Millington, "Responsibility in the Supply Chain," in Andrew Crane et al., eds., *The Oxford Handbook of Corporate Social Responsibility* (Oxford: Oxford University Press, 2008): 363–383.

59.   *increasingly attracted to companies* For evidence that a company's values attract employees, see Daniel Turban and Daniel Greening, "Corporate Social Performance and Organizational Attractiveness to Prospective Employees," *Academy of Management Journal* 40, no. 3 (1997): 658–672; and Heather Schmidt Albinger and Sarah Freeman, "Corporate Social Performance and Attractiveness as an Employer to Different Job Seeking Populations," *Journal of Business Ethics* 28, no. 3 (2000): 243–253. For an analysis of how companies explicitly use CSP activities as a competitive advantage in the context of the "war for talent," see C. B. Bhattacharya, Sankar Sen, and Daniel Korschun, "Using Corporate Responsibility to Win the War for Talent," *MIT Sloan Management Review* 49, no. 2 (2008): 37–44.

60.   *Values and principles may be invoked* Numerous studies offer a business case for CSP. In general, they fall into four major classes of arguments: cost and risk reduction, competitive advantage, reputation and legitimacy, and value creation. For a review, see Elizabeth Kurucz, Barry Colbert, and David Wheeler, "The Business Case for Corporate Social Responsibility," in Andrew Crane et al., eds., *The Oxford Handbook of Corporate Social Responsibility* (Oxford: Oxford University Press, 2008): 83–112.

63.   *IBM had given itself* Sam Palmisano, "The Globally Integrated Enterprise," *Foreign Affairs* 85, no. 3 (2006): 127–136.

66.   *in their statements of values* Lynn Paine, Rohit Deshpandé, Joshua D. Margolis, and Kim Eric Bettcher, "Up to Code: Does Your Company's Conduct Meet World-Class Standards?" *Harvard Business Review* 83, no. 12 (2005): 122–133. In their analysis of global demands for codes of conduct, they found that the underlying principles were remarkably similar, suggesting that a "world-class code" of business conduct had emerged.

72.   *Stories are important* The importance of stories lies not so much in basic memory processes but in a narrative's ability to integrate information and experience into coherent meaning. Cognitive, social, and personality psychologists have emphasized the central role narrative plays in memory processes, especially in relation to reality construction, collective and individual identity formation, and self-functioning. See Jerome Bruner, *Acts of Meaning* (Cambridge: Harvard University Press, 1990); Jerome Bruner, "The Narrative Construction of Reality," *Critical Inquiry* 18 (1991): 1–21; Lewis Hinchman and Sandra Hinchman, eds., *Memory, Identity, Community: The Idea of Narrative in the Human Sciences* (Albany: State University of New York, 1997); and

Dan McAdams, *The Stories We Live By: Personal Myths and the Making of the Self* (New York: William Morrow, 1993).

73. *P&G is among the companies* Thomas J. Peters and Robert H. Waterman Jr., *In Search of Excellence: Lessons from America's Best-Run Companies* (New York: Harper & Row, 1982). Other "excellent" companies from that book that are still functioning include IBM, Johnson & Johnson, McDonald's, Boeing, Hewlett-Packard, and Marriott.

chapter four

87. *innovation is stifled* Rosabeth Moss Kanter, "Innovating Against the Grain: Ten Rules for Stifling Innovation," in *The Change Masters: Innovation and Entrepreneurship in the American Corporation* (New York: Simon & Schuster, 1983), 69–101.

87. *and skills traps* Rosabeth Moss Kanter, "Innovation: The Classic Traps," *Harvard Business Review* 84, no. 11 (November 2006): 72–83.

87. *stay connected with colleagues* Rosabeth Moss Kanter, John Kao, and Fred Wiersema, eds., *Innovation: Breakthrough Thinking at 3M, GE, DuPont, Pfizer, and Rubbermaid* (New York: HarperCollins, 1997). See also James Utterback, *Mastering the Dynamics of Innovation* (Boston: Harvard Business School Press, 1994); Michael Tushman and Charles O'Reilly, *Winning Through Innovation: A Practical Guide to Leading Organizational Change and Renewal* (Boston: Harvard Business School Press, 1997); and Henry Chesbrough, *Open Innovation: The New Imperative for Creating and Profiting from Technology* (Boston: Harvard Business School Press, 2003).

88. *shook up his thinking* Rosabeth Moss Kanter, "Kaleidoscope Thinking," in Subir Chowdhury, ed., *Management 21C, Someday We'll All Manage This Way* (London: Financial Times/Prentice Hall, 2000), 250–261. See also Teresa Amabile, *Creativity in Context* (Boulder, CO: Westview Press, 1996).

94. *open innovation, in which customers* Henry Chesbrough, *Open Innovation: The New Imperative for Creating and Profiting from Technology* (Boston: Harvard Business School Press, 2003).

95. *classic seven skills* Rosabeth Moss Kanter, *Evolve! Succeeding the Digital Culture of Tomorrow* (Boston: Harvard Business School Press, 2001), 255–284. See also Rosabeth Moss Kanter, "Leadership for Change: Enduring Skills for Change Masters," Harvard Business School note 304–062.

95. *Lafley brought the Connect and Develop* See A. G. Lafley and Ram Charan, *The Game-Changer: How You Can Drive Revenue and Profit Growth with Innovation* (New York: Crown Business, 2008). See also Nabil Sakkab, "Connect and Develop Complements Research and Develop at P&G," *Research-Technology Management* 45, no. 2 (2002): 38–45; and

Larry Huston and Nabil Sakkab, "Connect and Develop: Inside Procter & Gamble's New Model for Innovation," *Harvard Business Review* 84, no. 3 (2006): 58–66.

96.   *but by extending conveniences* Kasturi Rangan, John Quelch, Gustavo Herrero, and Brooke Barton, eds., *Business Solutions for the Global Poor: Creating Social and Economic Value* (Hoboken, NJ: John Wiley & Sons, 2007).

96.   *the company's multiple engineering firsts* Omron is known for many innovations. In 1962, when Omron listed on the Kyoto and Osaka stock exchanges, its stock price soared amidst commentary that Omron was the western Japan competitor to eastern Japan's Sony. In the 1950s, it developed the solid-state relay and a solid-state (noncontact, transistor-based) proximity switch, called the dream switch. In 1960, it built an R&D laboratory at a cost of four times its capital. It introduced the first vending machine capable of dispensing several different items and accepting a variety of currencies, paving the way for it to develop one of the world's first ATM machines. It created its first health device, the stress meter in 1962; Japan's first automated traffic signal (in Kyoto in 1964); and the world's first fully automated train station (in 1967). Omron opened its first international R&D center in Mountain View, California, followed shortly by Omron Singapore in 1972, and launched the world's smallest calculator, the Calculet-1200.

97.   *brought to engineers* Studies of R&D effectiveness discover that when users are consulted, more and better innovation results. See Eric von Hippel, "Lead Users: A Source of Novel Product Concepts," *Management Science* 32, no. 7 (1986): 791–805; Eric von Hippel, *Sources of Innovation* (New York: Oxford University Press, 1988); and Eric von Hippel, *Democratizing Innovation* (Cambridge: MIT Press, 2005). However, Clay Christensen also found that talking to current customers could in some cases reduce the potential for breakthrough innovation. See Eric von Hippel, *The Innovator's Dilemma: When New Technologies Cause Great Firms to Fail* (Boston: Harvard Business School Press, 1997).

101.   *The least-advantaged places* Rosabeth Moss Kanter, "From Spare Change to Real Change: The Social Sector as Beta Site for Business Innovation," *Harvard Business Review* 77, no. 3 (1999): 122–132.

102.   *largest private sector bank* India's ICICI Bank was not immune to the global credit crisis. In October 2008, rumors spread about its foreign exposure, prompting its stock to fall 25 percent over a three-day period. Despite verbal reassurances from the company and the government, there were isolated runs on deposits, especially in southern India. ICICI filed a grievance, requesting the state to capture those responsible for spreading false bankruptcy rumors. Two major ratings agencies also

made public statements in support of the company, allowing ICICI to regain, in two days, its prerumor price. At the end of October, it reported a 27.5 percent drop in quarterly profit, stemming mostly from its UK subsidiary's exposure to Lehman Brothers bonds. See Nandini Lakshman, "Credit Chatter Snares India's ICICI Bank," *BusinessWeek*, October 16, 2008; and Erika Kinetz, "India's ICICI Bank Quarterly Profit Falls 27 pct," Associated Press, October 27, 2008.

111. *When the climate is right* Rosabeth Moss Kanter, "When a Thousand Flowers Bloom: Structural, Collective, and Social Conditions for Innovation in Organizations," in Barry M. Straw and L. L. Cummings, eds., *Research in Organizational Behavior,* vol. 10 (Greenwich, CT: JAI Press, 1988), 169–211.

chapter five

115. *investors often drive down* Researchers find that, on the whole, a target company's share price is positive and rises relative to that of the buyer firm. Returns for acquirers are mixed. A third lose financial value, a third maintain the share price, and a third realize gains. See Robert Bruner, "Does M&A Pay? A Survey of Evidence for the Decision-Maker," *Journal of Applied Finance* 12 (2002): 48–68.

115. *rally populist sentiment* After P&G announced its acquisition of Gillette in January 2005, the Massachusetts secretary of state opened an investigation into the deal, claiming that the sale price was too low and unfair. After several months of subpoenas, the case was dropped. See William Symonds and Robert Berner, "In a Lather over the Gillette Deal," *BusinessWeek*, June 16, 2005. On the public demand for good company conduct, see Rosabeth Moss Kanter, *America the Principled* (New York: Crown, 2007), 95–132.

115. *mergers and acquisitions continue* Since the 1980s, there have been three major merger waves: the leveraged finance era in the late 1980s and early 1990s, the Internet bubble era between the mid-1990s and early 2000s, and the industry consolidation era in the early 2000s until the 2008 financial crisis. All three were accompanied by an increase in the size of cross-border mergers and acquisitions (M&A), in line with rising globalization. The number of total global M&A transactions rose from less than 5,000 deals a year worth $500 billion in the late 1980s to a peak of 21,676 transactions valued at $2.2 trillion in 2000, before falling and rising again to 22,007 deals worth $1.8 trillion in 2007. Numbers were compiled from the Thomson Financial database.

115. *high proportion of mergers* The Boston Consulting Group study of nearly thirty-two hundred M&A transactions between 1992 and 2006 found that deals above $1 billion destroyed twice as much value as those below that figure. The relative size of the target and the acquirer

also mattered. The mergers of targets with half or more of the acquirers' value destroyed twice as much value as mergers of targets with 10 percent or less of the acquirers' value. See Kees Cools, Jeff Gell, Jens Kengelbach, and Alexander Roos, "The Brave New World of M&A: How to Create Value from Mergers and Acquisitions," Boston Consulting Group (July 2007). Interestingly, the role of M&A size seems to have risen in importance with time. A study of the fifty largest U.S. mergers between 1979 and 1984 found value creation. See Paul Healy, Krishna Palepu, and Richard Ruback, "Does Corporate Performance Improve after Mergers?" *Journal of Financial Economics* 31, no. 2 (1992): 135–175.

115. *strong values encourage leaders* For a collection of readings examining the cultural challenges faced during merger-and-acquisition situations, see Gunter Stahl and Mark Mendenhall, eds., *Mergers and Acquisitions: Managing Culture and Human Resources* (Stanford: Stanford Business Books, 2005).

118. *making North Korea* Robert J. Lifton, *Thought Reform and the Psychology of Totalism: A Study of "Brainwashing" in China* (Chapel Hill: University of North Carolina Press, 1989 [first published in 1961]); and Edgar Schein with Inge Schneier and Curtis Barket, *Coercive Persuasion: A Socio-psychological Analysis of the "Brainwashing" of American Civilian Prisoners by the Chinese Communists* (New York: W. W. Norton, 1961). For a recent update on the study of brainwashing, see Benjamin Zablocki, "Towards a Demystified and Disinterested Scientific Theory of Brainwashing," in Benjamin Zablocki and Thomas Robbins, eds., *Misunderstanding Cults: Searching for Objectivity in a Controversial Field* (Toronto: University of Toronto Press, 2001), 159–214.

124. *they formed a strategic alliance* Rosabeth Moss Kanter, "Collaborative Advantage: The Art of Alliances," *Harvard Business Review* 72, no. 4 (1994): 96–108. See also Rosabeth Moss Kanter, *World Class: Thriving Locally in the Global Economy* (New York: Simon & Schuster, 1995).

140. *Positive change with minimum resistance* Rosabeth Moss Kanter, *Confidence: How Winning Streaks and Losing Streaks Begin and End* (New York: Three Rivers Press, 2006).

chapter six

147. *People choose to do* People in general and workers in particular often respond more to self-regulatory environments built on intrinsic motivation than on command-and-control settings based on external pressures or extrinsic rewards. See, for example, Edward Deci and Richard Ryan, *Intrinsic Motivation and Self-Determination in Human Behavior* (New York: Plenum, 1985). For a model of motivation that empha-

sizes four internal human drives (acquire, bond, comprehend, and defend), see Nitin Nohria, Boris Groysberg, and Linda-Eling Lee, "Employee Motivation: A Powerful New Model," *Harvard Business Review* 86, no. 7–8 (2008): 78–84.

147. *This is where company values* The phrase *war for talent* was coined by McKinsey & Company consultants in a 1998 report. See Elizabeth Chambers, Mark Foulon, Helen Handfield-Jones, Steven Hankin, and Edward Michaels, "The War for Talent," *McKinsey Quarterly* no. 3 (1998): 44–57. See also Edward Michaels, Helen Handfield-Jones, and Beth Axelrod, *The War for Talent* (Boston: Harvard Business School Press, 2001). Christopher Bartlett and Sumantra Ghoshal take the argument a step further, arguing that human capital could serve as a company's strategic point of departure in "Building Competitive Advantage Through People," *MIT Sloan Management Review* 33, no. 2 (2002): 34–41.

148. *The growing importance of "connectors"* Malcolm Gladwell uses the term *connectors* to refer to those people who link people and groups. See Malcolm Gladwell, *The Tipping Point: How Little Things Can Make a Big Difference* (Boston: Little, Brown, 2000). The tipping point model was taken from research in network theory and threshold models. See Thomas Schelling, "Dynamic Models of Segregation," *Journal of Mathematical Sociology* 1 (1971): 143–186; and Mark Granovetter, "Threshold Models of Collective Behavior," *American Journal of Sociology* 83, no. 6 (1978): 1420–1443. The notion of people who act as "bridges" between groups was developed in social capital research. Those who link two networks occupy a more advantageous position than those who do not. Likewise, organizations that bridge structural holes gain a competitive advantage over those which fail to do so. See Ronald Burt, *Structural Holes: The Social Structure of Competition* (Cambridge: Harvard University Press, 1992). See also Ranjay Gulati, *Managing Network Resources: Alliances, Affiliations, and Other Relational Assets* (Oxford: Oxford University Press, 2007).

148. *reflection of the expectations* For an analysis of differences in attitudes and expectations between Generation X and Generation Y or "millennials," see Neil Howe and William Strauss, *13th Gen: Abort, Retry, Ignore, Fail?* (New York: Vintage Books, 1993); and Neil Howe and William Strauss, *Millennials Rising: The Next Great Generation* (New York: Vintage Books, 2000).

148. *images of toil, drudgery,* Daniel Bell, *Work and Its Discontents* (Boston: Beacon Press, 1956); and Harvey Swados, *A Radical's America* (Boston: Little, Brown, 1962), 111–120.

148. *reserve army of the unemployed* Neo-Marxist scholars made these arguments most forcefully. For classic studies, see Michael Burawoy, *Manufacturing Consent: Changes in the Labor Process under Monopoly Capitalism*

(Chicago: University of Chicago Press); Erik Olin Wright, *Class Structure and Income Determination* (New York: Academic Press, 1979); and Erik Olin Wright, *Classes* (London: Verson, 1985).

148. *only organized labor and government* Lawrence Mishel and Matthew Waters, "How Unions Help All Workers," *Economic Policy Institute Briefing Paper Series* (August 2003).

152. *evidence shows that people* Ellen Galinsky, James T. Bond, Stacy S. Kim, Lois Backon, Erin Brownfield, and Kelly Sekai, *Overwork in America: When the Way We Work Becomes Too Much* (New York: Families and Work Institute, 2005); and Sylvia Ann Hewlett and Carolyn Buck Luce, "Extreme Jobs: The Dangerous Allure of the 70-Hour Workweek," *Harvard Business Review* 84, no. 12 (2006): 49–59.

159. *people at all levels* The study of digital culture and its generational effects is a burgeoning field. In 2005, the MacArthur Foundation launched the five-year, $50 million Digital Media and Learning initiative. Part of the funds helped set up the Digital Youth Research project at the University of California, Berkeley. Findings will be published in Mimi Ito et al., eds., *Hanging Out, Messing Around, Geeking Out: Living and Learning with New Media* (Cambridge: MIT Press, forthcoming). The Pew Internet and American Life Project is also dedicated to understanding the emerging use of digital technologies and its impact on society. See http://www.pewinternet.org. For a study of e-mail etiquette in the workplace, see Joan Waldvogel, "Greetings and Closings in Workplace Email," *Journal of Computer-Mediated Communication* 12 (2007): 456–477.

160. *idea scouts, transfer agents* Rosabeth Moss Kanter, *The Change Masters* (New York: Simon & Schuster, 1983); and Rosabeth Moss Kanter, "Change Is Everyone's Job: Managing the Extended Enterprise in a Globally-Connected World," *Organizational Dynamics* 28, no. 1 (summer 1999): 7–23.

162. *"face time" a status symbol* Time, attention, and personal contact could become the new status symbol in an "attention" or "experience" economy when anyone can get information through impersonal means or own replicas if not originals of the same goods.

162. *With so many people* In the early 1990s, some analysts expected e-mail and other digital media to replace existing forms of communication. However, researchers have since discovered that such technologies as e-mail do not substitute for other media. Rather, they become complementary. See Adam Kleinbaum, Toby Stuart, and Michael Tushman, "Communication (and Coordination?) in a Modern, Complex Organization," *Administrative Science Quarterly* (under review).

163. *MBWA—management by walking around* This catchphrase was made famous in Thomas J. Peters and Robert Waterman's best-seller *In Search of Excellence* (New York: Harper & Row, 1982).

164. *resources must be acquired* Rosabeth Moss Kanter, *Change Masters* (New York: Three Rivers Press, 1983).

166. *Finding the resources to beg* The term *social capital* was first used and popularized by Pierre Bourdieu, James Coleman, and Robert Putnam. While they and others used the term in differing ways, it generally refers to people's social networks and the related group norms of reciprocity and trust. For elaborations of the concept, see Ronald Burt, *Structural Holes: The Social Structure of Competition* (Cambridge: Harvard University Press, 1992); and Nan Lin, *Social Capital: A Theory of Social Structure and Action* (Cambridge: Cambridge University Press, 2001).

167. *nature of the job* See Ronald Burt, *Brokerage and Closure: An Introduction to Social Capital* (Oxford: Oxford University Press, 2005). The case of interdivisional innovation also serves as an example. Unlike intradivisional innovation, which is driven by a firm's formal structure, managers can better achieve interdivisional innovation by encouraging employees to use existing contacts within their social network. See Adam Kleinbaum and Michael Tushman, "Building Bridges: The Social Structure of Interdependent Innovation," *Strategic Entrepreneurship Journal* 1 (2001): 102–122.

168. *organization-specific knowledge* The knowledge-based theory of the firm views knowledge as a firm's most important strategic asset because it is the major source of organizational capabilities and is not easily imitable. This knowledge can be wrapped up in rules, routines, tasks, systems, documents, language, people, and groups. See Robert Grant, "Toward a Knowledge-based Theory of the Firm," *Strategic Management Journal* 17, Winter Special Issue (1996): 109–122; and Bruce Kogut, "The Network as Knowledge: Generative Rules and the Emergence of Structure," *Strategic Management Journal* 21 (2000): 405–425. The knowledge-based theory stems from the resource-based theory of the firm. See Jay Barney and Delwyn Clark, *Resource-based Theory: Creating and Sustaining Competitive Advantage* (Oxford: Oxford University Press, 2007).

168. *also good for the mentors* Sarah Hezlett and Sharon Gibson, "Linking Mentoring and Social Capital: Implications for Career and Organization Development," *Advances in Developing Human Resources* 9, no. 3 (August 2007): 384–412.

170. *IBM and P&G are ubiquitous* Fortune ranked P&G and IBM as the "most admired" companies in their respective industries in 2008. In 2007, P&G was ranked 68 on Fortune's list of "best companies to work for." *Working Mother* magazine has consistently ranked P&G as the best company for female parents and inducted the firm into its "hall of fame" in 2005. In 2006, P&G was considered one of the top thirty best companies for women in Latin America. *DiversityInc* magazine also

placed the company in the global top five employers of diverse workers. The Great Place to Work Institute, which cosponsors the Fortune list as well as rankings in other regions, consistently placed IBM in its "best company to work for" lists in Brazil, Mexico, Peru, Portugal, and the United Kingdom. It has also won various diversity awards. IBM UK, led by GM Larry Hirst, who professes a particular passion for the importance of diversity, has pulled down numerous awards for its treatment of minorities in its workplace. Yet IBM and P&G are not alone among the vanguard. Since 2004, Shinhan has appeared among the top five "best companies to work for" in South Korea and placed second in 2007. Diageo also performs well, appearing annually among the top twenty-five and top one hundred lists in Argentina, Brazil, Colombia, Germany, Ireland, Italy, Mexico, Portugal, Spain, Uruguay, and Venezuela.

171. *new way of working* The "voice" issue is one raised by advocates of labor unions, who feel that even benign employers can give people less than they deserve by treating them as individuals or subgroups rather than letting them engage in collective bargaining. For evidence of a "union wage premium," see Richard Freeman and James Medoff, *What Do Unions Do?* (New York: Basic Books, 1984); and Richard Freeman and James Medoff, "The Impact of the Percentage Organized on Union and Nonunion Wages," *Review of Economics and Statistics* 63, no. 4 (1981): 561–572.

chapter seven

180. *In the past, international activities* Christopher A. Bartlett and Sumantra Ghoshal, *Managing Across Borders: The Transnational Solution* (Boston: Harvard Business School Press, 1998); and Sam Palmisano, "The Globally Integrated Enterprise," *Foreign Affairs* 85 (2006): 127–136.

180. *expats often lived* See M. Mendenhall and G. Oddou, "The Dimensions of Expatriate Acculturation: A Review," *Academy of Management Journal* 10 (1985): 39–47; J. S. Black, M. Mendenhall, and G. Oddou, "Toward a Comprehensive Model of International Adjustment: An Integration of Multiple Theoretical Perspectives," *Academy of Management Review* 16 (1991): 291–317; and J. S. Black and H. B. Gregersen, "The Right Way to Manage Expats," *Harvard Business Review* 77, no. 2: 52–62.

181. *Chinese refugees in Indonesia* For a now classic anthropological study of globalization and the transnational nature of the ethnic Chinese diaspora in Asia, see Aihwa Ong, *Flexible Citizenship: The Cultural Logics of Transnationality* (Durham, NC: Duke University Press, 1998).

181. *there has been continuing growth* In the 1950s, the International Labour Organization (ILO) passed two landmark conventions, the Equal Re-

muneration Convention, No. 100 (1958), and the Discrimination Employment and Occupation Convention, No. 111 (1958). At the time, there was relatively little explicit legislation against discrimination based on gender, race or ethnicity, religion, social origin, disability, or age. The United States passed its first major laws—the Equal Pay Act, the Civil Rights Act, and the Age Discrimination in Employment Act—in the 1960s, as did many European countries. By 1990, the two ILO conventions had been ratified by 109 and 106 countries, respectively. In 2000, the European Union passed two directives on racial and employment equality, which were later adopted by twenty-five member states. By 2005, the number of countries that had ratified the two ILO conventions had risen to 164 and 168, respectively. During that time, countries such as South Africa and Brazil made notable legal reforms addressing racial and ethnic discrimination. The countries that had not yet ratified at least one of the ILO conventions include Kiribati, Laos, Montenegro, Myanmar, Oman, Samoa, Solomon Islands, Suriname, Timor-Leste, and the United States. Liberia, Malaysia, Namibia, Qatar, and Singapore had accepted only one of the two. See International Labour Organization, *Equality at Work: Tackling the Challenges: Global Report Under the Follow-up to the ILO Declaration on Fundamental Principles and Rights at Work* (Geneva: International Labour Office, 2007).

181. *Yet differences are a matter* Social psychological research finds that people have an inherent tendency to identify themselves as members of a group, which can lead to stereotyping, misattribution, and discrimination. See Henri Tafjel and John Turner, "An Integrative Theory of Intergroup Conflict," in W. G. Austin and S. Worchel, eds., *The Social Psychology of Intergroup Relations* (Monterey, CA: Brooks/Cole, 1979), 33–47.

182. *major corporations were characterized* See Rosabeth Moss Kanter, *Men and Women of the Corporation* (New York: Basic Books, 1993 [first published in 1977]); and Donald Hambrick et al., "Top Executive Commitment to the Status Quo: Some Tests of Its Determinants," *Strategic Management Journal* 14 (1993): 401–418.

182. *But is there a business case?* These arguments are outlined and analyzed in an article by Robin Ely and David Thomas, "Cultural Diversity at Work: The Effects of Diversity Perspectives on Work Group Processes and Outcomes," *Administrative Science Quarterly* 46, no. 2 (2001): 229–273. See also David Thomas and Robin Ely, "Making Differences Matter: A New Paradigm for Managing Diversity," *Harvard Business Review* 74, no. 5 (1996): 79–90; and Freada Kapor Klein et al., *Giving Notice: Why the Best and Brightest Are Leaving the Workplace and How You Can Help Them Stay* (San Francisco: Jossey-Bass, 2007). Klein and her coauthors provide an astute analysis of the bias still present in the workplace and offer a framework for how to overcome the unconscious but persistent obstacles.

185. *Differences can also become* Postcolonial and cultural theorists have explored the effects cultural differences and power relations have on subordinate social, ethnic, and national groups and their accompanying mentalities. See, for example, the collection of classic texts contained in Simon During, ed., *The Cultural Studies Reader* (New York: Routledge, 2003).

185. *Groupings of any kind* The process of categorization and identification creates the ingroup/outgroup phenomenon, which leads to such effects as discrimination and stereotyping. For a review, see Michael Hogg, "Social Categorization, Depersonalization, and Group Behavior," in Michael Hogg and R. Scott Tindale, eds., *Blackwell Handbook of Social Psychology: Group Processes* (Oxford: Blackwell Publishers, 2001), 56–85. Georg Simmel was among the first to theorize ingroup/outgroup processes. See Georg Simmel, *Conflict and the Web of Group-Affiliations* (New York: Free Press, 1964); and Rosabeth Moss Kanter and Rakesh Khurana, "Position and Emotion: The Significance of Georg Simmel's Structural Theories for Leadership and Organizational Behavior," in Paul S. Adler, ed., *Organization Studies and Classical Social Theory* (Oxford: Oxford University Press, 2009).

186. *Identity is differentiation* Simone de Beauvoir, *The Second Sex* (New York: Alfred A. Knopf, 1993 [first published in 1953]).

186. *Social and linguistic differences* Nancy Adler, *International Dimensions of Organizational Behavior* (Cincinnati: South-Western, 2002). Cultural influences are also critical. For a promising new approach to cultural influences on individual psychology and behavior, see Shinobu Kitayama and Dov Cohen, eds., *Handbook of Cultural Psychology* (New York: Guilford Press, 2007). The approach takes the view that cultural meaning systems are integral for understanding psychological processes. For applications to consumer choice, see Donnel Briley and Jennifer Aaker, "Bridging the Culture Chasm: Ensuring that Consumers Are Healthy, Wealthy and Wise," *Journal of Public Policy & Marketing* 25, no. 1 (2006): 53–66.

187. *I call that one the "O"* Rosabeth Moss Kanter, with Barry Stein, *A Tale of "O": On Being Different in an Organization* (New York: Harper & Row, 1980). See also a companion video by the same authors, *The Tale of "O"* (Cambridge: Goodmeasure, Inc., 1993). The X and O concept grew out of an earlier study. See Rosabeth Moss Kanter, *Men and Women of the Corporation* (New York: Basic Books, 1993 [first published in 1977]).

189. *Diversity goals were communicated* Alexandra Kalev, Frank Dobbin, and Erin Kelly, "Best Practices or Best Guesses? Assessing the Efficacy of Corporate Affirmative Action and Diversity Policies," *American Sociological Review* 71 (2006): 589–617; and Frank Dobbin and Alexandra Kalev, "The Architecture of Inclusion: Evidence from Corporate

Diversity Programs," *Harvard Journal of Law & Gender* 30 (2007): 279–301.

191. *Awareness of others* Anthony Greenwald and Mahzarin Banaji, "Implicit Social Cognition: Attitudes, Self-Esteem, and Stereotypes," *Psychological Review* 102: 4–27; and Anthony Greenwald et al., "A Unified Theory of Implicit Attitudes, Stereotypes, Self-Esteem, and Self-Concept," *Psychological Review* 109 (2002): 3–25. Mahzarin and her colleagues show that people have many unconscious biases and an unconscious preference toward their own social group, but the same-group preference is not universal, and the biases operate in so many different ways that she and her researchers cannot generally predict the type of bias for any one subject or set of subjects in her rapid-fire quizzes called the Implicit Association Test, developed by her and two colleagues. Thus, this work serves mainly to confirm that biases exist, and for fruitful interactions to flourish, people should know themselves first.

191. *The goal is pluralism* Robert Dahl argued that American democracy is defined by pluralism, a situation in which political power does not reside in the electorate, as a pure conception of democracy holds, or in a small elite, as C. Wright Mills claimed. Rather, it sits within a polyarchy or multitude of interest groups who must compete, compromise, and ally in order to govern. See Robert Dahl, *Who Governs? Democracy and Power in an American City* (New Haven: Yale University Press, 2005 [first published in 1961]); and Robert Dahl, *Dilemmas of Pluralist Democracy: Autonomy vs. Control* (New Haven: Yale University Press, 1982). For a collection of lectures on citizenship diversity within American pluralist democracy, see Gary Jacobsohn and Susan Dunn, eds., *Diversity and Citizenship: Rediscovering American Nationhood* (Lanham, MD: Rowman & Littlefield, 1996). For a sociological examination of how cross-cutting ties operate, see Rosabeth Moss Kanter and Rakesh Khurana, "Position and Emotion: The Significance of Georg Simmel's Structural Theories for Leadership and Organizational Behavior," in Paul S. Adler, ed., *Organization Studies and Classical Social Theory* (Oxford: Oxford University Press, forthcoming).

192. *People in vanguard companies* Geert Hofstede, *Culture's Consequences: Comparing Values, Behaviors, Institutions, and Organizations Across Nations* (Thousand Oaks, CA: Sage, 2001); Geert Hofstede, *Cultures and Organizations: Software of the Mind* (New York: McGraw-Hill, 2005); and Fons Trompenaars and Charles Hampden-Turner, *Riding the Waves of Culture: Understanding Cultural Diversity in Global Business* (New York: McGraw-Hill, 1998 [first published in 1993]).

193. *Empathy of this sort* Experimental studies demonstrate that the ability to cognitively take the perspective of the other worked better than connecting emotionally with another in negotiation situations. See Adam Galinsky et al., "Why It Pays to Get Inside the Head of Your

Opponent: The Differential Effects of Perspective Taking and Empathy in Negotiations," *Psychological Science* 19, no. 4 (2008): 378–384. See also Daniel Goleman, *Emotional Intelligence: Why It Can Matter More Than IQ* (New York: Bantam Books, 2005 [first published in 1995]); and Daniel Goleman, *Social Intelligence: The New Science of Human Relationships* (New York: Bantam Books, 2006).

194. *Thus, to flourish under pluralism* For a critique of Hofstede's dimensional and national approach to understanding culture, see Rachel Baskerville-Morley, "Hofstede Never Studied Culture," *Accounting, Organizations, and Society* 28 (2003): 1–14; Brendan McSweeney, "Hofstede's Model of National Cultural Differences and Their Consequences: A Triumph of Faith—a Failure of Analysis," *Human Relations* 55, no. 1 (2002): 89–118; and Felix Tan and Michael Myers, "Beyond Models of National Culture in Information Systems Research," *Journal of Global Information Management* 10, no. 1 (2002): 24–32.

196. *Some observers hold* Early anthropologists studied African, Australasian, Amazonian, and Native American tribal societies as the first prototypical human organizational form. For early classics from the French and British anthropological traditions, see Emile Durkheim, *Elementary Forms of Religious Life* (New York: Free Press, 1995 [first published in 1912]); and A. R. Radcliffe-Brown, *Structure and Function and Primitive Society* (London: Cohen & West, 1952). While the anthropological discipline has moved its critical eye toward modern society, the notion of tribalism continues to permeate some works, especially those dealing with evolutionary themes. Robin Dunbar, an anthropologist and primatologist, argues that the number of people with whom a human can maintain social relationships has an upper limit of 150. The number was derived from primate research and was calculated as a function of the size of the human brain's neocortex region. Subsequent testing of "Dunbar's Number" against archeological and anthropological data suggests that this was, in fact, the approximate size of early human tribes and settlements. Dunbar subsequently extended his argument to claim that human gossip within small groups acted as the functional equivalent of grooming; both are done to create social bonds. See Robin Dunbar, "Neocortex Size as a Constraint on Group Size in Primates," *Journal of Human Evolution* 22 (1992): 469–493; Robin Dunbar, "Coevolution of Neocortical Size, Group Size and Language in Humans," *Behavioral and Brain Sciences* 16, no. 4 (1993): 681–735; and Robin Dunbar, *Grooming, Gossip, and the Evolution of Language* (Cambridge: Harvard University Press, 1997).

196. *In some U.S. communities, diversity* Robert Putnam, "E Pluribus Unum: Diversity and Community in the Twenty-first Century (the 2006 Johan

Skytte Prize Lecture)," *Scandinavian Political Studies* 30, no. 2 (2007): 137–174.

196. *Democratic pluralism works* Robert Dahl, *Dilemmas of Pluralist Democracy: Autonomy vs. Control* (New Haven: Yale University Press, 1982).

196. *They want people* Miriam Erez and Efrat Gati, "A Dynamic, Multi-level Model of Culture: From the Micro Level of the Individual to the Macro Level of a Global Culture," *Applied Psychology: An International Review* 53, no. 4 (2004): 583–598; Miriam Erez and Efrat Gati, "The Culture of Global Organizations," in Peter Smith, Mark Peterson, and David Thomas, eds., *The Handbook of Cross-Cultural Management Research* (Thousand Oaks, CA: Sage, 2008); and Efrat Shokef and Miriam Erez, "Shared Meanings Systems in Multicultural Teams," in Ya-Ru Chen, ed., *National Culture and Groups* (Boston: Elsevier JAI, 2006): 325–352.

196. *Helping people to work* Rosabeth Moss Kanter, "Creating Common Ground: Propositions About Effective Intergroup Leadership," in Todd Pitinsky, ed., *Crossing the Divide: Intergroup Leadership in a World of Difference* (Boston: Harvard Business School Press, 2009).

chapter eight

205. *One paradox of globalizing* See Rosabeth Moss Kanter, *World Class: Thriving Locally in the Global Economy* (New York: Simon & Schuster, 1995). This global/local paradox surfaced in responses to Thomas Friedman's treatise on globalization in his *The World Is Flat: A Brief History of the Twenty-First Century*, 3rd ed. (New York: Farrar, Strauss, & Giroux, 2007). Friedman argues that forces have leveled the global playing field to create new commercial and competitive challenges. Yet critics such as Pankaj Ghemawat assert that the world is not as flat as some believe. Much communication remains local, and differences continue to matter a great deal. See Pankaj Ghemawat, "The World Isn't Flat," *Foreign Policy* 159 (March/April 2007): 54–60; and Pankaj Ghemawat, *Redefining Global Strategy: Crossing Borders in a World Where Differences Still Matter* (Boston: Harvard Business School Press, 2007). The cultural argument about the interaction between global and local factors was made earlier by anthropologists. For an accessible example, see James L. Watson, "China's Big Mac Attack," *Foreign Affairs* 79, no. 3 (2000): 120–134.

206. *These stakeholders do not want* Rosabeth Moss Kanter, *World Class: Thriving Locally in the Global Economy* (New York: Simon & Schuster, 1995). Community and country demands on multinationals vary by industry. Oil and mining companies, for example, feel intense pressures to operate in an environmentally sustainable way. Emerging

market governments often make demands on pharmaceutical companies to license products for local markets at reduced fees. Consumer goods and other manufacturers must stay cognizant of labor conditions. For case studies of the varying effects of corporate citizenship programs on the formation of social capital in local communities, see Ian Jones, Michael Pollitt, and David Bek, *Multinationals in Their Communities: A Social Capital Approach to Corporate Citizenship Projects* (London: Palgrave Macmillan, 2007).

206. *It is corporate social innovation* Klaus Schwab, "Global Corporate Citizenship: Working with Governments and Civil Society," *Foreign Affairs* 87, no. 1 (2008): 107–118.

206. *companies show that they are acting* Rosabeth Moss Kanter, "From Spare Change to Real Change: The Social Sector as Beta Site for Business Innovation," *Harvard Business Review* 77, no. 3 (1999): 122–132.

211. *He focused IBM's philanthropy* Gerstner's interest in education reform predated his IBM years. See Louis Gerstner et al., *Reinventing Education: Entrepreneurship in America's Public Schools* (New York: Plume, 1995 [first published in 1994]). But it was not just Gerstner's interest in education that led to the IBM initiative. IBM surveys showed that K–12 public education was the issue that employees and customers cared about the most.

223. *Corporate citizenship has become* Bradley K. Googins, Philip H. Mirvis, and Steven A. Rochlin, *Beyond Good Company: Next Generation Corporate Citizenship* (New York: Palgrave Macmillan, 2007); and Sandra Waddock, *The Difference Makers: How Social and Institutional Entrepreneurs Created the Corporate Responsibility Movement* (Sheffield: Greenleaf Publishing, 2008).

223. *bigger and more visible* Company visibility often rests on how recognizable its brands are, making it the target of consumer boycotts, liability suits, and negative press. For this reason, many NGOs target companies with the most recognizable brands. See David Vogel, *The Market for Virtue* (Washington, DC: Brookings Institution Press, 2005), 52–53.

229. *Diageo was recognized* In an impact study of the Senator project, Diageo found economic and health benefits. Its evidence suggests that the initiative has created employment opportunities and reduced alcohol poisoning mortality. The Marketing Society of Kenya awarded Senator best product innovation in 2006, and its brand manager, Lemmy Mutahi, twice received the Africa Hero award from Diageo for Senator-related activities in 2006 and 2008.

chapter nine

237. *they are exposed to attack* NGOs, in the attempts to give their causes greater publicity, often target those companies with well-known

brands. Firms that specialize in intermediate goods or the production of generic products often manage to avoid NGO "naming and shaming" campaigns. See David Vogel, *The Market for Virtue* (Washington, DC: Brookings Institution Press, 2005), 52–53, 106–107.

238. *Their endurance and generally stellar* P&G's net income margin rose from 11 percent in 2003 to 13.5 percent in 2007, which included the Gillette integration, allowing it to surpass in size archrival Unilever. IBM's revenue grew from $89 billion in 2003 to $99 billion in 2007 despite selling its large PC business to Lenovo. Shinhan's stock performance outperformed its Korean competitors between 2003 and 2007, and it was named a top one hundred global financial institution. Banco Real registered 21 percent annual growth between 2001 and 2006. Publicis Groupe's operating margins as percentage of revenue reached nearly 17 percent in 2007, the highest among its holding group competitors. From September 1 through December 1, 2008, all the companies in my research faced declines in their stock prices, but IBM was a star; Publicis Groupe, P&G, Shinhan, and Diageo outperformed their competitors, which meant smaller declines; and Omron was even with its competition. Cemex was an underperformer, as was ICICI Bank, but its comparison was a government-owned bank. We used Hoovers, OneSource, and company information to make these calculations. Banco Real was the recipient of plans for new investment by Grupo Santander, indicating satisfaction with its performance at the start of the crisis.

240. *Furthermore, some problems* Al Gore has dedicated much of his public life to placing global warming on the public agenda, especially in the United States. See Al Gore, *Earth in the Balance: Ecology and the Human Spirit* (Boston: Houghton Mifflin, 1992); Al Gore, *Our Purpose: The Nobel Peace Prize Lecture, 2007* (New York: Rodale, 2008); and his Oscar-winning documentary, *An Inconvenient Truth* (2006). The Union for Concerned Scientists, an advocacy group, has also fought to raise political awareness, taking issue with George W. Bush and his administration's politicization of the scientific study of global warming. See Union for Concerned Scientists, "Scientific Integrity in Policymaking: An Investigation into the Bush Administration's Misuse of Science," http://www.ucsusa.org/scientific_integrity/abuses_of_science/ investigations_and_surveys/reports-scientific-integrity.html (accessed November 24, 2008).

240. *Public health issues threaten* Laurie Garrett, a Pulitzer Prize–winning journalist and senior fellow at the Council on Foreign Relations, has written extensively on public health threats associated with globalization. See Laurie Garrett, *The Coming Plague: Newly Emerging Diseases in a World out of Balance* (New York: Farrar, Straus & Giroux, 1994); and Laurie Garrett, *Betrayal of Trust: The Collapse of Global Public Health* (New

York: Hyperion, 2000). In later works, she has written about sudden acute respiratory syndrome, the avian flu, and other health threats. See Laurie Garrett, "The Next Pandemic?" *Foreign Affairs* 84, no. 4 (2005): 3–23; and Laurie Garrett, "The Challenge of Global Health," *Foreign Affairs* 86, no. 1 (2007): 14–38.

240. *Income inequality is widening* Richard Newfarmer et al., *Global Economic Prospects 2007: Managing the Next Wave of Globalization* (Washington, DC: The World Bank, 2007).

240. *A wage premium for education* The wage premium for skills, human capital, or education is a robust finding in labor economics. For a historical analysis of changes in the education wage premium in the United States, see Claudia Goldin and Lawrence Katz, *The Race Between Education and Technology* (Cambridge: Harvard University Press, 2008). For evidence of education wage premiums internationally, see Richard Newfarmer et al., *Global Economic Prospects 2007: Managing the Next Wave of Globalization* (Washington, DC: The World Bank, 2007), xviii.

241. *leaders say that something more* Joseph Bower et al., "Is Market Capitalism Sustainable? A Summary of Views of Participating Global Leaders," HBS Centennial Project on the Future of Market Capitalism, Faculty Symposium Overview Paper, June 2008.

241. *Detractors cover a contradictory range* For a critical and balanced analysis of potential CSR shortcomings, see David Vogel, *The Market for Virtue: The Potential and Limits of Corporate Social Responsibility* (Washington, DC: Brookings Institution Press, 2005).

245. *join associations espousing* Global, regional, and national corporate social responsibility associations have expanded since the 1990s. Business for Social Responsibility included over 250 global companies by 2008. The CSR-Europe network, founded in 1995, consists of roughly seventy-five multinationals and twenty-five partners and focuses on the European region. The Ethos Institute, founded in 1998, serves Brazil with its network of over nine hundred members. The Keidendran in Japan, the largest industry association, has an explicit focus on corporate citizenship.

245. *vanguard companies not only fail* André Sobczak, "Are Codes of Conduct in Global Supply Chains Really Voluntary? From Soft Law Regulation of Labour Relations to Consumer Law," *Business Ethics Quarterly* 16, no. 2 (2006): 167–184. The realization that companies could devolve corporate responsibility to suppliers is in part what led to the movement for "ethical supply chain management." As Nike and Mattel found out, the price for not maintaining close surveillance of supplier production conditions was steep. However, the tendency to target visible brands allows others to fall through the accountability cracks, especially in cases where suppliers are not exclusive, as in the case of

Nike and Mattel, and serve multiple buyers. See David Vogel, *The Market for Virtue: The Potential and Limits of Corporate Responsibility* (Washington, DC: Brookings Institution Press, 2005), 106–109.

246. *Transparency will reign* See Warren Bennis, Daniel Goleman, and James O'Toole, *Transparency: Creating a Culture of Candor* (San Francisco: Jossey-Bass, 2008).

246. *Banco Real asks NGOs* The Ethos Institute is a Brazil-based corporate social responsibility NGO dedicated to the management of the country's sustainability initiatives. Its nine-hundred-plus members account for roughly 30 percent of Brazil's GDP.

246. *IBM, starting in 2002* IBM was among the first companies to issue environmental reports, doing so in 1990. Prior to 1993, fewer than one hundred companies published responsibility reports of some kind. The figure rose to five hundred by 1999 and over two thousand in 2005. See David Vogel, *The Market for Virtue: The Potential and Limits of Corporate Responsibility* (Washington, DC: Brookings Institution Press, 2005). A major driver was the Global Reporting Initiative, begun in 1997 by two nonprofit organizations (CERES and Tellus Institute) with the support of the United Nations Environmental Program (UNEP). Together, they created a worldwide standard for nonfinancial reporting. The first guidelines were released in 1999 and by 2008 had gone through three iterations.

247. *Elkington and his organization* John Elkington made TBL a centerpiece to his popular 1997 book *Cannibals with Forks: The Triple Bottom Line of 21st Century Business* (Oxford: Capstone, 1997). A survey of Corporate Social Responsibility and Sustainability Development frameworks between 1997 and 2001 found that the use of TBL skyrocketed between 1999 and 2001. See John Elkington, "Enter the Triple Bottom Line," in Adrian Henriques and Julie Richardson, eds., *The Triple Bottom Line: Does It All Add Up?* (London: Earthscan, 2004), 1–16.

247. *The concern is also raised* Some evidence supports a "slack resources" theory of CSP, which suggests that the degree of CSP commitment is related to previous financial performance. If times are good, companies dedicate more discretionary spending to CSP activities, but when times get tough, firms pull back. See Sandra Waddock and Samuel Graves, "The Corporate Social Performance–Financial Performance Link," *Strategic Management Journal* 18, no. 4 (1997): 303–319.

247. *Exceptions can prove the rule* Jerry Sternin, "Positive Deviance: A New Paradigm for Addressing Today's Problems Today," *Journal of Corporate Citizenship* 5 (2002): 57–62; and Jerry Sternin, "Practice Positive Deviance for Extraordinary Social and Organizational Change," in Louis Carter et al., eds., *The Change Champion's Fieldguide: Strategies and Tools*

for Leading Change in Your Organization (Boston: Best Practice Publications, 2003): 20–37.

248. *twin forces* Joseph Bower et al., "Is Market Capitalism Sustainable? A Summary of Views of Participating Global Leaders," HBS Centennial Project on the Future of Market Capitalism, Faculty Symposium Overview Paper, June 2008.

248. *The trend in practically every part* Vito Tanzi and Ludger Schuknecht, *Public Spending in the 20th Century: A Global Perspective* (Cambridge: Cambridge University Press, 2000). Country governments grew, on average, 22 percent between 1937 and 1960 and then accelerated to 54 percent between 1960 and 1980, at which point government expansion stopped, registering declines until the end of the century. However, there are indications that national governments may be expanding once again as has occurred with growing U.S. government expenditure during the George W. Bush administration and the renewed focus on state interventions in the face of the 2008 financial crisis.

248. *But does the increased action* Robert Reich, a former U.S. secretary of labor, has criticized "responsible" companies for a potential distortion of public policy. See Robert Reich, "The New Meaning of Corporate Social Responsibility," *California Management Review* 40, no. 2 (1998): 8–17; and Robert Reich, *Supercapitalism* (New York: Alfred A. Knopf, 2007). See also David Vogel, *The Market for Virtue: The Potential and Limits of Corporate Capitalism* (Washington, DC: Brookings Institution Press, 2005), 162–173; and Jeremy Moon and David Vogel, "Corporate Social Responsibility, Government, and Civil Society," in Andrew Crane, Abagail McWilliams, Dirk Matten, Jeremy Moon, and Donald Siegel, eds., *The Oxford Handbook of Corporate Social Responsibility* (Oxford: Oxford University Press, 2008), 303–323.

249. *U.S. Bush Administration ties* The term *military-industrial complex* was coined by U.S. president Dwight D. Eisenhower when he warned citizens against it in his farewell address to the nation on January 1961. "In the councils of government, we must guard against the acquisition of unwarranted influence, whether sought or unsought, by the military-industrial [*sic*] complex," he said. See http://avalon.law.yale.edu/20th _century/eisenhower001.asp (accessed November 17, 2008). Sociologists had earlier warned of the interlocking government, military, and business interests. In 1936, a French historian and anarchist described the close relationship between the rise of fascism in Italy and Germany and big business. See Daniel Guerin, *Fascism and Big Business* (New York: Monad Press, 1973 [first published in 1936]). C. Wright Mills, however, offered the most complete analysis of the phenomenon as it applied to the United States in the 1950s, in his *The Power Elite* (New York: Oxford University Press, 2000 [first published in 1956]). The publication sparked a wave of studies. See Fred Cook, *The*

Warfare State (New York: Macmillan, 1962); John Swomley, *The Military Establishment* (Boston: Beacon Press, 1964); and others. The thesis also sparked a major debate between Mills and Robert Dahl, who argued that the elites were not a singular and narrow group but consisted of various groups who came into conflict and compromised to create policy. See Robert Dahl, *Who Governs? Democracy and Power in an American City* (New Haven: Yale University Press, 2005 [first published in 1961]).

249. *and let governments run the schools* The statement was made at "Future of Market Capitalism" Centennial Colloquium held at Harvard Business School on June 9, 2008.

250. *They do not want to get* Many companies actively use CSP, especially during its inception, to reduce risk before stakeholders. See, for example, Shawn Berman, Andrew Wicks, Suresh Kotha, and Thomas Jones, "Does Stakeholder Orientation Matter? The Relationship Between Stakeholder Management Models and Firm Financial Performance," *Academy of Management Journal* 42, no. 5 (1999): 488–506.

251. *CEOs use shareholders' money* Larry Summers has made this argument verbally. It is a variant of the principal-agent critique of social responsibility first outlined in Milton Friedman, *Capitalism and Freedom* (Chicago: University of Chicago Press, 1962); and Milton Friedman, "The Social Responsibility of Business Is to Increase Its Profits," *New York Times Magazine*, September 13, 1970. He argues that the manager is an agent of owners or shareholders who act as principals. The agent's duty is to maximize shareholder interest. If he or she uses the position to act as a civil servant to the detriment of shareholder interest, then the principal-agent contract is violated. The same holds if the CEO, as Summers argues, uses shareholder capital to pursue individual causes and then takes personal credit for the contribution.

251. *some economists define "corporate social responsibility"* The classic treatment of CSP as actions taken by businesses at the cost of profit maximization is contained in Milton Friedman, "The Social Responsibility of Business Is to Increase Its Profits," *New York Times Magazine*, September 13, 1970.

251. *In 2006, total U.S. corporate* This figure does not include the Bill and Melinda Gates Foundation because it is considered private. Total philanthropic giving in the United States reached $295 billion in 2006. See the National Foundation Trust website (www.ntrust.org/philanthropy/philanthropy_stats.asp [accessed November 23, 2008]). The most generous corporate givers in 2008 were Aventis Pharmaceuticals Health Care Foundation, Bank of America Charitable Foundation, and Wal-Mart Foundation, the same order as in 2006.

251. *Even the Bill and Melinda Gates Foundation* The Bill and Melinda Gates Foundation is the world's largest philanthropy, and individually its

three trustees—Bill Gates, Melinda Gates, and Warren Buffett—rank
as the world's most generous givers, according to *BusinessWeek*. As of
October 1, 2008, its total trust endowment was $35.1 billion (a $3.6 billion loss since December 31, 2007). The Gates Foundation has made
$17.3 billion in grants since it began in 2000. In 2007, it paid out $2
billion in funds, roughly equivalent to the nominal gross domestic
product of Suriname and larger than thirty other countries, according
to 2007 World Bank figures. See Bill and Melinda Gates Foundation,
Fact Sheet, found at www.gatesfoundation.org (accessed November 17,
2008).

252. *If a U.S. company* This argument is made in David Vogel, *The Market
for Virtue: The Potential and Limits of Corporate Capitalism* (Washington, DC: Brookings Institution Press, 2005), 4–6.

252. *Companies whose own practices* Public business support for the Kyoto treaty
was greater in Europe than in the United States. The European Business
Council for a Sustainable Energy Future led the e-Mission 55—Business
for Climate initiative, gathering more than one hundred companies (including Deutsche Telekom and Credit Suisse) from Europe, Japan, and
the United States to publicly support ratification. See Greenpeace Briefing, "Corporate America and the Kyoto Climate Treaty," http://archive
.greenpeace.org/climate/climatecountdown/documents/corporate
_america.pdf (accessed November 17, 2008).

253. *IBM filed a brief* A record number of amicus briefs were submitted in
support of the University of Michigan prior to the Supreme Court's
ruling on two affirmative action cases filed against the university. One
brief was filed jointly by leading companies, including Steelcase, 3M,
Abbott Laboratories, Bank One, Du Pont, Dow Chemical, Eastman
Kodak, Eli Lilly, General Mills, Intel, Johnson & Johnson, Kellogg,
KPMG, Lucent, Microsoft, PPG, Procter & Gamble, Sara Lee, and
Texaco.

253. *ABN AMRO stimulated the World Bank* The first ten financial institutions to sign on to the Equator Principles were ABN Amro, Barclays,
Citigroup, Crédit Lyonnais, Credit Suisse First Boston, HypoVeriens-
bank, Rabobank, Royal Bank of Scotland, WestLB, and Westpac.

253. *studies show that voluntary codes* See, for example, Richard Rothstein,
"The Starbucks Solution: Can Voluntary Codes Raise Global Living
Standards?" *American Prospect*, November 30, 2002; and Jeffrey Hol-
lender and Stephen Fenichell, *What Matters Most: How a Small Group
of Pioneers Is Teaching Social Responsibility to Big Business, and Why Big
Business Is Listening* (New York: Basic Books, 2004).

254. *vanguard companies also win* A list of awards won by the vanguard companies in this study would fill several pages. Highlights include IBM's
receipt of the Partner in Progress Award from the United Way of
America and the Nationwide Corporate Impact Award from the

American Cancer Society, not to mention the honors the company has received in Brazil, China, Spain, Taiwan, and the United Kingdom, just to name a few. P&G won the 2008 Cannes Advertiser of the Year Award, the highest of honors, as well as numerous accolades for its diversity, marketing, and R&D activities. Cemex has won various global CSP awards, including a 2006 World Business Award given by the International Chamber of Commerce and the United Nations Development Program. Shinhan has received "best places to work" awards and has won the 2005 Korean Ethical Management Award, an honorable achievement in a country that has struggled to infuse greater transparency in the corporate governance of its *chaebols*. Omron took home eight iF Product design awards in 2008, a top industry honor given by the German-based International Forum Design. Diageo consistently wins medals in the San Francisco World Spirits competition, the most comprehensive of its kind, and in 2006 was honored as Importer of the Year. And the list goes on.

254. *That is the strategy* Klaus Schwab, the founder and president of the World Economic Forum, has made an explicit call for corporate social entrepreneurship at forum events and in print. See "Global Corporate Citizenship: Working with Governments and Civil Society," *Foreign Affairs* 87, no. 1 (2008): 107–118. IBM's vice president of corporate citizenship and corporate affairs has added his voice to this; see Stanley Litow, "Peace Through Commerce: Responsible Corporate Citizenship and the Ideals of the UN Global Compact," in Oliver Williams, ed., *Peace Through Commerce: Responsible Corporate Citizenship and the Ideals of the United Nations Compact* (Notre Dame, IN: University of Notre Dame Press, 2008).

chapter ten

257. *Finding symbols that create meaning* Joel Podolny, Rakesh Khurana, and Marya Lisl Hill-Popper, "Revisiting the Meaning of Leadership," *Research in Organizational Behavior* 26 (2005): 1–36.

261. *the best characteristics of leaders* Howard Gardner, *Five Minds for the Future* (Boston: Harvard Business School Press, 2006).

262. *Effective leaders have always possessed* Warren Bennis, *On Becoming a Leader* (Cambridge: Perseus Publishing, 2003); Warren Bennis and Bert Nanus, *Leaders: Strategies for Taking Charge* (New York: Harper Business Essentials, 2003); James O'Toole, *Vanguard Management: Redesigning the Corporate Future* (Garden City, NY: Doubleday, 1985); Daniel Goleman, *Emotional Intelligence: Why It Can Matter More Than IQ* (New York: Bantam Books, 2005 [first published in 1995]); Daniel Goleman, Richard Boyatzis, and Annie McKee, *Primal Leadership: Learning to Lead with Emotional Intelligence* (Boston: Harvard Business

School Press, 2004 [first published in 2002]); and Robert Goffee and Gareth Jones, *Why Should Anyone Be Led By You? What It Takes to Be an Authentic Leader* (Boston: Harvard Business School Press, 2006).

262. *Ensuring sufficient human talent* Meira Levinson, *The Demands of Liberal Education* (New York: Oxford University Press, 1999).

263. *To encourage companies to change* All the companies studied have been honored for their corporate citizenship activities. Every year, IBM receives corporate social responsibility awards (see http://www.ibm.com/ibm/ibmgives/awards/index.shtml), as does P&G and Cemex. In 2007, P&G won two accolades for Children's Safe Drinking Water, including a Gold Medallion Award from the Johns Hopkins University Bloomberg School of Public Health. Cemex was honored in 2006 with a World Business Award given by the International Chamber of Commerce and the United Nations Development Program.

263. *companies featured in this book* See the notes for chapter 9 for a sample of the awards.

263. *indices such as the Financial Times'* Created in 2001, the FTSE4 good index assesses globally listed companies based on environmental, social and stakeholder, human rights, supply chain and labor, and countering bribery criteria. It is intended to provide market transparency for responsible investors. The other two leading ethical fund indexes are the Dow Jones Sustainability World Index and the Domini 400 Social Index.

263. *Some companies offer sabbaticals* The 2008 Families and Work Institute "National Study of Employers" found that workplace flexibility was on the rise and that 38 percent of companies in the United States with a hundred or more workers offered employees the chance to take six months or more of paid or unpaid leave with the opportunity to return to a comparable position. See Ellen Galinsky et al., "2008 National Study of Employers," Families and Work Institute (2008), http://familiesandwork.org/site/research/reports/2008nse.pdf (accessed November 20, 2008).

267. *American and European companies* A benchmark annual corporate relocation survey, conducted by GMAC Global Relocation Services in association with the National Foreign Trade Council, found a trend toward younger, unmarried expatriates. They also detected a greater relative movement between nonheadquarters locations than to and from the headquarters country. In 2007, 56 percent of employees transferred to and from headquarters, compared to the historical average of 65 percent. See GMAC Global Relocation Services, "Global Relocation Trends: 2008 Survey Report," http://www.gmacglobal relocation.com/insight_support/global_relocation.asp (accessed November 20, 2008). As companies become more multinational and talent ever scarcer, companies are shifting managers from emerging

market countries between their global offices. Another trend is that of the "halfpat," a person who travels alone and ends up in a foreign location as a student, intern, or traveler and begins a career in that country. See Alan Paul, "Younger, Nimbler, Cheaper: 'Halfpats' Are the New Expats," *Wall Street Journal*, September 9, 2008. In general, multinationals have begun to reduce their reliance on expats, especially in an effort to cut costs in the face of the 2008 financial crisis. See, for example, Kala Vijayraghavan, Lijee Philip, and Chaitali Chakravarty, "MNCs Relieve Expats from India Posts," *Economic Times*, November 20, 2008.

ACKNOWLEDGMENTS

Saying thank you can be a greater pleasure for the thanker than the thankee, because it is a reminder of warm acts of generosity.

First I should thank the people from the companies featured in this book for their inspiring examples of ways to transcend the bureaucratic grind. By temperament, I tend to be a can-do, action-oriented, confident optimist (thus, typically American, people from other places have told me, or hopelessly idealistic and naive). I cannot wallow in problems for very long without wanting to find solutions. I am grateful for the chance to work with other can-do problem solvers and tell their stories.

A big thanks to the Harvard Business School Division of Research and Faculty Development (DRFD) for the resources to hire research associates and get us in the air. (Like the leaders in this book, I have managed by flying around.) Debora Spar and Srikant Datar were generous supporters on behalf of DRFD. *Harvard Business Review* editors, including Tom Stewart and Julia Kirby, provided encouragement and magazine space for early versions of some of the ideas in this book and performed heroic acts of editing, plus a great video interview that ended up on YouTube. Eric Hellweg and Josh Macht at Harvardbusiness.org offered a cyberspace home on the Web (I'm still blogging), and Josephine Schmidt at the New York Times International Syndicate helped my global print columns play in translation. I should also thank Klaus Schwab, founder and chairman of the World Economic Forum, for many invitations to Davos, where I could meet leaders and exchange ideas about businesses in their broader vision and mission.

The effervescent Douglas Raymond laid some of the groundwork as an MBA student doing a field study project for me in Egypt, where he tracked down social contributions by Procter & Gamble Egypt; after graduation, he became a valued, highly skilled research associate before departing for Alcoa, Google, and Obama's Washington. Champion swimmer Ryan Raffaelli dove into project waters to visit Shinhan in Seoul, South Korea, and then stayed with me for two stimulating years to work on Publicis Groupe, then Banco

acknowledgments

Real (along with Ricardo Reisen in São Paulo), and he also helped me initiate the full field research with three successive short trips to Mexico, Europe, and Egypt. Pamela Yatsko, a wonderful writer and shrewd analyst, came out of my "alumni association" to juggle baby and Cemex case, Cemex case and baby; she had worked with me years earlier on a different Publicis venture. Lance Pierce graciously picked up on numerous pieces and conducted informative interviews en route to his current post working on climate change initiatives for the Union of Concerned Scientists. Ethan Bernstein returned to HBS as a doctoral student five years after taking my MBA course and, using his knowledge of Japan and his Japanese language skills, became the lead researcher and analyst on Omron, while doing dozens of other things.

Matthew Bird deserves particular thanks and praise. He joined me as a full-time professional research associate in October 2007 with a doctorate almost completed from the University of Chicago. His intellectual curiosity and experience conducting field research were immediately useful. He became an instant expert on Procter & Gamble, going to many countries while working on the Brazil case and then the full inside story of the Gillette acquisition and integration, as well as conducting many other interviews at other companies and literature reviews, doing it all with enthusiasm, intelligence, and constant good cheer. Some of the interesting commentaries in the chapter notes come from Matthew's eye for valuable intellectual connections.

Brilliant colleagues and friends provided support, encouragement, platforms for discussion, and key pieces of their own work. These include Rakesh Khurana, Nitin Nohria, Rob Kaplan (for his comments at the leadership colloquium), David Thomas, Robin Ely, Herminia Ibarra, Michael Tushman, Ranjay Gulati, and Jordan Siegel. I am especially grateful to Nitin for his truly insightful comments and brilliance and to Rakesh for his abiding friendship, generosity of spirit, wide-ranging intellect, and collaboration on papers and ventures, including academic articles revisiting classic social theorists whose insights about modernity nearly a century ago stimulated my thinking about the transitions now under way in the world.

Among a wonderful set of friends who are extended family and are too numerous to name but please don't feel left out, there are a few deserving of name recognition: Connie and Dominique Borde, Laura Delano Roosevelt, Charlie (Dr. Charles) Silberstein, Drs. Randy and Michael Wertheimer, who offered conversations and encouragement (Michael is also my title doctor). Add to those Tom and Corrie Dretler, Corinne Ferguson, Swanee Hunt, Michael Brown and Charlotte Mau, Phyllis Segal, Noah Kindler, Matthew Morgan, Marsha Feinberg, and Rakesh and Stephanie Khurana; they were the chief strategists for an almost-surprise party under Charlie's direction at just the right moment. Michael Brown is also the inspiring leader of City Year, the youth corps he cofounded with Alan Khazei, which operates in twenty cities in the United States and South Africa; I am happy to be a longtime board member, deriving insights that help me see the power of positive change.

acknowledgments

Anna Porter, Klara Prachar, and Cheryl Daigle were my faculty assistants during the years of research and writing, and each one was a high-quality professional with organizational and diplomatic skills. Anna Porter also stepped up to take responsibility for portions of projects that still had to be done even while I was trying to write a book, such as the exciting new Advanced Leadership Initiative (www.advancedleadership.harvard.edu), which I have been leading with faculty from five of Harvard's professional schools, aimed at some of the same world-changing goals as vanguard companies have. My findings about innovation and organizational change came to life as we guided this new venture in an established organization. Thanks are due to Harvard collaborators Charles Ogletree (Barack Obama's mentor at Harvard Law School), David Gergen, Fernando Reimers, Howard Koh, Jim Honan, David Bloom, "America's Best Leaders" Don Berwick, Allen Grossman, Bill George (former Medtronic CEO), Rakesh Khurana, and Nitin Nohria, among others, all of whom taught me important things.

Thanks are also due to the senior executives who have been innovators, pioneers, and big thinkers about business and society, because my insights in this book have been built on their actions. I also thank them for opening doors in their companies. CEOs cited in the book are high on this list, such as Sam Palmisano at IBM, A. G. Lafley at Procter & Gamble, Maurice Lévy at Publicis Groupe, and Fabio Barbosa at Banco Real. I also want to thank Bob McDonald at P&G and especially Stanley Litow at IBM, who is a very smart contributor to his company's way of making a difference in the world and has become a good friend. I am also grateful to numerous others, too many to list, who were willing to take time and facilitate contacts. Many of them will find themselves quoted in the book.

John Mahaney at Crown and the wonderful Crown team worked their usual magic during tough times for book publishing. John deserves repeated thanks for being an editor who actually edits and thus is willing to help an author untangle confused thoughts and find the central idea.

And, of course, thanks always go to family. Matthew and Melissa Stein graciously allowed us to buy them dinner on Sunday nights, which served as a welcome relief from the grind. Boswell (the dog who is the pontificator's best friend) restrained the barking at the right moments; he accompanied Charlie Silberstein and me (and Bino and sometimes the goats) on renewing beach walks. Barry Stein and I have named a number of small boats after my books. I finished first drafts of chapters 9 and 10 of this book on my laptop while on board *Confidence*. I suppose that impending publication of this book means changing the boat name to *SuperCorp*.

—Rosabeth Moss Kanter, Boston, Cambridge, and Edgartown, Massachusetts, March 2009

INDEX

index

index

Rosabeth Moss Kanter holds the Ernest L. Arbuckle Professorship at Harvard Business School, where she specializes in strategy, innovation, and leadership for change. She cofounded and serves as chair and founding director of the Harvard Advanced Leadership Initiative, an innovative university-wide program to help successful leaders at the top of their professions apply their skills to addressing challenging national and global problems—a new stage of higher education for a new stage in life. The first Advanced Leadership Fellows started their year at Harvard in December 2008.

Dr. Kanter's strategic and practical insights have guided leaders of large and small organizations worldwide for over twenty-five years, through teaching, writing, and direct consultation to major corporations and governments. The former editor of *Harvard Business Review* (1989–1992), she has been named in lists such as the "50 most powerful women in the world" (*Times* [of London]) and the "50 most influential business thinkers in the world" (Accenture and Thinkers 50 research). In 2001, she received the Academy of Management's Distinguished Career Award for her scholarly contributions to management knowledge, and in 2002, she was named "Intelligent Community Visionary of the Year" by the World Teleport Association.

SuperCorp is Dr. Kanter's eighteenth book, elaborating on her recent *Harvard Business Review* articles "Transforming Giants" and "Innovation: The Classic Traps." Her eighteen books have been translated into seventeen languages. Her recent book *Confidence: How Winning Streaks and Losing Streaks Begin and End* (a *New York Times* business bestseller and #1 *BusinessWeek* best-seller) describes the culture and dynamics of high-performance organizations as compared with those in decline and shows how to lead turnarounds, whether in businesses, hospitals, schools, sports teams, community organizations, or countries.

Her classic prizewinning book *Men and Women of the Corporation* (which won the C. Wright Mills Award for the year's best book on social issues) offered insight to countless individuals and organizations about corporate careers and the individual and organizational factors that promote success; a spin-off video *A Tale of "O": On Being Different* is among the world's most widely used diversity tools; and a related book *Work and Family in the United States* set a policy agenda (in 2001, a coalition of university centers created the Rosabeth Moss Kanter Award in her honor for the best research on work/family issues). Another awardwinning book, *When Giants Learn to Dance*, showed how to master the new terms of competition at the dawn of the global information age. *World Class: Thriving Locally in the Global Economy* identified the rise of new business networks and analyzed dilemmas of globalization. *America the Principled: 6 Opportunities for Becoming a Can-Do Nation Once Again* provided a new direction for the United States after the 2008 presidential election.

She has received twenty-three honorary doctoral degrees, as well as numerous leadership awards and prizes for her books and articles; for example, her book *The Change Masters* was named one of the most influential business books of the twentieth century (*Financial Times*). Through Goodmeasure, Inc., the consulting group she cofounded, she has partnered with IBM on applying her leadership tools from business to other sectors; she is a senior adviser for IBM's Global Citizenship portfolio. She advises CEOs of large and small companies; has served on numerous business and nonprofit boards and national or regional commissions, including the Governor's Council of Economic Advisors; and speaks widely, often sharing the platform with presidents, prime ministers, and CEOs, at national and international events, such as the World Economic Forum in Davos, Switzerland.

Before joining the Harvard Business School faculty, she held tenured professorships at Yale University and Brandeis University and was a fellow at Harvard Law School, simultaneously holding a Guggenheim Fellowship. She lives in Cambridge, Massachusetts, where she can walk to work along the Charles River and get to Logan Airport in fifteen minutes, and in Edgartown, Masschusetts, where she can get away to the ocean, accompanied by her husband, a strong-willed cocker spaniel, her son, daughter-in-law, extended family, a wonderful community of loving friends who are adopted family, and way too many phone lines and computers.